DIESTERWEGS
NEUSPRACHLICHE
BIBLIOTHEK

W0409784

Sindiwe Magona

Mother to Mother

edited and annotated
by Rudolph F. Rau

Diesterweg
westermann

© 1998 Sindiwe Magona, reprinted with permission

Bildnachweis
|Imago, Berlin: ZUMA/Keystone Titel. |laif, Köln: Basso Cannarsa/Opale/Leemage 159.

Wir arbeiten sehr sorgfältig daran, für alle verwendeten Abbildungen die Rechteinhaberinnen und Rechteinhaber zu ermitteln. Sollte uns dies im Einzelfall nicht vollständig gelungen sein, werden berechtigte Ansprüche selbstverständlich im Rahmen der üblichen Vereinbarungen abgegolten.

westermann GRUPPE

© 2016 Bildungshaus Schulbuchverlage
Westermann Schroedel Diesterweg
Schöningh Winklers GmbH, Braunschweig
www.diesterweg.de

Das Werk und seine Teile sind urheberrechtlich geschützt. Jede Nutzung in anderen als den gesetzlich zugelassenen Fällen bedarf der vorherigen schriftlichen Einwilligung des Verlages.

Für Verweise (Links) auf Internet-Adressen gilt folgender Haftungshinweis: Trotz sorgfältiger inhaltlicher Kontrolle wird die Haftung für die Inhalte der externen Seiten ausgeschlossen. Für den Inhalt dieser externen Seiten sind ausschließlich deren Betreiber verantwortlich. Sollten Sie daher auf kostenpflichtige, illegale oder anstößige Inhalte treffen, so bedauern wir dies ausdrücklich und bitten Sie, uns umgehend per E-Mail davon in Kenntnis zu setzen, damit beim Nachdruck der Verweis gelöscht wird.

Druck A[7] / Jahr 2019
Alle Drucke der Serie A sind im Unterricht parallel verwendbar.

Redaktion: Rudolph F. Rau, Angela Wesser
Layoutkonzeption: Harald Thumser, Frankfurt am Main
Druck und Bindung: Westermann Druck GmbH, Braunschweig

ISBN 978-3-425-**04971**-7

Table of Contents

preface [ˈprefəs] *Vorwort*

outrage great anger
unprecedented never having happened before
subsequent coming afterwards
deprivation *Entbehrung*
aspiraton strong desire to achieve s.th.
reverse opposite
benevolent wishing to do good
to nurture (here): to support, to help to develop
entity (here): individual, organisation
malice hatred so great that one is willing to commit violent acts
glimpse quick look
callousness heartlessness
legacy *Vermächtnis*
to breed, bred, bred (fig.) to generate, to produce
nefarious [nɪˈfeəriəs] (formal) criminal, immoral
to promote *fördern*
through the warped (distorted) **prism** *(Prisma)* (fig.) from a subjective viewpoint that prevents you from seeing the truth
overarching (here): serving as a general term to describe several things in common
to label *kennzeichnen*
bewildered confused
grief-stricken extremely sad because of a tragic incident
to dredge (fig.) to search from deep down
to ease to make less painful

Author's Preface

Fulbright scholar Amy Elizabeth Biehl was set upon and killed by a mob of black youth in Guguletu, South Africa, in August 1993. The outpouring of grief, outrage, and support for the Biehl family was unprecedented in the history of the country. Amy, a white American, had gone to South Africa to help black people prepare for the country's first truly democratic elections. Ironically, therefore, those who killed her were precisely the people for whom, by all subsequent accounts, she held a huge compassion, understanding the deprivations they had suffered.

Usually, and rightly, in situations such as this, we hear a lot about the world of the victim: his or her family, friends, work, hobbies, hopes and aspirations. The Biehl case was no exception. And yet, are there no lessons to be had from knowing something of the other world? The reverse of such benevolent and nurturing entities as those that throw up the Amy Biehls, the Andrew Goodmans, and other young people of that quality? What was the world of this young women's killers, the world of those, young as she was young, whose environment failed to nurture them in the higher ideals of humanity and who, instead, became lost creatures of malice and destruction?

In my novel, there is only one killer. Through his mother's memories, we get a glimpse of human callousness of the kind that made the murder of Amy Biehl possible. And here I am back in the legacy of apartheid – a system repressive and brutal, that bred senseless inter- and intra-racial violence as well as other nefarious happenings; a system that promoted a twisted sense of right and wrong, with everything seen through the warped prism of the overarching *crime against humanity*, as the international community labelled it.

In **Mother to Mother**, the killer's mother, bewildered and grief-stricken, dredges her memory and examines the life her son has lived ... his world. In looking for answers for herself whilst talking to the other mother, imagining her pain, she draws a portrait of her son and of his world, and hopes that an understanding of that and of her own grief might ease the other mother's pain ... if a little.

Chapter One

Mandisa's lament

My son killed your daughter.

People look at me as though I did it. The generous ones as though I made him do it. As though I could make this child do anything. Starting from when he was less than six years old, even before he lost his first tooth or went to school. Starting, if truth be known, from before he was conceived; when he, with total lack of consideration if not downright malice, seeded himself inside my womb. But now, people look at me as if I'm the one who woke up one shushu day and said, Boyboy, run out and see whether, somewhere out there, you can find a white girl with nothing better to do than run around Guguletu, where she does not belong.

And hey, while you're at it, Sonnyboy, hey, if she's American, all the better! As though that were something - a badge or label - she would have worn on her face. As though he would go out there, weigh the pros and cons, and carefully choose her for her sake, for being who she truly was.

My revilers seem to think that, with such perfect understanding between mother and son, I wouldn't have had to say one word more. Naturally, he'd've just known what it was I wanted done ... what I wanted him to do.

I should have such an obedient son! Why do they think he did what he did if he were such a lamb, a model child?

Let me say out plain, I was not surprised that my son killed your daughter. That is not to say I was pleased. It is not right to kill.

But, you have to understand my son. Then you'll understand why I am not surprised he killed your daughter. Nothing my son does surprises me any more. Not after that first unbelieving shock, his implanting himself inside me; unreasonably and totally destroying the me I was ... the me I would have become.

I have known for a long time now that he might kill someone some day. I am surprised, however, it wasn't one of his friends or even one of my other children he killed. Mind you, with his younger brother, he was wise not to try. That one would have killed him with his bare hands first. And perhaps that would have been for the better. If it had happened, your child would still be alive today. Except, of course, there is always the possibility she might have got herself killed by another of these monsters our children have become. Here in Guguletu or in Langa or Nyanga or Khayelitsha. Or, indeed, in another, far-away township in the vastness of this country.

But, let me ask you something: what was she doing, vagabonding all over Guguletu, of all places; taking her foot where she had no business? Where did she think she was going? Was she blind not to see there were no white people in this place?

Yes, the more I think about this the more convinced I am that your daughter must have been the type of person who has absolutely no sense

lament expression of sorrow or regret

to be conceived to begin to exist as a fetus

malice *Bosheit*

to seed oneself to allow the female ovum to be impregnated by a male sperm

womb [wu:m] *Gebärmutter*

shushu (Xhosa [ˈkɔ:sə]) hot

badge *Abzeichen*

label *Etikett*

for her sake *ihr zuliebe*

reviler [rɪˈvaɪlə] a person who severely criticizes another person with abusive language

plain (here): clearly

to implant to become fixed in the womb

to vagabond to wander about aimlessly without a job or home

to hamper to prevent s.o. from doing s.th.
to be bent on doing s.th. to be determined to do s.th.
all-consuming completely taking up your mind
fierce passionate
compulsion drive, urge, obsession
to blinker (fig.) to make narrow
perception *Wahrnehmung*
hue [hju:] **and cry** public protest
breadth *Breite*
to burden to weigh down
to stoop to bend downwards
to crucify *kreuzigen*
unease anxiety
period Full stop!
sin *Sünde*
to wring, wrung, wrung to twist

of danger when she believes in what she is doing. That was your daughter's weakness, I can see. How many young white South African women were here in Guguletu that day she was killed? Do you see them driving up and down this township as though they are going to market? But people like your daughter have no inborn sense of fear. They so believe in their goodness, know they have hurt no one, are, indeed, helping, they never think anyone would want to hurt them.

I bet you anything, if she ever thought she might be in danger ... she probably saw that coming from the authorities, who might either hamper and hinder her in what she was bent on doing, or in some way stop her altogether from doing it.

To people like your daughter, doing good in this world is an all-consuming, fierce and burning compulsion. I wonder if it does not blinker their perception.

And, if he had killed one of the other women who were with your daughter, d'you think there would be all this hue and cry? He'd be here now; like the hundreds of killers walking the length and breadth of Guguletu. But then he never did have any sense. No sense at all in that big head that burdens his shoulders till they stoop. Full of water, it is. What a shame. For the years he has lived, hasn't he learnt anything at all? Did he not know they would surely crucify him for killing a white person?

And your daughter; did she not go to school? Did she not see that this is a place where only black people live? Add to that, where was her natural sense of unease? Did she not feel awkward, a fish out of water, here? That should have been a warning to her ... a warning to stay out. Telling her the place was not for her. It was not safe for the likes of her. Oh, why did she not stay out? Why did she not stay out?

White people live in their own areas and mind their own business – period. We live here, fight and kill each other. That is our business. You don't see big words on every page of the newspapers because one of us kills somebody, here in the townships. But with this case of Boyboy's, even the white woman I work for showed me. The story was all over the place. Pictures too.

It's been a long, hard road, my son has travelled. Now, your daughter has paid for the sins of the fathers and mothers who did not do their share of seeing that my son had a life worth living.

Why is it that the government now pays for his food, his clothes, the roof over his head? Where was the government the day my son stole my neighbour's hen; wrung its neck and cooked it – feathers and all, because there was no food in the house and I was away, minding the children of the white family I worked for? Asked to stay in for the weekend – they had their emergency ... mine was just not being able to tell my children beforehand that they would be alone for the weekend ... not being able to leave them enough food for the time I was away ... not being able to phone and tell them of the change of plans. Who was on the phone, in Guguletu then? And why would the awarding of phones have started with a nobody such as I am?

Why now, when he's an outcast, does my son have a better roof over his head than ever before in his life? … living a better life, if chained? I do not understand why it is that the government is giving him so much now when it has given him nothing at all, all his life.

God, you know my heart. I am not saying my child shouldn't be punished for his sin. But I am a mother, with a mother's heart. The cup You have given me is too bitter to swallow. The shame. The hurt of the other mother. The young woman whose tender life was cut so cruelly short. God, please forgive my son. Forgive him this terrible, terrible sin.

awarding granting

outcast *Ausgestoßene(r)*

to swallow to make food or drink go down your throat

tender gentle and delicate

Chapter Two

Mowbray – Wednesday 25 August 1993

A clear autumn morning. The room, window facing east, awash with the thin August light. The window is open. Your daughter slept with it like that all night through.

What thoughts filled her mind as she woke! What dreams were hers the night just past! What hopes did she harbour in her breast for the day just born! What, for the homing morrow!

The shrill cry of the telephone jolts her. It dredges her from deepest sleep. Is the call expected or does it come as a complete surprise? I can't say. But she is very happy talking on the phone.

She tells the person, 'See you soon!' her voice, a swan's at break of day. As she puts the receiver down, her face is bathed in radiant smile.

She lies back and hums a tune, the smile lingers on, lighting her eyes. Mother? Or … boy-friend?

Whoever it was has made her happy. A little while later, singing still, she leaps out of bed and jumps into the shower.

Body, tall and strong, every sinew and limb fully awake, alive, tingling, she steps out of the big, white bathtub, with cracks and chips over its bone-coloured surface from which all gloss has long evaporated. The house is one of those old, decaying structures students love so much.

A big, fluffy towel wrapped around her, barefoot, she heads for the kitchen. Long thick dark strands of hair plastered down her back, in quick, efficient movements, she fixes herself breakfast. Hurriedly, she gulps down cold-milk cereal. Chases it down with black coffee, piping hot. And a slice of wholewheat bread. Toasted. Butter and a dash of Marmite. As an afterthought, she grabs a thick slice of cheese.

Still unclad except for the white towel, back to bed she pads on her long thin feet, pink against the deep brown, almost black carpet. Back to bed. To read, scribbling notes as she goes along, the hand holding the pen wagging furiously like the tail of an over-eager puppy. A little frown pleats her forehead.

She stops. Cocks her head. Hears the shower gurgling. That tells her one of her room-mates is up. Lisa? Tess? For a moment she listens. Smiles. Then her eyes go back to the book that lies open against her chest.

What is the last act of her morning routine this day? Does she shout, 'See you, later!' to her roommates? Briskly, she walks to the car parked out in the open yard. Key turns. Door opens. She slides in behind the wheel and her eyes automatically leap to her wrist. The big round watch that looks like a man's tells her: seven fifty-five.

Twenty kilometres away, in Guguletu, that is exactly the time I leave the house.

awash flooded

to harbour (fig.) to keep secretly

homing morrow (literary) going home the next day

to jolt to give s.o. a sudden shock

to dredge (fig.) to bring s.th. up from the bottom

radiant [ˈreɪdiənt] bright with happiness

to linger on to continue longer than expected

sinew [ˈsɪnjuː] *Sehne*

limb leg or arm

to tingle *kribbeln*

chip a small area with a piece broken off

gloss shiny smooth surface

to evaporate (here): to disappear

decaying shabby, falling apart

fluffy soft

plastered (here): sticking on the skin

to gulp to swallow quickly

to chase (here): to drink s.th. immediately after having drunk s.th. else

piping hot very hot

wholewheat *Vollkorn*

dash small amount

Marmite ™ a spread made of yeast and vegetable extract

unclad unclothed

to pad to walk with quiet steps

to scribble to write quickly

to wag *wedeln*

frown worried expression

to pleat to form folds

to cock to raise

briskly quickly

'You go on sleeping,' I'd said earlier to the silent, inert log in the smaller of the two bedrooms. 'It's nearly eight o'clock, if you care to know. I'm about to leave.' My daughter had mumbled and turned to face the wall.

The ritual is unchanging. First I try her, then I go to her brothers, both older than her. Standing at the back door, the kitchen door, facing the back yard, where the boys sleep in the tin shack, the *hokkie* (you know these one-size-fits-all houses of Guguletu don't expand as the children come), I holler:

'Hey, you two! Time to get up!' As usual, no response came from the *hokkie*.

'Mxolisi!' (That's the older boy, circumsized just last year) He prides himself on his ability to stay up half the night. What he has not learnt, in all his many years, is that there is a direct relationship between when one goes to bed and when one wakes up. He will readily acknowledge his inability to get up in the morning, but sees no cause and effect, no link, between that daily difficulty and the hours he keeps. He insists that his condition is natural, just as some people have soft voices while others' voices are gruff.

'Lunga! Lunga, get up and wake your brother up! Hurry, before the water I've heated for you gets cold.'

'Yes, Ma!' Although Lunga's voice sounds as though he has cotton wool in his mouth, I am reassured, deeply gratified that, once again, my power has worked, I possess the ability to raise the dead.

Soon he and Siziwe are in the kitchen, having coffee and bread with jam.

'Sit down! Sit down!' Why my children never sit down to eat, especially mornings, is beyond me. Of course, now, they are in a hurry; you should see how they wolf the food down. Why do they never get up on time?

'Is your *bhuti* still in bed?'

Just then, a scratchy voice says from the door, 'Can we have some money for eggs, Mama?' My heart lurches. Some days Mxolisi sounds so much like his father I forget the years and think I will see China standing there when I raise my eyes.

Giraffelike, knees semi-genuflected while neck flops head down to escape scraping the top of the door frame, he comes in. Soon he will be shaving, I see. Tall and muscular. Suddenly, Lunga, next to him, seems small for his age … or a lot younger than the six years between them.

'Did we all sleep in the same room?' I throw at him.

'Good morning, Mama! Morning, Siziwe!' in a voice gone loud and serious, he says; hand, palm up, stretched out toward me.

'I'll bring eggs when I come back from work.'

At that, he turns his attention to his sister, 'What're you having?'

Her mouth choc-a-block full, Siziwe mumbles something and shows him her bread.

inert lifeless
log *Baumstamm*
to holler to shout
to circumsize *beschneiden*
gruff deep and rough
beyond me difficult to understand
to wolf down (coll.) to quickly eat
bhuti (Xhosa) brother
scratchy rough
to lurch to suddenly leap
semi-genuflected (formal) half-bent
to flop down to cause to move down awkwardly
to escape (here): to avoid
to scrape to rub by accident
palm inside surface of the hand below the fingers
choc-a-block (coll.) full of things pressed together

'Ma,' he says, rummaging around the cupboard, 'can we have the pickled fish?'

'There is plenty of fruit,' I tell him. 'There's bread, jam and the peanut butter, too.'

'Bread's running out,' grumbles Mxolisi, holding up what is left of the loaf, about a quarter.

'So am I,' I say, smiling at him, '... running out. Or else, I'll be late.' There is no answering smile on his face. Instead, he says, '*Wayeka nokusenzel' isidudu, Mama!* You've even stopped making us porridge, Mother!'

'You're old enough to make that for yourselves!'

'But we miss your hand,' says Lunga. I swallow my guilt. What would happen if I stayed home doing all the things a mother's supposed to do? We couldn't possibly survive just on what Dwadwa makes ... we hardly make it as it is, with me working full time.

As I step out of the door minutes later, I hastily throw out a couple of reminders: what they're supposed to do for me that day around the house, what food they're not to touch. 'And remember, I want you all in when I come back!' Not that I think this makes any difference to what will actually happen. But, as a mother, I'm supposed to have authority over my children, over the running of my house. Never mind that I'm never there. Monday to Saturday, I go to work in the kitchen of my *mlungu* woman, Mrs Nelson; leaving the house before the children go to school and coming back long after the sun has gone to sleep. I am not home when they come back from school. Things were much better in the days when I only had Mxolisi. I took him to work with me ... did that till he started school. But what *mlungu* woman will allow my whole crèche into her home? Besides, the children are all big now, they go to school. To remind them of my rules therefore, each morning I give these elaborate, empty instructions regarding their behaviour while I am away. A mere formality, a charade, something nobody ever heeds. The children do pretty much as they please. And get away with it too. Who can always remember what was forbidden and what was permitted? By the time I get back in the evening, I am too tired to remember all that. I have a hard time remembering my name, most of the time, as it is. But, we have to work. We work, to stay alive. As my people say, *ukulunga kwenye, kukonakala kwenye*, the righting of one, is the undoing of another (problem). Life is never problem free.

Does your daughter drive with others to school or is she by herself? Is the car radio on or does she put in a cassette, play a song that brings to mind her young man so far away? What plans does she have for the evening?

Traffic is light as she leaves Mowbray. So is her heart. Light. Soon. Soon, she will be home. Strange how she was able to bear it – bear being away. Until now. With a day to go, it has suddenly become unbearable. Since that party on Saturday night. Smashing send-off

---

to rummage around to search for s.th., moving things carelessly around
pickled *eingelegt*
to grumble to complain
porridge *Haferbrei*
to swallow (here): to try to forget
mlungu (Xhosa) white
crèche [kreʃ] (ironic) (here): *Kita*
elaborate complicated
charade [ʃəˈrɑːd] absurd act
to heed to pay close attention to s.th.
smashing (old-fashioned, BE) great

political

psychological + feministic

these lovely people gave her. Really smashing. So, why is she feeling so blue? Ah, well, she thinks to herself, I've always had a problem, saying goodbye.

She hardly has a moment to breathe through the day. So busy. Her very last day at this place she has called home these ten months past. Here at the university too, many people want to talk about her trip back home. If only they knew. If only they knew. Excited as she is about the prospect of seeing her family, of going home, seeing her friends, with all that ... still, saying goodbye is not easy. Never has been for her. That is what she's doing now. How she wishes everybody would just forget she was going back home. But no. People insist on saying goodbye, on giving her party after party. Therefore, she is forced to take leave of her friends, to acknowledge the pain of parting. Bitter sweet. How she wishes she were home already. But, of course, before that can happen, she has to say goodbye to all these dear, dear friends, these people of whom she has grown so fond. But perhaps she will come back. Of course, she will come back, one day. A not too far-away day too, that's for sure.

Yes, I can see how torn she must have felt. Excited and grieving. Happy and sad. At one and the same time. For the same, the very same, reason.

Wednesday is a school day. However, not one of my children will go to school. This burdensome knowledge I carry with me as a tortoise carries her shell. But, it weighs my spirit down.

Two days ago, the Congress of South African Students (COSAS) ordered the school children to join Operation Barcelona, a campaign they say is in support of their teachers who are on strike. Students were urged to stay away from school, to burn cars and to drive reactionary elements out of the townships. Flint to tinder. The students fell over each other to answer the call. Now, anyone who disagrees with them, the students label 'reactionary.' This has struck stark fear in many a brave heart. One student leader has publicly announced, 'We wish to make it clear to the government that we are tired of sitting without teachers in our classes.' These big-mouthed children don't know anything. They have no idea how hard life is; and if they're not careful, they'll end up in the kitchens and gardens of white homes ... just like us, their mothers and fathers. See how they'll like it then.

As for Mxolisi, I'm not sure we didn't make a mistake, sending him to the bush, last December. But, he was of age. Was old enough. However, since coming back, instead of showing improvement, he has grown lazier than ever. Whatever they removed from him at circumcision, it certainly wasn't laziness or letting his foot hit the road. Although he is always but always the last to get out of bed, Mxolisi is always the first to leave the house. And the way he bullies his brother and the girl, he hardly does any of the chores. Often, unless the others throw it out for him, my husband and I have come back from work only to find the basin in which he washed himself in the morning still

post-colonial + political

burdensome *belastend*

tortoise [ˈtɔːtəs] *Schildkröte*

historical + political

flint grey stone whose sparks are used to start a fire

tinder dry material that burns easily

stark great

bush area of wild land far from civilisation

letting his foot hit the road wandering aimlessly

to bully *tyrannisieren*

chore household task

basin *Schüssel*

to gad about (coll., BE) to go about aimlessly searching for pleasure
blessed (here): damned
daily round daily route
to survey [sə'veɪ] to inspect
to jerk to cause to make a sudden movement
to saunter to walk in a relaxed way
to hail to greet
lithe [laɪð] *geschmeidig*
frame (here): body
many-limbed with many legs or arms
millipede *Tausendfüßler*
to dawdle to take your time doing s.th. or going somewhere
hunched bent forward and raised
to swagger to walk in an extremely proud manner
cohesive forming a united whole
dim dark
pang sudden pain
to stab to push s.th. sharp into s.th.
scholarship *Stipendium*
demeanour [dɪ'mi:nə] (formal) appearance
loath [ləʊθ] (formal) unwilling
to boast to offer what is impressive
zest enthusiasm

holding that dirty water of his. Lazy boy. Forever gadding about. Oh, yes! That is the one thing he is never lazy to do: going from the home of this friend or acquaintance to the home of that one ... on and on and on ... the whole blessed day. Seeing him do his daily rounds, one would be excused in thinking he delivers milk to these houses and gets paid for it.

This day, Mxolisi leaves the house. He stands at the gate and takes a long look at the street. Like a general surveying his armies, up and down the street he looks.

A whistle.

That jerks his head up.

From the corner, a wave of arm.

He waves back and slowly saunters out the gate.

'Yes, *Bajita*!' he hails his friends.

'Ja, *Mjita*!' the others reply in chorus. The group opens up and swallows him. In their midst, he is lost. You couldn't tell him from the others now. Although they are not wearing their school uniform, the clothes they have on are so similar in colour, cut, and the way they hang on their long, lithe and careless frames that the boys appear as though they are wearing a uniform of sorts.

Like a gigantic, many-limbed millipede, the group swells as it moves up NY 1. There is neither haste nor dawdling in the manner in which its numerous feet eat up the distance. Hunched shoulders and uniform long, swaggering strides say much about the common purpose that binds the group together, cements the members into one cohesive whole. By the time it reaches its destination, St Mary Magdalene, corner of NY 2 and NY 3, the group has split into two enormous branches.

Your daughter is in the University cafeteria. She is surrounded by friends. Many friends. Among these friends are three young African women, girls from the townships.

'I guess this is the last time we see you?' one of her black friends asks. Smiling eyes dim as a pang of sadness stabs her heart. Such a kind heart, this friend from overseas. Has she not promised to look into the possibility of scholarships for them? Might be going to the US of A, next year ... if all goes well. A good person. She deserves better than tears. Far better. The very next moment, the girl's demeanour brightens. This is her friend's last day with them. It must not be sad ... she must send her away with good memories: laughter, not tears.

But, 'So, this is goodbye!' says yet another of the girls. The hearts of the young women, your daughter included, are heavy. They're all loath to say goodbye. Your daughter has been a very good friend, full of enthusiasm and eager to learn: the Xhosa language, the African dances, and the ways of the people here. She learnt to appreciate the foods the country boasts ... everything. Not a trace of arrogance in her ... so full of childlike zest. A good person, her friends will say of her, later.

Your daughter knows the problems her friends from the townships face. Also, she would like to extend this moment of saying goodbye to them a little longer. Where they stay, there are no phones and when she says goodbye to them now, it will be for good. Letter writing is so tedious. Moreover, with postal delivery such an iffy affair in the accursed townships, who knows whether they'd ever get any letters were she to write them? The scholarships will have to be arranged through UWC ... only way to keep in touch with the townships gang. She hears herself blurt:

'I'll take you home.' She cannot believe she has said that. 'You will?' asks one of her friends, in disbelief.

'Sure!' answers your daughter, convinced now this is something she should do. 'But I can't stay. I'll just drop you guys off.'

'I don't think so,' says Lumka, another of the Guguletu trio. 'You said you have lots to do still.'

'But taking you to Gugs will only take a few minutes, it's just a detour.'

'No! No! we can take a taxi,' Lumka is adamant. She is uneasy about your daughter, a white person after all, going to the townships at this time of day - late afternoon, when people return from work and wherever else their day had taken them. Earlier, perhaps. But not this late. No, not this late.

'I insist! You cannot refuse me this last wish,' your daughter jokes.

'Okay, then,' Lumka acquiesces. She doesn't want to be a spoilsport. Since the other two girls from Guguletu do not help her in declining the offer, she understands that they want to be driven home. They want to be with this friend, who is leaving them, just a little longer.

Your daughter's generosity has endeared her to many. She knows she should not be doing this ... not with all the packing she still has to do. Packing. And all the innumerable last-minute things she has to see to: call and confirm her flight and transport arrangements to the airport; call the friends she has not been able to see for the last time; disconnect the telephone; pay bills; buy the few outstanding presents (she had no idea how many people back home she counted as friends who should get and were probably expecting her to bring them something from South Africa). Briefly, she wonders what some would say were she to tell them of the less romantic and downright hard, hard life of many of the people about to get the vote in this country? Worse than anything they could possibly imagine ... far worse than she had imagined before coming here. She shakes her head, blocking off that trend of thought. Strides were being made. There was hope. Universal franchise was all but guaranteed.

'Let's go, now!' she says, taking a peek at her inner left-hand wrist.

'Why, thank you,' the three girls say in unison.

A flurry of hugs follows, for most of the people around the table will not be seeing your daughter again. She leaves with the three Guguletu women and another friend, a young man who stays not far

to extend to lengthen
for good permanently
tedious ['ti:diəs] boring
iffy (coll.) unreliable
accursed [ə'kɜ:sɪd] *verflucht*
to blurt to suddenly say
Gugs (slang) Guguletu
detour a somewhat longer route
adamant determined
to acquiesce (formal) to accept s.th. you don't agree with
spoilsport *Spielverderber, -in*
to decline to refuse
generosity *Großzügigkeit*
to endear yourself to s.o. to cause yourself to be beloved by s.o.
innumerable great number of
to confirm *bestätigen*
outstanding (here): not done yet
downright clearly
strides (plural) (here): progress, improvements
universal franchise the right of all adults to vote
peek quick look
wrist *Handgelenk*
flurry sudden burst of activity

from where your daughter stays. He'll ride out of the township with her … the two will ride back to Mowbray together.

reverend title of a church minister

No, my friends,' Reverend Mananga said to the group of students. 'I'm afraid today, the Young Women's *Manyano* is meeting there this afternoon. Always does, Wednesdays.'

'There', was the hall at St Mary Magdalene, the Anglican Church in Guguletu.

'Every Wednesday,' he reiterated.

to reiterate (formal) to repeat

to put s.o. in a quandary to put s.o. in a difficult position

The minister's refusal put the group in a quandary. They'd already been refused the use of the halls in the three local high schools. Even had they forced their way in (something they have successfully done before) this time, they'd have failed. In each school, a police blockade barred them entry to the grounds.

They knew the minister was telling the truth. Most of their mothers belonged to the Women's *Manyano*, which met Thursdays. A few had sisters who belonged to the organization the minister alluded to. But still they tried to reason with him.

to allude to s.th. (formal) to mention in an indirect way

No, the minister said. He could not change the meeting place of the Young Women's *Manyano*. Nor could he change the day or hour of their meeting. It was not up to him to change church programmes and procedures. No, it would not do to let them use the hall for even the half hour there was before the girls' meeting. These boys could be unruly and it took time to arrange the seats and put everything in order once turned upside down.

unruly rowdy, uncontrollable, wild

'Reactionary!' – someone lost in the crowd, hollered. At which the man of God hastily whispered something to Mxolisi's ear, before he beat a retreat.

to beat a retreat to leave quickly to avoid a conflict

rectory building where a church minister lives

'We can meet here, tomorrow morning!' Mxolisi told the group, even as the minister disappeared into the rectory.

There were some half-hearted grumbles, nothing serious. Taking the time of day into account, many agreed that meeting early the next day might be more profitable, in any event.

'Nine o'clock, then?'

'Nine!'

'Nine!' the chime rang.

chime bell

toyi-toyi a protest dance with chants

premises (plural) a piece of land with its buildings

lichenous ['lɪtʃənəs] *mit Flechten*

squatting (fig.) low to the ground

amorphous (formal): shapeless

to splinter to break into thin, sharp pieces

to facilitate to make a process easier

Thereafter, the crowd broke into song: *Siyanqoba*! We overcome! Doing the toyi-toyi, they half- marched, half-danced away from the premises.

A little while later, the song changed to a call and response chant:

Ngubani lo? NguMandela!

Uyintoni? Yinkokheli!

The cry and counter-cry was repeated and the sound swelled and boomed over the low, lichenous roofs of the squatting houses of Guguletu. The amorphous group split into two. To facilitate mobility the amoeba divided itself. Over and over again, it splintered, broke off, as little groups reached their part of the road and branched off, heading in different directions, some going home.

Mxolisi's group toyi-toyied its way along NY 3, towards NY 1. As the vanguard neared NY 1, all at once, it came to an abrupt halt; hit by familiar cacophony: the crackling of hungry tongues of fire, busy devouring a house or a vehicle. The accompanying hoarse-voiced cheering of spectators. The loud thud-thudding of running feet.

Galvanized by the commotion, the group stopped singing. It stopped toyi-toying. And ran, surged forward as though pulled by a gigantic powerful magnet. The forest of stamping feet and airsawing arms hurtled along NY 3 till it came to an abrupt halt; stopped by the all-too-familiar but highly thrilling spectacle.

At the corner of NY 1 and NY 3, a big van was doing a slowmotion dance to the shimmering rhythms of orange and red flames caressing it. On closer look, though, the van was still. The movement, mirage, an optical illusion. Only the eager orange tongues frolicked all around it, licking it, consuming it, making it look as though it were shaking and shivering. Even as the spectators held their breath, eyes popping, the van appeared to sway, teeter and falter drunkenly. Then, trembling still, with a deep crackling sigh, down it went, slowly lowered itself till it fell on its knees as though in prayer. By this time, the front wheels were completely gone while those at the back remained intact. However, a moment later, they too caught flame.

& SONS.

Now and then, swathes of blue and white letters peeped and winked from between the busy, eager tongues of flames. A long silent scream issued from the gaping, savaged doors – two in number; the erstwhile doors someone had wrenched open and through which now thick black smoke belched and intimate tongues caressed, darted and leapt, searching the most hidden corners and crevices of the fallen vehicle; lashing, licking. From the debris all around the furnace, it was obvious that whatever the van had carried had long ago been looted.

'What d'you think this van was delivering?' asked Sazi, a lieutenant in the group.

'Ask the driver,' retorted Lwazi, one of Mxolisi's staunch followers.

Those who heard this laughed. The driver of a delivery van was the first target in these cases of looting and burning. Drivers either fled or stood in grave danger of being fried alive inside their vehicles. The driver of this van, it was clear, had chosen the first option, discretion.

'Probably making a delivery to the TB clinic here,' said another member of the group, flicking his head toward the white building standing not far from the scene. This was the Guguletu Anti-Tuberculosis Clinic.

'They're good about giving us medicine to fight TB,' said Lwazi. 'But not books or good teachers.'

'TB is catching, don't you know that?' asked Sazi. 'The Boers are scared we'll give it to them. Since our mothers work in their houses, if we all get TB, then they will get it too.'

Just then, police sirens sounded.

vanguard *Vorhut*
premises (plural) piece of land together with its buildings
cacophony [kəˈkɒfəni] mixture of loud, unpleasant sounds
to crackle *knistern*
to devour to eat hungrily
hoarse rough and unpleasant
to galvanize to shock
to surge to move with force
to hurtle to rush
to caress to touch gently
to frolick to move about in a happy way
to sway to move from side to side
to teeter to stand unsteadily
to falter to stumble
swathe [sweɪð] large strip
to peep to look quickly
to wink to quickly open and shut an eye
to issue to come forth
gaping wide open
savaged heavily damaged
to wrench open to open with force
to belch to come out in large amounts
crevice crack
lieutenant leader
TB tuberculosis
to flick to move with a quick movement
Boer [bɔː] white South African of Dutch ancestry

Mxolisi's group needed no further warning. The police would shoot first and ask questions later – that is, if they asked any questions at all. To the police, whoever was within sneezing distance of the burning van would be suspect number one.

Fast, the group made itself scarce, leaving behind the crackling of burning metal as the van seemed to melt and all colour disappear. There it stood, a blank-faced shimmering hulk painted gun-metal grey, streaked black by the eager licks of the fiercely intimate flames. '& SONS' too was gone. Had totally disappeared. Vanished from its charred flanks. On closer look, though, it could be seen, blanched like the picture on a photographer's negative.

blank-faced with a surface with nothing on it
hulk gigantic object
streaked *gestreift*
lick (fig.) movement like a tongue
charred burnt and black
flank side
to blanch to make white

The two groups had earlier arranged that those still walking south reconnoitre at the NY 7 Sports Field. That is where what remained of Mxolisi's group headed. As did the remnants of the other group, whose members had fared much better. As it happened, they had also come across a vehicle that had been hijacked. But, in their case, they were able to scavenge from the victim, a meat delivery van.

The groups then held a brief, informal meeting and shared what intelligence they had gathered on their way to this rendezvous. Several members of the second group also shared the prized spoils. Thereafter, the whole once more split, this time, according to which way the members' homes lay.

to reconnoitre (military) to inspect the surrounding area
remnants (plural) remains
to fare to manage, to get on
to scavenge to search through and take
prized spoils valuable goods stolen by thieves or soldiers in a battle won

Some walked south, others pointed their noses eastward. As these splinters went along, they divided and subdivided even further as here and there a few broke away to channel themselves through the by-ways and other insubstantial side streets of Guguletu.

splinter (here) small group
byway small road
insubstantial unimportant

Mxolisi's group, much diminished now, continued southward. Suddenly energized, they went back to the earlier toyi-toyi:

Ngubani lo? *NguMandela!*
Ngubani lo? *NguSobukhwe!*
Baziintoni? *Ziinkokheli!*

Singing and half-marching, half-dancing, they wended their way down in the direction of the Police Station, always an exciting, tantalizing occurrence. Who knew what mood the pigs might be in? There was always the possibility of sporting with them.

to wend your way to move slowly somewhere
tantalizing making you expect that s.th. exciting will happen
pigs (slang) police
to sport with s.th./s.o. to amuse yourself with s.th./s.o.

Your daughter and her four friends reach the car. She opens her door, sidles sideways in, reaches over and opens the passenger doors.

'All aboard?'

The car glides out of the parking space. She manoeuvres it out, turns, levels off and slowly pushes forward.

As she drives out of the campus, a sudden hush falls in the car. This is unrehearsed leave-taking. It was not planned. But each of the five young people in the yellow Mazda silently gazes at the passing scene; taking stock and measure of what it is the eye records; deliberately holding the image, letting it linger long in the mind's eye, tucking it safely away, storing it. For always.

to sidle to move along sideways
to level off to move along a level surface
unrehearsed spontaneous
to take stock and measure of s.th. to closely observe s.th.
to tuck s.th. away to put s.th. in a small space to keep it safe

They reach the highway. A silent letting off, an easing of shoulders, a private, inaudible sigh. For each. Another day is done. Only, for all, this is a marked day. A day with a singular reason. A day that spells closure. Heavy as a prison door.

Mxolisi's group rounds a bend in the road. A sprawling greyish-white building hits the eye.

'*Yekelela! Yekelela, Mjita!* Ease off, brother, ease off!' Lumko, a lanky, solemn-looking young man of Mxolisi's age and one of his mates in the bush, the year just past, cautions.

At once, the fervour of the dance step dies down. So does pitch of song. The warning has dredged rumours of horrific deeds in that building. Unconscious memory takes reign. In the middle of the night, blood-curdling screams have been heard coming from it. Awful things were said to happen to those dragged there by the police. Terrible, terrible things, some, worse than death. Of course, death too happened there. Of course.

There is a slight pause at the lights, a few metres past the Police Station. The group is splitting for the night. The Langa crowd discusses, bus or train? The rest have but their feet to see them home. From this point on, no one lives more than fifteen minutes away, at the very outside.

Of the Langa group, a significant number is left at this corner. They have opted for the bus. Those who are taking the train continue walking with the Guguletu Section 3 crowd, down NY 1 and towards Netreg, the nearest train station at this juncture.

The two groups will split at the next corner.

The yellow Mazda enters Guguletu, over the south bridge near the coloured township of Montana. As the moment of separation approaches, conversation falters. To ward off the awkwardness and threatening tears, the girls break out into song, the mood of the moment giving license:

We have overcome! We have overcome!
We have overcome, today-a-a-aay!
For deep, in our hearts, We did believe
We would overcome, one day!

After two or three rounds, however, the song peters out and the group is silent once more, each person mulling over private thoughts.

Mxolisi's group has reached the point of final separation. One block north of the approaching car, at the corner of NY 1 and NY 109, most of the young people break off and make a left turn. The station lies that way. However, they have hardly walked ten steps when a cry yanks them back to NY 1.

Back they run, the magnet too powerful for their stomachs, hungry for excitement.

letting off reduction of tension
easing relaxation
inaudible cannot be heard
to spell (here): to signify
closure (here): sense of s.th. being concluded
sprawling spreading
to ease off to slow down
lanky tall and thin
mate (coll. BE) close friend
fervour enthusiasm
pitch high tone
to take reign to become dominant
blood-curdling terrifying
at the very outside at the most
to opt for s.th. to decide on s.th.
at this juncture at this point of time
coloured with people of mixed race
to falter (here): to begin to stop
to ward off to prevent from happening
awkwardness *Verlegenheit*
to give license to s.th. to allow, to permit
to peter out to gradually end
to mull over s.th. to ponder over s.th.
to yank to pull with force

swarm (fig.) a large group of people
abuzz (here): full of excitement

to eclipse (here): to completely cover

They reach the corner they'd but so lately left. Down NY 1, to the left, a swarm is abuzz. In its midst, right in the middle of the road, they see what looks like a car. Difficult to tell, the way it is completely surrounded; the swarm growing even as they run towards it. In the tumult, patches of yellow peep and wink; appear, disappear and reappear. Only to blink away again.

The car is small.

The crowd totally eclipsing it is wild and thunderous, chanting and screaming, fists stabbing air. Fists raised towards the blue, unsmiling heavens.

Chapter Three

5.15 pm – Wednesday 25 August 1993

'Mandy!' Mrs Nelson screams.

That is what the white woman I work for calls me: Mandy. She says she can't say my name. Says she can't say any of our native names because of the clicks. My name is Mandisa. MA-NDI-SA. Do you see any click in that?

Anyway, this day, here she comes, her eyes on stalks.' Grab your bag, I'm taking you to the station: she says. Now it is my turn to be astonished. What has come into her head?

'But, Madam,' I say, 'I'm still cooking.' I am not a little surprised, I can tell you. After all, this is Wednesday, a day on which I do not get to leave this place till as late as eight o'clock most times. I cannot imagine what has come over her, for her to tell me I should leave work early. On Wednesday, too. Usually, on this day she makes sure I not only cook and serve dinner but wash the last dessert spoon before I can leave. Be that as it may, I am not complaining, though. In some ways, this is also the best day of my work week.

Wednesday's my *mlungu* woman's 'day off,' if you can imagine that. A woman gets a day off when she never does any work around this house. But I'm not complaining. Indeed, I look forward to her day off almost as much as I welcome mine on Sunday. Wednesday, I can breathe instead of having Mrs Nelson breathing down my neck every minute of the blessed day: Mandy, do this! Mandy, do that! Mandy, come here! Mandy, go there!

However, on Wednesdays, all morning long I am free as air. First, she goes to the gym. She says it's a big hall where everybody jumps up and down so they will not get old or sick or fat. Madam's very scared of getting old. And she thinks she can stop old coming to her. She doesn't know it comes quietly, when she's fast asleep, or when she's busy eating all those *zimuncumuncu* that she likes so much.

She doesn't even take the two girls to school. Mrs Thompson from up the road does that, and brings them back after school. Madam does the same for her on Fridays. I guess that's Mrs Thompson's day off.

Madam tells me that after all that jumping up and down and her running, she gets so hungry she could eat a horse. So what does she do? This person who is so afraid of getting fat? Why, she has breakfast with her best friend, Miss Joan, who never married. Miss Joan is just the same as the no-marry women of the church, the nuns.

But, ag shame, it's so sad about Miss Joan. So sad. Madam told me how Miss Joan's young man got killed in the war of the Boers. On the last day too, the poor thing. So Miss Joan stayed Miss Joan even though all her hair is goat-hair white, like she's put it in Jik or Javel, the stuff you use to bleach your whites snow white. And she has a restaurant all her own. A nice one too, Madam says. Of course, I wouldn't know anything about that. How could I? Unless we work

eyes on stalks *wie Stielaugen*

gym [dʒɪm] (coll.) *Turnhalle*

zimuncumuncu (Xhosa) delicious things

nun *Nonne*

ag (coll.) (South African English) *verdammt*

goat *Ziege*

Jik ™, Javel ™ brands of bleach (*Bleichmittel*)

whites bed sheets and towels

there, we never go to restaurants or hotels or any nice places like that. But the food in Miss Joan's restaurant must be nice. Very good. Look how fat Miss Joan is and look how happily unhappy the food makes my *mlungu* woman.

One day I told her she must get nice and fat like Miss Joan. Madam was so angry she stamped her foot. 'Mandy!' she said, 'I will never get *that* fat!' That is when she told me about the young man Miss Joan was going to marry but who was killed in the war.

After breakfast, Madam and her friends meet and go shopping. They have lunch, and play bridge when they're done with that. That is her day off. She never sees her home that whole long day. That is also where her day off and mine are alike.

By the time she gets home, it is dinner time. 'Wheew!' she will say, throwing herself down on the living-room sofa, 'Am I exhausted!' Always, she comes back exhausted from her day off. Always. Me? I just give a grunt, shrug my shoulders, and go on with the real and exhausting work I have to do. If she wants to see exhausted, she should see me on my day off. Indeed, on my day off, I think I work hardest and longest of all week.

grunt short, low sound in the throat

This Wednesday, however, here is Mrs Nelson butting in with her strange and silly talk of my going home just as I am busy laying the dinner table. Fresh flowers from the garden: 'It makes the house cheerful,' she always says. And a man comes twice a week to do nothing but the garden. It is practice that I put a fresh vase on the dining-room table even if all there is in that vase is leaves.

to butt in to interfere, to intrude

it is practice it is the usual thing

I'm almost done cooking. Dinner is at six sharp, rain or shine. Going to the cupboard for the raisins, I look at the grey-faced clock on the wall and think: Master should be back any minute now. Then Madam will come puffing and huffing, flustered, just before dinner. She's always late from her bridge. Except today.

to puff and huff to breathe heavily

flustered nervous and confused

It is just as I pour out a cup of raisins over the rice in the colander, telling myself that Master will be here any minute now, that the clang-clang! of the gate as Madam's car goes over the iron grate hits my ears. The raisins spill onto the counter. Quickly, I gather up the strays and stuff them in my apron pocket. She hates waste. But did I hear right? Is that her car? I'm quite surprised at this. Both her coming back before Master and the hurry the grate's cry betrays. Ordinarily, she lets the car glide easily over it. Not today. Today, she is positively flying. One would think someone told her the house was on fire. But before I have finished that thought, hasty footsteps beat a staccato on the long woodfloor passage leading to the kitchen. This is another surprise, for I did not hear the car door close. Next thing I know, Mrs Nelson comes sailing into the kitchen. And she does not ask about the children. She always asks about them. Did Mrs Thompson bring them over? Are they all right? Is everything all right? She always asks about the children first – before anything else. Even before she asks about her telephone messages, she asks about the chil-

colander *Sieb*

grate frame of metal bars

strays (plural) loose pieces

apron *Schürze*

to betray *verraten*

to glide to move smoothly

dren or goes to them first. Not today. It is then that I notice that the engine of the car is still running. My, I think, my, she sure is in one big hurry ... she sure is ... not to even turn the car engine off.

Now, no doubt, seeing the look of utter stupefaction that has painted itself on my face at these goings on, Madam nods her head several times and rather vigorously. Then she puffs:

'Trouble in Guguletu, my girl! I think you'd better go.' Even as she is saying that, she is already turning around and making for the door.

'Come!' she says, striding along the passage, her shoes going *klap-klop! klap-klop*! on the wooden floor. 'I'll run you down to the station!'

Now all doubt leaves me. I know there must be big, big trouble, for Madam is not complaining at all. Not about how much food she ate. Or how tired she is. Or all the work I'm leaving her with. On her day off too.

'What trouble, Madam?' My voice sounds strange to my ears. Too high. Squeaky. My mouth is bone dry. But she is calling out to the children. 'Hey, Gang!' she shouts. She does not wait for their reply or appearance, however, but scoots to the car.

In a matter of minutes, she has bundled me into the kombi. 'Tell your father I've taken Mandy to the station,' she yells as she reverses the car down the driveway, over the grate, out of the gate. I hope the children heard her.

It is a grim-faced woman sitting behind the wheel. I watch her: a small marble is playing hide and seek along her jawline. I've never seen Madam quite like this. She is upset each time something happens in Guguletu. And these days, something is always happening in Guguletu. Or in Langa. Or Nyanga. Since the schoolchildren started boycotting classes, way back in '76, when the riots in Soweto came down to Cape Town. August of '76.

Madam is not taking me to Guguletu, the township where I live. She never takes me to Guguletu. White people are not allowed to go there. We reach the bus terminus near the station and find pandemonium king.

The queues were gigantic columns of ants disturbed into disarray. In a frenzy, people pushed and shoved, trying every which way to make their way into the buses. The very activity revealed a desperation, a deep distrust on the part of those waiting on the bus lines. They did not believe they would be adequately served. Or served timeously. Or served at all. The queue was a messy affair, not unlike the intestines of a pig that children are roasting over an open fire: jumbled and confused and everywhere all at once. Snatches of conversations conveyed the same anxiety and restlessness. The woman next to whom I was standing, a tall, large woman, black-skinned and small-eyed, yellow turban on her head, turned to me and, slowly shaking her head, volunteered, '*Bekuse kukudala kakade!* Two whole weeks with no trouble in Guguletu.'

my (here): *Meine Güte!*
utter complete
stupefaction surprise or shock
to nod to move up and down
vigorously energetically
to puff to speak with short, quick breaths
squeaky with a high, short sound
to scoot to go in a hurry
kombi (South African English) van for transporting people
marble *Glasperle*
jawline *Kieferpartie*
terminus last station
pandemonium chaos
ant *Ameise*
disarray state of confusion
in a frenzy in a state of wild confusion
timeously (South African English) timely
intestines (plural) *Eingeweide*
jumbled mixed in an untidy way
snatch short part
to convey to reveal, to show
to volunteer (here): to tell s.o. s.th. without being asked

news bulletin news report
to plop to fall like s.th. falling into water
to propel to force
to scuff to rub
unmatched not of the same pair
ankle *Fußknöchel*
to scour to rub with s.th. rough
Lion Lager a brand of beer
matted wet and dirty
roughened no longer smooth
threadbare old and thin from use
volition (formal) ability to decide on s.th.
to bump to continuously hit s.th. while moving along
stint period of time working somewhere
to staple *befestigen*
casing skin covering
minced meat *Hackfleisch*
piecemeal bit by bit
ensconced comfortable and safe
to stagger to walk unsteadily almost falling
to scowl to look at s.o. angrily
circulation (here): movement
to protrude to stick out
sundry various

'What has happened, now?' I returned, fishing for information. She might know more than I did, which was next to nothing. Madam's 'Something's happened in Guguletu!' was hardly a news bulletin.

'I don't know,' the woman said and added that people getting off the Guguletu buses, who'd just come from there, said the schoolchildren were rioting.

So, what's new? The thought plopped itself into my mind. Haven't we lived with these children's riots since '76? What are they rioting for now? I was not a little upset. And angry. More angry than upset, if truth be known. These tyrants our children have become, power crazed, at the drop of a hat, they make these often absurd demands on us, their parents.

No Going to Work!
No School!
Stay Away from the Grocery Shops!
Don't drink white man's liquor!
Don't buy red meat!

I, for one, have had it up to here, with all this nonsense.

Pressed and pushed from all sides, I allowed the crowd to propel me forward, my feet hardly touching the ground. As I rode on tight-packed bodies, the feet scuffed unknown and unmatched ankles. Hands grabbed others' elbows and dug into unfriendly shoulders. They were scoured by sweaty beards smelling of Lion Lager beer, greasy and matted hair, the roughened surfaces of threadbare coats. They were cold-slimed by the unwiped noses of little children on the backs of mothers. Thus did I slide my way forward. Passed along from bodies to bodies, with no volition or direction on my part. On and on I went, floating and bumping my way forward and nearer and nearer to the bus. Inch by bumpy inch. I clutched my bag tight against my bosom. Hugged it as though it were a new-born babe. Or a lover newly returned from a long stint in the gold mines of Johannesburg. If, in the pandemonium, the bag should fall, I might as well kiss it goodbye.

Finally, I gained the bus. Was hurtled, headlong, onto the doorway. With my right hand, I grabbed the pole at the door for support, my bag flat against my chest still, the left arm securely stapling it there.

The long narrow passage between the two rows of seats had become a tube, a giant sausage casing and we, minced meat, stuffed piecemeal down it. Shoved to the back. Shoved against the knees and elbows sticking out of those who, miraculously, had managed to find themselves ensconced in seats. Down the passage we staggered the best we could. We definitely were no smooth stuffing: lumpy, irritable, hard-edged and scowling at one another. A distinctly uneasy mix.

Everywhere but everywhere, something takes up room, fills the gaps, arrests all circulation. Elbows, far flung from their bodies, heads that appear similarly grotesquely dislocated, tired and torn plastic bags from which protrude and spill sundry items of groceries: hard-edged bars of soap, bottles of cooking oil, packets of candles that are now broken and caking and flaking and crumbling so that the thin white wick in the middle is revealed dangling, limp and lifeless, packets of beans and stamped mealies rain out and onto the floor. On the rare occasion I can move a foot, the shoe scrunches on granules on the floor of the bus. Sugar? No, bigger. Samp? Can't be, much smoother. Amazing how much one can tell ... just from feeling the surface of things beneath one's be-shod foot. Clever they are, aren't they? The feet, I mean. Never knew they could tell me so much. Never realized so much could be conveyed in this manner.

Mxolisi's eggs! My heart sank. In the flurry of my leaving, I'd clean forgotten my promise of the morning. Just as well. Where would these eggs be in this mess?

The packed bus groans under the weight of all these sweaty bodies.

'They say Guguletu is completely surrounded ... Saracens everywhere!' The bus driver yells above the din of discordant voices. Does he really hope to be heard? But he is persistent and, indeed, soon gets results. There is a lull in the buzz and many faces strain in his direction.

'When did all this start?' asks a faceless man in that crowd.

'When we left, just now,' says the driver, 'the police were at every entrance in Guguletu ... Big trouble there, I tell you.'

The driver's words brought back madam's '... trouble in Guguletu, my girl.' Trouble is, there is always trouble in Guguletu ... of one kind or another ... since the government uprooted us from all over: all around Cape Town's locations, suburbs, and other of its environs, and dumped us on the arid, windswept, sandy Flats. My first impressions of the place are still vivid in my mind, etched inside my eyelids, fresh today as they were all those many years ago when I was still but a child, not even ten ... No big, smiling sign welcomes the stranger to Guguletu. I guess even accomplished liars do have some limits. This place is like a tin of sardines but the people who built it for us called it Guguletu, Our Pride. The people who live in 'Our Pride' call it Gugulabo – Their Pride. Who would have any *gugu* about a place like this?

It was early morning when my family got here, early in 1968. How my eyes were assaulted by the pandemonium. People choking the morning streets. People everywhere you looked. Stray dogs. Peddlers. Children roaming the streets aimlessly even in that early hour. And then the forest of houses. A grey, unending mass of squatting structures. Ugly. Impersonal. Cold to the eye. Most with their doors closed. Afraid.

Guguletu is both big and small. The place sprawls as far as eye can see. It is vast. That jumps right at you when you see Guguletu for the first time. All that space. But even as you look you suddenly realize that it will be hard for you to find any place where you can put your foot down. Congested.

As far as eye can see. Hundreds and hundreds of houses. Rows and rows, ceaselessly breathing on each other. Tiny houses huddled close together. Leaning against each other, pushing at each other. Sad small

to cake to harden into a mass
to flake to fall off in small, thin pieces
to crumble to break into small pieces
wick *Docht*
to dangle to hang loosely
limp loose, not stiff
mealie maize
to scrunch to make a loud sound when walking on s.th.
granule small, hard piece of s.th.
samp crushed maize seeds
be-shod (literary) wearing shoes
flurry excitement
clean (coll.) completely
Saracen Armoured (*gepanzert*) Personnel Carrier
din loud, unpleasant noise
discordant unpleasant sounding
persistent *hartnäckig*
lull quiet period
to strain (here): to move with effort
environs surrounding area
to dump to get rid of and leave somewhere
arid very dry
Flats the Cape Flats area south-east of central Cape Town
to etch to clearly print
accomplished skilled
to assault to attack
to choke (here): to completely fill
stray homeless
peddler *Hausierer*
squatting low and broad
to sprawl to spread in an untidy way
congested overcrowded

houses crowned with gray and flat unsmiling roofs. Low as though trained never to dream high dreams. Oppressed by all that surrounds them ... by all that is stuffed into them ... by the very manner of their conception. And, in turn, pressing down hard on those whom, shameless pretence stated, they were to protect and shelter.

The streets are narrow, debris-filled, full of gullies alive with flies, mosquitoes, and sundry vermin thriving in the pools of stagnant water that are about the only thing that never dries up and never vanishes in Guguletu. From morning till night, ragged-clothed children wade these pools, playing in them, muddying each other, dredging them for precious treasure, the toys of the children of the streets: bottles, cans, the pits and peels of fruit and vegetable, scraps of food and anything else they can lay their hands on. For most, this is their only school, their playground.

From the very first days in this place, how different everything appeared. Different from how we had been in Blouvlei, how we had done things in that beloved place we called home. Here, everything changed. It was not as if people didn't try. But how can one welcome a neighbour and show her the ways of a place when one is also new there? That was part of the problem: this throwing together of so many, many people, all at once, into a new place. All of them new in the place. All of them still grieving, yearning for the places they were forced to leave. All of them with no heart for the new place, having left their hearts in their erstwhile homes: Blouvlei; Vrygrond; Addersvlei; Windermere; Simonstown; Steenberg; District Six; as well as many pockets of real suburbs, where predominantly white people lived. From now on, only white people would live in those places, places from which Africans and Coloureds and Indians had been driven off. The government had decided that residential areas would be segregated, strictly so, and by law. Nonetheless, people tried to follow the rules by which they had lived before coming to this place. At least, in the beginning they did. It was hard though.

When we arrived here, it was to find that not enough houses had been built. Many families had to put up shacks on the white, white sand that said the sea had withdrawn from this area only yesterday. Bleak. Unable to hold down anything, not even wild grass. In no uncertain terms, the coarse, unfriendly sand told us nothing would ever grow in such a place. It would take a hundred years of people living on it to ground the sand and trample some life into it so that it would support plant and animal.

My family was among the many, many unfortunates, people from whose shacks nothing could be salvaged. At the first touch of hammer, our shack had simply disintegrated, just turned to rubble. Unusable rubble which the trucks of the government continued to flatten like so many birds' nests torn off bough and flung down by a tornado.

You will eat what I eat and sleep where I sleep, so say our people, making the stranger feel he is never burdensome to the family. Saddest of all was Vuyo's mother, Sis' Lulu. On the day of the move

conception planning
pretence false claim
debris ['deɪbri] rubbish left somewhere
vermin rats, insects
stagnant not moving
ragged-clothed with old and torn clothes
to wade to walk through water
to dredge (here): to remove mud and stones from the bottom
peel skin
scrap small piece
to grieve to feel sad about s.th.
to yearn for to long for
Blouvlei, etc. communities in and around Cape Town
Indians (here): people originally from India and their descendants
bleak *öde*
coarse rough
to ground (here): to fix
to disintegrate to fall apart
rubble broken pieces of a building
bough (formal) branch
burdensome *belastend*

she had given birth to twins and her husband was away, at sea. Sis' Lulu's little family had to be split as she had nowhere to stay. I was very happy that Mama took her son, Vuyo, to stay with us. It was like having a little brother. Tat' uNonjayikhali, who had neither wife nor children, agreed to give his bed up for Sis' Lulu and the little twin boys, so she stayed in his shack. Meanwhile, her furniture and other things she didn't need as a matter of urgency, were divided among several people, all her former neighbours. They would keep them for her till she could build her own shack or she got a Council house, whichever came first.

And where were people supposed to build those shacks for themselves? Where?

Here, said the government pointing to the periphery of the new concrete township, where in its building, the Council workers had dumped refuse and surplus matter. Here, it said, put up your shacks and wait in them until more houses have been built for you.

The authorities had underestimated the numbers of Africans in Cape Town and the resulting housing shortage aggravated an already untenable situation. Of course, the government was not paying for the folly of its miscalculation. That, and the hope of an early escape ensured that the hastily-built shacks would be even more rickety than those we had left ... forced to leave. Who would invest his hard-earned wages in the building of a shack the government would soon force him to tear down?

Thus did my family, alongside thousands of families from Blouvlei as well as other parts of Cape Town, find its lot far from improved in the wake of the government's 'Slum Clearance' project. Were we not still living in shacks? Moreover, where before we had been members of solid, well-knit communities, now we were amongst strangers, people we did not know from a bar of soap.

However, in the eyes of the government the problem belonged squarely on the shoulders of the African. There were just too many Natives, said the government. How was that its fault?

To add to the hardship of living in shacks, a vicious, gale-force wind blew ceaselessly through the area. By day, it whipped sand till it bit into skin on face, arms and legs; got into hair, into eyes, into food, into the clothes on the line, into each and every nook in house or shack. By night, it howled and wailed and shrieked like the despairing voices of lost souls. In fact, some said what we heard of nights were the voices of Malay slaves lost in a ship wrecked hereabouts, when the area was still all sea.

Whatever it was, the relentless wind blew the sand everywhere. Day and night, it blew. We swept and swept and swept, but still the sand would not leave us alone. We shared our fragile homes with it. Every day. A reminder of how we had been swept into this howling place against our will. Yes ... much against our will.

No sooner had we settled in, so to speak, than a new problem cropped up when schools reopened, late that September.

as a matter of urgency as s.th. absolutely necessary
Council house house provided by the local government (Council)
periphery outer edge
to underestimate *unterschätzen*
to aggravate to make even worse
untenable indefensible
folly stupidity
rickety likely to fall apart
lot situation
in the wake of resulting from
well-knit closely tied together
squarely completely
vicious violent
gale-force extremely strong
ceaselessly never stopping
nook corner
to howl *heulen*
to wail *jammern*
to shriek to scream
relentless ceaseless
fragile *gebrechlich*
to crop up to unexpectedly appear

to boast to feature, to have
to entail to require
to assign (here): to send to a particular place to work
to reign *herrschen*
to flock to move in great numbers
rejection *Absage*
to exceed to be greater than a certain amount
to designate *zuweisen*
to see fit to consider to be suitable
mercifully luckily
to sneak s.o. in to secretly get s.o. in
to trust (here): to hope
to enroll to register
to relieve *erleichtern*
turn of events how everything concluded
rude awakening unpleasant surprise
bewildered confused
hither and thither (literary) *hin und her*
to strew, strewed, strewn to scatter
chaff *Spreu*
winnower a person or machine that blows air through grain to remove the chaff
blessing *Segnung*

Blouvlei had boasted but one school. Guguletu had, at least, a dozen. In Blouvlei, registering a child for school had always only entailed taking that child by the hand to school, come opening day. Here, our inexperienced mothers assumed that their children would automatically go to whichever school the teachers from their old school had been assigned. And perhaps this should have been so, had the Department of Bantu Education, under which those teachers served, had a system. At the best of times that department was run in a chaotic manner and these were not the best of times. The influx of thousands of families into Guguletu would have been problematic to the most systematic of organizations. No one had ever accused the Department of Bantu Education of being that.

Pandemonium reigned on schools opening day. Blouvlei mothers flocked to Vuyani Higher Primary School and Songeze Lower Primary School. And that was because most of the teachers from Blouvlei had been assigned to those two schools.

When they were met with rejection, the teachers there saying they had already exceeded the number permissible under government regulation, the mothers were alarmed. They out and out panicked, when they were turned away by teachers they did not know, teachers with strange names from other parts of Cape Town. Blouvlei residents had assumed they would be able to keep their community, more or less, intact. It was a shock to them to find that, while it was true for most, not all their teachers were in these two schools, in their minds designated for Blouvlei children. Indeed, there were teachers from Blouvlei who had been taken to other schools, as the Department saw fit.

From school to school our parents went, roaming the streets of Guguletu, looking for schools on streets they'd never before set foot. From school to school, only to be given the same unwelcome news: *kugcwele kwesi sikolo* – It is full in this school.

Mercifully, because both Khaya and I were such good students, our teachers sneaked us in, trusting that, as things settled, some of those enrolled would fall away. Mama was greatly relieved at the turn of events and that my brother and I were able to be in the same school, and with our teachers, at Vuyani.

However, when I came to school the next day, a rude awakening awaited me. Very few of the children from Blouvlei were in my new school. None of them, in my class. As none of my friends lived anywhere near where we lived, I had lost all my friends. My new school, ten times bigger than the school in Blouvlei, had hundreds of children more, none of whom I knew. I was completely bewildered. Lost. In that sea of strange faces, I was alone. I did not belong. Hither and thither, a gale-force wind had strewn us, chaff at the hands of a mad winnower.

Mama did not want to hear any moaning about my not having friends at school.

'Count your blessings,' she said. 'Do you know how many children would just love to change places with you?'

Change places with me? Change places with me? I'd have done anything to change places with them.

Mama's lack of sympathy only added to my misery. I hated school and envied those children she pitied. What had they done to be that lucky? To me, the prospect of loafing the rest of the year away was quite appealing. What I didn't know then, of course, was that some of those children would never go back to school again. Others who, like Khaya and me, were lucky enough to gain admission to a school, soon found the newness too much and played truant. From this group too, there were those who would gradually drift away from school ... and eventually leave for good.

To this day, there are not enough schools or teachers in Guguletu to accommodate all the children. You heard me talk about Operation Barcelona, just now. There never has been enough of anything in our schools. Therefore, many of the children, even today, do not go to school. There are not enough mothers during the day to force the children to go to school and stay there for the whole day. The mothers are at work. Or they are drunk. Defeated by life. Dead. We die young, these days. In the times of our grandmothers and their grandmothers before them, African people lived to see their great-great-grandchildren. Today, one is lucky to see a grandchild. Unless, of course, it is a grandchild whose arrival is an abomination - the children our children are getting before we even suspect they have come of child-bearing age.

Good things are scarce in Guguletu. The place boasts not tree, nor flower, nor animal – except the mangy, discarded and ownerless dogs that roam the length and breadth of the township by day and by night, upsetting refuse bins as they forage for scraps of food. But those too are hard to come by. There is no harder luck for a dog than to be a stray in a place of poor people. What is such a dog to benefit, when the people themselves gnaw and chew bones to powder, suck in the last bit of juice therefrom before spitting out the useless pulpy matter? What can its desperate scavenging ever yield the poor mutt?

I know that for years my heart yearned for Blouvlei. Mama Mandila's *vetkoek*. The Storm Breakers, our rugby team, and the games Khaya took me to watch. Tata Mapheka's *isityhwentywe*. My dear friends with whom I played *ikula*, jump rope, and *poppie huis*. For years, I mourned the loss of my friends and erstwhile playmates with whom I went swimming in the dam on hot summer days, and with whom I shared gossip in the shelter of the corners of our homes on frosty winter evenings. My heart bled for myself and what I'd lost, and for all those millions that had lost their homes. All those lives rudely disrupted, mercilessly plucked from hearth and the familiar. That sea of shacks forever silenced. To this day, I still remember how we laughed when the rumour of mass removals first circulated among us. The rumour that came softly, whispered with stark-naked disbelief, taken as the ravings of a man not altogether there, lightly dismissed.

to loaf to spend your time doing nothing
to gain admission to be admitted
to play truant to stay away from school without permission
to accommodate to provide enough places
abomination s.th. that causes hatred and disgust
child-bearing age old enough to get pregnant
mangy having a skin disease
to discard to get rid of s.th. no longer wanted
to forage to search for food
stray (here): homeless dog
to benefit to be useful
to gnaw [nɔː] to continuously chew
pulpy soft and wet
to yield to provide
vetkoek (Afrikaans) small cakes fried in fat
poppie huis (Afrikaans) doll house
to mourn to feel sadness
dam (here): small artificial pool
mercilessly *gnadenlos*
to pluck to pull
hearth [hɑːθ] (literary) home
rumour *Gerücht*
stark-naked (here): completely naked
ravings (plural) *Hirngespinste*
not altogether there (coll.) mad

to dismiss *abtun*
incredulity doubt
scope *Rahmen*
strain (here): type
ruthlessness *Rücksichtslosigkeit*
forlorn miserable
bereft sad because of loss
aggrieved distressed
no pretence no attempt to impress
no fooling nothing done to make you believe s.th. is true
whim sudden impulse
means money available
to worship to go to church
confounded confused
to perish to be destroyed
drabness cheerlessness
harsh brutal, cruel
allocation act of granting s.th. to s.o.
to dwell to live
to lacerate (fig.) to rip through
to penetrate to go through with force
boesman (Afrikaans) ethnic group related to the Xhosa
Bellville suburb of Cape Town
to apportion to divide, to share blame or responsibility for s.th. bad
gravelly harshly
to scold *ausschimpfen*

Yet, even today we still laugh sad laughs, remembering our innocent incredulity. Our inability to imagine certain forms of evil, the scope and depth of some strains of ruthlessness. We laugh, to hide the gaping hole where our hearts used to be. Guguletu killed us ... killed the thing that held us together ... made us human. Yet, we still laugh.

We left Blouvlei in tears, forlorn and bereft in our loss. We were aggrieved anew when we came to Guguletu, for worse awaited us here. Blouvlei was an honest-to-goodness tin shacks place. No pretence. No fooling. Guguletu would have you think it is a housing development, civilized, better – because of being made of concrete, complete with glass windows. But we lived in Blouvlei because we wanted to live there. Those were shacks we had built ourselves, with our own hands ... built them where we wanted them, with each put together according to the wishes, whims and means of its owner. The people there, a well-knit community. Knowing each other: knowing all the children, knowing whose wife a woman was, knowing where each man worked, where he worshipped, what drink he preferred.

We came here and were confronted and confounded by all these terrible conditions: the loss of our friends, the distances our parents had to travel to and from work, the high fares we had to pay going to and from places with decent food shopping. And then there was the deadening uniformity of Guguletu houses. Had it not been for the strength of the human spirit, we would all have perished. The very houses – an unrelieved monotony of drabness; harsh and uncaring in the manner of allocation, administration and maintenance – could not but kill the soul of those who inhabited them. For some, though, the aridity was to be further aggravated: for some reason, the small, inadequate, ugly concrete houses seemed to loosen ties among those who dwelled in them.

'Save your fighting strength for the township!' An anonymous voice lacerates the silence in the bus.' There is real fighting there, today,' it flings out.

'Who's fighting?' asks another, also unknown and unknowable in that jungle of bodies. The exchange penetrates the fog. My ears antennae, I come up for air.

'Appears there was a fight. The schoolchildren beat up the students from the university ... this one of the *boesmans*, in Bellville.' I cannot figure out what the man is telling me. Why would the schoolchildren fight with coloured university students? Where was the connection?

A heated debate follows, people apportioning blame as presents from loving grandparents.

'It's not like that at all,' shrilled one voice. A young man this time, from the sound of it.

'What's not like that?' asks a woman's voice. Gravelly. She must be the mother of many children, I tell myself. Whole day long, she has to scold them and now her voice has grown like that. Like the sound of the words her mouth must throw out many, many times each day.'

Are you telling us the driver's lying? He's just come from Guguletu, why should he lie to us?' Gravel-voice has gone shrill as though she were excited or angry or both.

'I'm not saying he's lying,' the young man replied. 'But I was there ... I saw what happened.'

The whole bus stopped breathing. Heads turned. Hands holding on to the supporting rods fell or were replaced as people readjusted their bodies the better to see the source of the knowledgeable voice.

'*Khawutsho*! We are all ears,' several voices said at once. Then another silence fell. A hush.

'The trouble is in Section 3,' ventured the young man. 'A car carrying UWC students was stoned, overturned and set alight.'

'Who did the stoning?' Gravel-voice was back.

'I didn't take down their names,' the youth threw back.

'*Awu*!' the woman ejaculated. 'Today's children have no respect at all for their elders,' she said, clearly fishing for sympathy from the other passengers, where adults were the vast majority. 'Such insolence!' she finished, to accompanying communal clucking of tongues and sucking of teeth. But that was as much support as she got.

'Where, in Section 3?' an old man's slow, high-pitched voice asks. Good question. My breath held back, I listen. My ears were burning. Rivulets ran in the palms of my hands. Section 3. That's the part of Guguletu in which I live.

'Right by the garage near the bridge going out of the township,' replied the young man. Instead of easing my anxiety, the answer plunged me deeper into the hell of uncertainty. The description fitted two bridges. Did he know what he was talking about? Which of the two? Which bridge? Which? My mind turns to my children. Did they go to school, today? No. Were they home? All three? I was particularly worried about the boys, especially Mxolisi. He is the one who seems always to forget to get back from his wanderings before their father returns from work. What does he want, roaming the streets of Guguletu by day and by night? This is what Dwadwa often asks me. Asks me, as though I go around Guguletu with the boy. But then, I know that is his way of telling me I spoil him. Don't ask me where everybody gets that idea from.

We round a bend.

A building, granite-grey and forbidding, looks back unblinkingly. Stern. Silent. To the front, several sinister-looking vehicles stand. They remind one of some of the frightening movies we used to see when we were children. Grotesque. Humongous. Reminiscent of a cross between a farm-fattened pig and a bed bug – if such a thing existed. Only huge ... a thousand times larger than any hog could ever hope to be. Enormous. Appearing without legs, wheels, or other means of locomotion. Saracens. Deadly, bullet-spitting contraptions. The menacing building before which the Saracens stand is the Guguletu Police Station.

to venture to say in spite of possible criticism
to set alight to set on fire
to ejaculate (here): to say excitedly
vast very great
insolence lack of respect
communal collective
to cluck to make a sound with your tongue to show you disapprove of s.th.
rivulet (here): very small stream of sweat
to plunge to cause to fall quickly
to spoil *verwöhnen*
unblinkingly (here): in a manner showing no expression
sinister suggesting s.th. evil
humongous (coll.) enormous
reminiscent of reminding you of
contraption strange device
menacing threatening

Dear God, I pray, let my children be safe. Keep them safe, all of them ... but especially Mxolisi. Immediately the thought leaves my control, as soon as it manifests itself, I catch my breath. No, I love them all ... all three of them. My children. A niggling doubt persists till I ask myself whether, indeed, I loved him more or whether I was paying, compensating for the earlier rejection. But, quickly, I ask myself, Is that what that was? Rejection? My heart hastens to say NO. Bewilderment. Anger. Resentment even ... But not rejection. Never any bad feeling towards him, directly. No.

'Last stop!' bellowed the driver.

'What do you mean?' some of the passengers demand. The driver doesn't immediately answer. His Walkie-Talkie is crackling. He listens then barks back, 'Roger!' Then turns his head around, 'Didn't you hear me?' he yells, 'I said to get off this bus! Are you people deaf?'

At that, a muffled grumble rises from the passengers. 'What about refunding our fare?'

'Refunding? What refunding?' answers the driver crossly. 'I bring you here all the way from Claremont and now you want your money back?'

'Well, we still have to walk the rest of the way, past the train station, some of us. I live in NY 132, that's a long walk from here and I'll have to take a taxi.'

'Ask these children of yours who have nothing better to do than start trouble to give you your money back,' the driver retorts. 'Now, go on! Get a move on and get off my bus! I have work to do.' From the roar of the engine, the driver has plastered his foot firmly on the accelerator, virtually flattening the latter to the floor.

Not a cloud in sight. The tight-stretched blue dome above looks down pityingly as the sun boasts, 'Buy me if you can!' - knowing full well that not all the gold that has yet to be mined in the world can do that. Low down in the far west, where the sky reaches down to kiss the earth, furious reds and golden yellows mingle and marry and striate the horizon, eye-blinding spectacle. The breath of approaching evening brushes softly against my cheek as I step off the bus. However, as soon as my feet hit the ground, it is as though I have walked into a cave or a gigantic pot. The crowd engulfs and swallows me whole. I can hardly breathe. But I am nearly there, I console myself ... I am nearly home.

Poor people. My house is a stone's throw away from the police station so I am not unduly worried. However, a few steps after I get off the bus, I find I cannot take one step without putting my foot on a policeman. They are like ants on a saucer of raspberry jam.

In that jungle, careless and uncaring bodies milling around, pushing and shoving, my thoughts did a three-hundred-and-sixty degrees turn-around. I froze. The proximity of my house, a source of delight

to manifest itself to appear
niggling not going away
to persist to still continue
to bellow to yell
Walkie-Talkie *Funkgerät*
roger (radio communication) 'Understood!'
muffled *gedämpft*
to refund *zurückerstatten*
crossly angrily
to retort to quickly reply to a comment
to plaster (here): to push down heavily
accelerator *Gaspedal*
to boast *prahlen*
to mingle to mix
to striate to mark with lines
to engulf *umringen*
to console yourself to comfort yourself
unduly excessively
raspberry *Himbeere*
to mill around *herumlungern*
proximity (formal) nearness

a minute before, had become a curse, cause for great concern. With the swiftness of laser, fear zapped the anticipated pleasure of not having much distance to walk. In place of that consoling thought, now cold and naked fear coiled, gnawing at the very strings of my heart. Where was my daughter? In the midst of all this havoc, this bedlam, where was Siziwe?

The safety of girl children has become a burning issue in Guguletu and all places like Guguletu. Every day, one hears of rapes. Rapes, not a rape. Rapes. Which means that, each day, more than one woman or girl or child is accosted. Each day. In this place. Surely, the crowd, if anything, heightened the chances that such an evil thing could happen. Happen for that reason. The mere gathering of so many people at the same time and place can precipitate inexplicable evil ... unleash latent demons. That could happen. Happen right here, where so many mindless people thronged. Crowds are mindless. Walking heads where all thought is suspended. They are to be feared.

My mouth, bone dry; heart pounding, the folds beneath my arms crawl with ants. Tiny, tiny ants. Lord, up above – I found myself doing something I had not known I still remembered. Please, Good Lord, keep her safe. Protect my baby and keep her safe!

Then swiftly, to more practical, more feasible sources of help my mind turned, dumping the celestial. Oh, I only hope her brothers are home with her. Preferably both. But if I had to choose between the two, I'd go with Mxolisi. Lunga is a bit on the soft side. Gentle. Although, when provoked, he can be just as efficient in a fight as his older brother. But for the job of scaring the unsavoury off, I'd pick Mxolisi. Any day of the week. He is a pit bull where Lunga is a Dalmation.

A thin, hard and very sharp elbow dug into the soft unboned part of my side between the rib cage and hip bone. Hot flashes erupted and rapidly radiated in a jumble of tiny, wrinkly, wavy lines of fire. I tripped on a body prone on the ground. Dead? I didn't wait to see. I couldn't look down as, even as I stumbled, my leg buckling on hitting the unexpected obstacle, the wave of harried humanity behind me pushed. Then suddenly, concrete. Hard on naked foot. Hard, grazing the now-naked sole. Cold. Shocked, my mind takes in the fact that my left foot is bare. How had I lost the shoe? There was no time to ponder the mystery. Can't look for the shoe right now. Can't. Didn't remember it saying goodbye. I pushed. I shoved. Stupid rabble. More of them should be on the ground to allow me passage to my home. So near. So near, without their blocking my way I would have been home by now. Oh, I hated each and every person in that crowd. Right then, I loathed the stupid, mindless hodge-podge of unthinking, unfeeling, stupid riffraff with all my might. Hated them. Bitterly. 'Move!' I screamed. At the top of whatever remained of my lungs. My lungs, bursting as though I were in a furnace, forced to breath in and out although I knew perfectly well that the air had been oven baked. But

curse *Fluch*
to coil to wind into tight circles
to gnaw to keep chewing
havoc destruction
bedlam noisy and confused place
to accost to approach and attack sexually
to precipitate *auslösen*
to unleash to let loose
to throng to gather in large numbers
to suspend to cause to stop
fold *Falte*
feasible likely to succeed
celestial (ironic) heavenly
unsavoury sickening, repulsive
pit bull *Kampfhund*
rib cage *Brustkorb*
to erupt to burst forth
to radiate to spread out from a centre
wrinkly with folds
prone lying face down
to stumble to trip
to buckle to bend
harried agitated
to graze to break the skin by scraping
to ponder to think about s.th.
rabble mob
hodge-podge jumbled mixture
riffraff rabble
furnace *Heizung*

push I did. I had to get out before I was trampled to my death by the brainless throng.

scores a great number
morrow (literary) the next day

People forget who they are when surrounded by scores of faces they do not know, eyes that do not recognize them and would not know them in the morrow, mouths that have never said their names. There is a comforting anonymity, a freeing facelessness, when one finds oneself surrounded by strangers. Such people have no connection to one's past or future, and the present is a fleeting blur, never to be remembered.

fleeting blur (here): brief, vague event

apprehension anxiety
to swamp to overwhelm
to ford to cross
stubborn *stur*

Apprehension swamped me, giving me the strength of an ox. Blindly, I fought my way, pushing and shoving and screaming for people to get out of my way. Fording a mighty river would have been easier. Scared people are like blind-starving donkeys – stupid and stubborn.

In what felt like a year but was, in all probability, perhaps just a few minutes, ten at most, I finally came within shouting distance of my house. Siziwe, my youngest and the only girl, was standing at the door when I eventually got there.

'Where are your brothers?' I said as I reached the gate.

Chapter Four

7.30 pm

'Where are your brothers?' again I asked, for I had received no answer from Siziwe, who was standing at the door, looking at me as though she had seen a ghost. I know I looked a sorry sight, but right then, all I wanted was the knowledge, the certainty, that all three of my children were home. That they were all right. That nothing had happened to them. They were safe. I know that earlier, if anyone had asked me, I would have said my concern was for her, for Siziwe. A girl-child, she is more vulnerable than the other two children. However, now that I had seen her, seen that she was in no immediate danger, my secret worry resurfaced, variegated and magnified a thousand fold. Anxiety over the safety of the other two assailed me. But, deep down my heart, I knew I was more worried about Mxolisi. Perhaps it is because we were all alone, the two of us, all those years after his father deserted us. Or, it could be the unusual way in which he came to this world that has created this bond between us that is unlike any other ... certainly unlike what I feel about my other two children ... I really don't know. And sometimes, I don't even know whether the whole thing isn't knitted and sewn in my imagination.

'Where are they?'

My daughter shrugged her shoulders. 'Lunga is here; she said, 'but where *bhuti* Mxolisi is; there was a slight pause. Then, raising her shoulders up to her ears, she said, 'Who can say?' With a careless shrug, she dropped the shoulders back to their accustomed place. This display of lack of concern for Mxolisi irritated me. She should care. Mxolisi, I knew ... I was certain ... would care very much were she the one who was not at home and whose whereabouts we could not account for at a time like this. He would be worried about her safety.

'When last did you see him?'

Siziwe gave me such a look as would be hard to describe. A disquieting look. A cheeky look? But then again, an I'm-sorry-for-you-look: Brow raised, ever so slightly. Cheeks mounded, just a little. Lips stretched sideways, carelessly, as though she were not aware she had done this. The overall effect was that the eyes, instead of widening because of the raised eyebrows, were narrowed. Baleful. Then, with calm deliberateness, slowly, ever so slowly, she turned away. Turned away and went inside even as I walked up the *stoep* toward her.

What was that all about? I wondered. Wasn't that just the welcome I needed? Here I had worried myself sick about her, and what do I get for welcome? How does my daughter receive me? A sour face. Yesterday's custard left outside the fridge.

'I asked you a question,' I yelled after the receding back.

'Mama?' I wasn't fooled by the tone of innocence. I'd seen that sinister look. Moreover, I was quite sure Siziwe had heard me the first time. I repeated my question nonetheless. By this time I was inside

vulnerable ['vʌlnərəbl] weak and easily hurt
variegated (formal) in many different forms
fold times
to assail (here): to severely upset
to knit *stricken*
to sew *nähen*
bhuti (Xhosa) brother
to account for to explain
disquieting upsetting
cheeky (coll., BE) *frech*
mounded rounded
baleful (literary) threatening
deliberateness careful consideration
stoep (Afrikaans) raised veranda
custard *Vanillepudding*
to recede to move gradually away

the house, in the dining-room. She stood in the middle of the kitchen, looking at me. Gone, however, the look that had so unsettled me a minute ago – the incongruous marriage of haughty indifference and naked pity that had sat on her brow.

'Mama,' she said, her tone much subdued, softer and without the brashness of a few seconds ago, 'I have not seen him, today.' Abruptly, she turned around, wrenched the back door open and left. I was a little puzzled by the brusqueness of her exit. What could be the matter with her? I wondered as I made for my bedroom.

What is eating Siziwe? again I asked myself as I kicked the remaining shoe right off my foot. Fancy that, I thought, she never even noticed that I was limping ... never noticed that I am walking without one shoe. How could she have missed such an obvious thing? Here I brave a veritable war, concerned for her safety, and she doesn't even ask me what happened to my other shoe? I don't believe she missed seeing that I was bedraggled, dishevelled, and totally worn out. Rattled by all the turmoil I'd been through.

What bothered me more than that, though, was her attitude, her nonchalance and lack of concern for Mxolisi, who loved her so much. That is the trouble with womb siblings, it's not blood and blood that binds them but blood and water. Besides, both Siziwe and Lunga often accuse me of favouring Mxolisi because I will let him do things I forbid them. But he is older than them. Is that my fault? I also knew that were the positions reversed, were it Mxolisi who was home, he would go in search of whoever was missing, his sister or brother ... more so his sister.

incongruous not fitting together
haughty arrogant
subdued quiet, sad
brashness aggressive behavior
to eat (here): to bother
to limp *hinken*
to brave to confront
veritable real
bedraggled wet and untidy
disheveled unkempt
to rattle to make anxious
turmoil confusion
nonchalance *Gleichgültigkeit*
womb [wu:m] *Gebärmutter*
sibling brother or sister

7.45 pm

Bang! Bang! Fists pound on the back door. Could only be Skonana, my next-door neighbour. What does she want? Must have been lying in wait for me, watched me behind her new seethrough curtains.

'*Ndiyeza, Mmelwane*! I'll be right there, neighbour!' I had just put my bag down and kicked off the offending shoe but had not rid myself of the light spring jacket I wear when the South Easter's a little too crisp for comfort. I reached under the bed and pulled my *veldskoene*, the old leather slippers Mrs Nelson had given me for Christmas five years ago. I liked shuffling in them around the house.

'Yes!' I called out as I stepped out of the bedroom. Skonana had started banging the door again. '*Ndiyeza*! - Coming!' I shouted.

Lunga was either asleep or reading a book. The house could burn down before that one noticed the fire, his eyes were forever buried in something he was reading. Or, exhausted from all that reading, he'd be snoring away, still in his seat, his head to the side, lolling against his shoulder.

I shambled out of the bedroom, past the dining-room and into the kitchen. The door was slightly ajar. Skonana, leaning over the barbed

offending (here): annoying
South Easter strong south-east wind
crisp (here): cold
veldskoen (Afrikaans) light, leather shoe
to shuffle to walk without lifting your feet
to snore *schnarchen*
to loll to hang
to shamble to shuffle
ajar open

wire fence that separates the two houses, saw me as I emerged from the dining room.

'*Malo, Mmelwane*! Hello, Neighbour!' I said as I opened the door wider and stepped outside.

'Mama *ka*Siziwe,' she shouted, totally skipping the customary greeting. 'But what happened to you?' She did not give me time to answer her question before saying, 'I see you're limping. And whatever did you do with your other shoe?' Does the woman have eyes even at the back of her head? Trust her to notice each and everything that happens to me ... or to the children ... or to Dwadwa. I swear she sees even when she is fast asleep.

'Forgive me for not letting you rest over a cup of tea first,' she said. And while I was still groping for a response, deciding which of her questions to answer first, she continued, 'but I ... '

'That's nothing,' I said, knowing there was no escape. She would not rest till her hunger for knowing had been fed. 'I lost my shoe getting off the bus,' I lied. 'Now, you know what happens when anyone walks bare foot on these streets, on which people break bottles every day. I stepped on a bottle neck.'

'Oh, no!'

'Ag!' I said, 'Don't let's worry about that shoe. It was an old thing anyway.' I looked her straight in the eye. 'But, tell me,' I said, 'what has been happening here? What have you people been doing to our lovely township while we were busy sweating at work?'

'My Sister,' she shook her head.

'What is it?' I said, painting on my face a look that said I was duly sobered by her solemnity.

'*Sukuhlekisa ngathi, sizigugele*, Don't mock us, we are old,' Skonana said. 'Have our children not killed a *mlungu* woman?'

'One?'

'You don't think killing ONE white woman is enough bad news for the whole of Guguletu?'

'No! No! No!' hastily, I said. 'I'm only saying that because, on the bus we heard so many conflicting stories.' I did not reveal the figure I'd heard on the bus. It would only compound the confusion if my information was inaccurate. But my neighbour's words brought some relief ... not much, but definitely some ... more than I had had reason to hope. That thin shaft led to a fluttering, then an awakening, a resurgence. Was it not possible? Perhaps only one person had died. Perhaps no one had died. Serious injury, perhaps ... even that would be something.

Rude reality pulled me back to the here. 'I don't know what you've heard,' Skonana was saying. 'But Mzonke, my cousin who's a policeman, told me himself that a white woman was killed here in Guguletu, today. A young woman, he said.'

Guguletu is a violent place. Every day one hears of someone who was killed ... or nearly killed. Often more than one. Every day – rape, robbery, armed assault and other, more subtle forms of violence. Ev-

Mama kaSiziwe (Xhosa) Siziwe's mother
to skip (here): to leave out
to grope to search with difficulty
duly quite
to sober to make s.o. behave in a serious manner
solemnity seriousness
figure number
to compound to make even worse
thin shaft (*Schacht*) (fig.) small bit of hope
resurgence rising to new life
assault crime of using physical violence
subtle ['sʌtl] not obvious

ery day. Guns are as common as marbles were when we were growing up. But, a white woman? To kill a *mlungu* woman? Where would we sleep? What would the police do to us?

The police are not our friends. They are to this day worse than ineffectual. Here in Guguletu we do not like the police. They are an endless source of irritation, at best. At worst, a presence we dread, an affliction. We know that many innocent people have died in their hands. Their blood-stained hands. Died. Killed by the police. With impunity they killed our people in the past. Therefore the perpetrators of evil, those who have made crime a career, live in the benign atmosphere cultivated by that corruption. As warm wet dirt breeds maggots ... so have criminals thrived. Sheltered by the police who conducted deeds even worse than theirs. Thus, crime thrives. But killing a white woman was quite another thing. Quite another thing.

Young and old alike, men and women, no one is exempt from the scourge. Violence is rife. It has become a way of life. When a husband leaves for work of a morning, there is no guarantee he'll safely find his way back home come night. Nor is there such casual certainty about children going to school. Between drunk drivers of stolen cars, the police, *tsotsies* and those who kill those with whom they do not see eye to eye in matters political – safety has become quite, quite fragile.

I woke up as from a deep sleep. But the nightmare would not leave me alone. It was there in my neighbour's eyes. It was not going to leave me alone. Real and tangible as the fingers on my hand.

'What is the matter with our people? Don't they know the police will pull this township apart? Is it not enough we kill each other as though the other is an animal and one is preparing a feast? Is that not evil enough? A white woman? Are people mad? Have they lost their minds?' My voice was shrill to my own ears and I saw that my hands shook. Indeed, my whole body was trembling.

'It's schoolchildren who did that,' said my neighbour.

I gasped, memories of the debate on the bus returning to haunt me. Words I'd taken not quite seriously, now wore a ghastly sinister shade of meaning.

'Who else would do such a mad thing?'

I thought I detected a note of gloating in her voice. Skonana has no children and somehow manages to make that seem such a virtue. 'I have no children and no worries', is her favourite saying, whenever any one of us complains of some misdeed one of our offspring has sprung on us. Skonana seems to equate child with problem. Mind you, looking at what scraps our children do get into these days, she could have a point. But I wasn't going to be the one to tell her that.

'Murderers are countless as the trees of a forest in this Guguletu of ours,' I told her. 'Most of them, I'd say, are well over thirty and do not attend any school.' I was fed up with her and wanted to go back into the house. Close the door to her face and go about my own business – change into something comfortable, which is what I was doing in

to dread to greatly fear
affliction cause of pain and suffering
with impunity without fear of punishment
perpetrator person who does s.th. evil
benign [bɪˈnaɪn] favourable
to breed, bred, bred to produce, to generate
maggot *Made*
to thrive to flourish
to shelter to protect
exempt not affected by
scourge cause of trouble and suffering
of a morning (S Afr E) in the morning
rife widespread
casual (here): slightest
tsotsies (Xhosa) criminals, thugs
tangible having real substance
to gasp *die Luft einziehen*
to haunt to keep coming back to your mind
ghastly awful
sinister shade (fig.) evil aspect
to detect to notice
to gloat to display happiness about s.o.'s misfortune
virtue *Tugend*
misdeed misconduct, wrongdoing
offspring children
to spring on s.o. (coll.) to do s.th. that is an unpleasant surprise
to equate to regard as the same
scrap (coll.) fight
countless too many to be counted

the first place before she called me out, the meddlesome gossip. But I was also curious as to what, exactly, had happened. Skonana is a very busy, very successful Shebeen Queen and a useful source of information about the goings on in the township during the day. My curiosity got the better of me.

'On the bus, people were saying that cars were stoned here in Section 3?'

'What Section 3?' she asked, her brows shooting up and writing semi-circles. What was she going to say happened to bring this pandemonium to our street? How account for the masses mobbing our very gates? We have no market anywhere near this street. And the Saracens. What were all those Saracens doing at the Police Station? Taking a vacation?

'The thing happened right here on our street!' my neighbour said conspiratorially. 'Right here, on this same NY 1.' Each word rolled off her tongue as a bullet from a gun: bang! bang! bang! bang! 'Over there,' she said, pointing toward the bridge further down NY 1, in a southerly direction.

At that, I gave her a sharp look that asked a thousand questions. She nodded her head, eyes widened knowingly.

'Oh, no!' Now I understood. Her negative was irony, to emphasize the positive. Leave the rest of Section 3 out of it, she was saying. Only our thin slice of it is affected this time.

'Ja!' again she nodded her head. 'And it wasn't even one settler, one bullet, my friend.' How could a person die from the car she's in being stoned? Terrible visions of necklacing flared before my eyes. Oh, no! No! Not that! Dear God, not that!

'What happened? How ... ?' I couldn't finish the sentence. Couldn't come out and say out loud – how did the children kill this woman? as though I were talking about the slaughter of a chicken. Wringing its neck. *Nkq*! Done.

'Knife,' she said quietly. Her right fist, thumb up, plunged into the cupped palm of the left hand, making a noise softer than that produced by two hands clapping against each other. Softer and duller than a smack or fist hitting hand. Harder, though. A thunk, lacking sharpness but heavy as hell. 'They stabbed her.'

meddlesome always interfering
gossip *Tratschbase*
Shebeen Queen (coll. South Africa) person who runs a place where illegal alcoholic drinks are sold
to mob to gather in large numbers
conspiratorially in a manner suggesting s.o. is fully informed about a secret plan
to flare (here): to explode
to wring to twist
to plunge to move quickly downwards
dull not intense, not sharp
smack the act of hitting s.o./s.th. with the open hand
thunk dull sound
to stab to push a sharp instrument such as a knife into s.o.

Chapter Five

My stomach turned. Skonana's eyes softened. 'Come over, let me put the kettle on.' I shook my head, closed my eyes for a moment, took a deep breath and said, 'I've had quite a time getting here, I can tell you that. Let me lie down for a while.' For some inexplicable reason, I felt weepy, like bawling my head off. My knees were giving notice of their intent to give up the duty of carrying me, of holding me upright. They were trembling and felt weak and wobbly as though someone had spun me round and round and then abruptly let go of me.

'Thanks, *Mmelwane*,' I said, my voice feathery, barely above a whisper. 'Why don't we have our tea on Sunday, when I'll be off?' Not waiting for her reply, I dragged myself back into the house. My head was reeling.

Guguletu? Who would choose to come to this accursed, God-forsaken place? This is what I want to know – what I can't begin to comprehend. I keep asking myself the same question, over and over again. What was she doing here, your daughter? What made her come to this, of all places? Not an army of mad elephants would drag me here, if I were her.

As for myself, I came to Guguletu borne by a whirlwind ... perched on a precarious leaf balking a tornado ... a violent scattering of black people, a dispersal of the government's making. So great was the upheaval, more than three decades later, my people are still reeling from it.

It was on a Friday that the rumour of removals first surfaced in Blouvlei. Although we went to school five days a week, on no day were my nine-year-old feet as light as on Friday to take me there. They were lighter still bringing me back. Things happened on Friday. Good things. Lovely things. Delicious things. Everything seemed expanded and carefree, the parents relaxed and more generous than on any other day.

Sure, there were more chores to do on Fridays, from early morning till late at night. But there was more play-time too, mother sending Khaya and me up and down the location: 'Get me *skaapkop* from Mandaba! Get me *isityhwentywe* from Mapheka! Go to Mavuthengatshi's shop and get me some sugar. Better still, she would send us to the shops over by the Main Road, where cars and buses zoomed up and down the busy streets that were tarred and where *abelungu* lived in their big, lovely houses with electric lights. When that happened, we were likely to be given a cent or even a whole five cents to spend as we pleased. With all the toing and froing of a Friday, Mama was not as particular as on other days about keeping time. She didn't notice when I went in or out of the house. And that was just fine with me, for then I could play outside as much as Khaya did ... play outside and not come inside till well into the night.

to put the kettle on *Wasser aufsetzen*
weepy about to cry
to bawl your head off to cry loudly
wobbly shaky
to drag yourself to move with great effort
to reel to spin
accursed damned
to drag (here): to pull s.th. heavy
to bear, bore, borne (here): to carry
perched resting
precarious likely to break or fall
to balk to oppose successfully
scattering movement in many directions
dispersal the process of being spread over a large area
upheaval strong, sudden, violent disturbance
to reel (here): to stagger under the shock of s.th.
skaapkop (Afrikaans) head of sheep
abelungu (Xhosa) white people
toing and froing going from one place to another

Mama worked half day, so she was always home when Khaya and I returned from school. This Friday, I hadn't even taken off my gym dress when she urged me:

'Run to Mandila's and get me a ten cent's *vetkoekies*. Here,' she said, fishing out money out of her overall pocket.

'Put the kettle on first, and run!'

I knew what that meant. She wanted me back before the water boiled. That was a test that I hadn't dawdled on the road. I ran out of the house, across the field of scraggy grass, past the little dam fringed with a thin crop of straggling reeds and *oonongobozana*, so delicious to the taste. This day, however, I completely ignored the fare. On the other side of the dam, beckoned Mama Mandila's little *pondok*, where could be found the best, the most scrumptious, cookies in all Blouvlei.

Even before I reached her door, the warm, tangy smell of *vetkoek* frying hit me. My mouth watered and I swallowed several times. Swallowed, although there was nothing but good, fat hope in my mouth.

Inside the house, Mama Mandila sat on a little wooden bunk. Next to her, on the floor, a big pan, silver shiny as new, sat plonk on a Primus stove that purred softly, stirring the pond of oil in the pan. Like ships on choppy seas, golden-brown peaked-shaped balls bobbed cheerfully in the turbulent oil. Now and then, Mama Mandila deftly turned one of these over with a fork, making the oil leap up and sizzle and gurgle, singing itself hoarse.

At the sight of the *vetkoek*, the watering inside my mouth become quite unruly, the swallowing noisy. I could hardly get the words out of my mouth. 'Ten cent's worth, please, Mama Mandila.'

Mama Mandila not only gave me the ten *vetkoekies* my ten cents bought, but an extra one just for me. An extra one she did not put with the others in the brown bag but handed directly to me.

'Here's one for my little good customer!' she said, smiling.

'Thank you, Mama,' I said, brown bag at my feet, freeing my hands to cup in humble acceptance. Those days, it was the height of rudeness for a child to take from an adult. A child accepted, with both hands cupped, when given anything by anyone older.

Good intentions are one thing, a warm, soft *vetkoek* in one's hand, just begging to be swallowed, quite another. The water had not only boiled by the time I reached home but Mama, pouring out her second cup of tea, was waiting impatiently for her *vetkoek*.

'Ah, I see,' she said, looking at the tell-tale oily hands. 'I hope my *vetkoeks* are still as hot,' she added as she put two on a small plate. 'Good,' she said, munching on a *vetkoek* and chasing it down with her tea. 'Good!' her eyes closed, she nodded. I could see that she was enjoying Mama Mandila's *vetkoek*.

'Don't tell me you want another one?' Mama teased, looking at me with one eye, the corresponding eyebrow raised.

'Yes, Mama,' I said, hoping I was right that she was only teasing me. I would not have put it past Mama to turn around and tell me one

vetkoekies (Afrikaans) small cakes fried in fat
to dawdle to walk slowly on purpose
scraggy thin and unhealthy looking
fringed having along the edge
crop growth
straggling spread irregularly
reeds *Schilfgras*
fare (old-fashioned) food
pondok (Malaysian) hut
to beckon (here): to attract
scrumptious (coll.) delicious
tangy refreshing, fresh
bunk narrow bed fixed to the wall
plonk (coll.) squarely
Primus stove™ small portable cooker
to purr to make a low, continuous sound
to stir to cause a liquid to move about
choppy with small waves
peaked shaped pointed at the top
to bob to move up and down
deftly skillfully
to sizzle the make the sound of food frying
hoarse (here): to the point of no longer being able to sing
unruly rebellious
humble respectful
rudeness *Unhöflichkeit*
to beg to ask earnestly
tell-tale revealing s.th. that is expected to be hidden
to munch to chew steadily
to tease *necken*
corresponding matching
to put it past s.o. to not be surprised about a person's reaction

vetkoek was enough for me, with supper coming shortly. 'Yes, I'd like one very much, if I may,' I told her in my sweetest voice.

After tea, it was back to the endless Friday chores. Fortunately, Mama made sure that most of these were done in the morning. After she'd seen to it that the house was tidied up in readiness for Friday's business, Mama soaked the laundry while I strained and bottled the ginger beer, which was the family business.

to soak to leave in water for a while
laundry [ˈlɔːndri] dirty clothes, sheets, towels, etc.
to strain to pour through a sieve (*Sieb*)
ginger beer *Ingwerbier*
to rinse to remove the soap with clear water
to scrub to clean by rubbing

Now, refreshed, we went out to attack the laundry. Mama did the washing while I rinsed the clothes and hung them up. When we were done, I took the used soapy water and scrubbed the floor. Then it was time for Mama's last cup of tea before the workers came home.

Early that evening, as was usual during the summer, a group of men, money in their pockets because Friday was Pay Day, came to cool themselves and wash away the cares of the work week with Mama's ginger beer. I helped her serve them and then went off to play.

'Mandisa!' Mama called out a while later.

'Mama,' I answered, galloping back into the house. I prayed that whatever she wanted me for, would take so little time that I'd be able to go out to play again.

'Get the empties from outside and put two bottles out for Nonjayikhali,' said Mama. 'He's already paid for them,' she added.

I grabbed two bottles from the forest of ginger-beer bottles under the table flush against the wall on which stood our pail of water, the Primus stove on which Mama cooked, and a few other sundries besides, and hurried outside.

flush right next to
sundries (plural) various other items

'Here, Tata,' I said, putting the bottles in front of Tat'uNonjayikhali, right between his feet planted on the gray-black sand.

'*Enkosi, Ntomb'am*, Thank you, My Daughter,' he said, giving me a whole five cents piece. Tat'uNonjayikhali was easily the most generous of Mama's customers. All the children in Blouvlei knew how warm-handed he was and were eager that he send them to the shop, especially Fridays.

Thus encouraged in my duties, I proceeded to gather the empty bottles scattered around the semi-circle of men and took them inside. This brought me endless praise from the mostly beoveralled workers, lunch pails beside them. I would keep a very good house when I grew up, they said, making me beam from ear to ear, as the compliments soaked through to the marrow in my bones.

to beam to smile broadly
to soak through (here): to enter
marrow *Knochenmark*

Tat'uNonjayikhali left, his bottles of ginger beer, heads together, held firmly in the grip of one hand. The other men grumbled playfully that he was leaving them dry-throated, going away with their drink.

'You all have people to make you tea, in your homes,' he replied laughingly. 'This is my tea.'

A moment later, as I was going back out, the hot clapping of hands beckoning, calling me to the game of *ikula*, I overheard Tat'uSikhwebu say:

'*Urhulumente, bonk'abantw'abamnyama kule ngingqi yeKapa, uza kubofudusela eNyanga*. The Government is going to move all Africans in the Cape Town area to Nyanga!'

'Wha-aat! What are you saying?' said several voices, all at once. 'How can such a thing be true?'

'I heard this from someone we all trust,' Tat' uSikhwebu replied.

'Ah,' said one of men, ' lies! lies! lies! All lies, if you ask me,' I recognized the voice of Bhelekazi's father, a neighbour.

'You're right, Bhele,' said Rhadudu, also a neighbour. 'Nothing like that can ever happen.' He sounded quite convinced of what he said. He sounded quite convincing too. Then everybody started shouting. The voices were so many and so loud I couldn't make out what was being said. I decided to go about my business; besides, the game of *ikula* was calling me outside.

In any event, even had I continued listening, I would have gained but little. At that time, the words that were being thrown about, words that generated the heated debate, to me, merely registered as fantastic. To my bent-on-play mind, they were in the same category as all the other unfathomable mysteries of the adult world, like taxes, *tikoloshes*, gold in the mines and God in Heaven - nothing which had anything to do with me.

However, a few days later, I heard the same rumour from other children. And one day, I even heard Tata, who seldom concerned himself with location talk, say something about it to Mama.

When I told Khaya about the rumour that we were going to be moved to Nyanga, he replied that he knew all about that. He bragged he even knew who had started the rumor: 'The unreliable Tat' uNonjayikhali,' he sneered.

'It's all over the location,' brows raised, eyes half closed with a haughty knowing, he whispered.

Everybody knew Tat'uNonjayikhali was not reliable. He didn't even have a wife, to say nothing of children. Who could trust such a man? The people of Blouvlei would be crazy to do so, according to Khaya, the wise.

Others, though, said the rumour was based on some truth and, although Nonjayikhali might have stretched that truth here and there, it was nonetheless still the truth. This group claimed he'd heard about this at his job, the big Post Office in Cape Town, where he worked. He'd mentioned it to his good friend, Tat'uSikhwebu, who'd whispered it to the ear of Mavuthengatshi, the store owner, who told his brother, the preacher, who passed it on to his son, the principal. From the principal, the rumor grew fast. Like wild fire, it spread. From person to person it went, with each embellishing it, stamping it with detailed individual whims and fears. Like the rollings of the dung beetle, merely passing it along carried within itself the mechanism for its own augmentation and it grew until it became the hoarse roar of a river greedily drinking down the first rains after a long, hard-hitting drought.

to gain (here): to obtain more useful information
to generate to cause
to register (here): to be considered
bent-on-play only interested in playing
unfathomable incomprehensible
to brag *angeben*
to sneer to smile in a nasty manner
principal headmaster
to embellish to add interesting details
whim sudden, fanciful idea
rollings of a dung beetle *(Mistkäfer)* the roll of dung *(Mist, Dünger)* that a dung beetle pushes before it
augmentation (formal) increase
greedily *gierig*
drought [draʊt] long period of little or no rain

The government is going to move all Africans to Nyanga.

All? To the last one? Our parents laughed. Obviously, the government didn't know what it was talking about.

For several weeks thereafter, this was the favorite topic of the men who sat outside our house, evenings and weekends. As we were not the only family selling ginger beer, others selling even stronger fare, the scene outside my home was, in all probability, replicated over and over again, throughout the location. In similar scenarios or variations thereof – one thing all had in common, was people refuting the unpalatable.

On upturned empty four-gallon paraffin tins, on the grimy dirt outside the houses, drinking ginger beer or beer and smoking their pipes, our fathers bared their teeth, stabbed the sand with long strong jets of tobacco spit, black-brown as tar, and shook their heads. Each little group of men – sitting as the horns of a bull, a friendly formation to lock the conversation within the breast – shared common, all too familiar, tales of the weeklong ordeal at the places of their harness.

Our mothers, to or from the communal water-tap that served the whole sprawling location, drums and big tins of water on their heads, clapped their hands and took them to chin and hip in gesture of incredulous amazement. Splotches of water from the buckets darkened uproariously giggling shoulders and stained the shawls wound around their waists like peplums. There were so many of us in Blouvlei, the tin-shack location where I grew up. Millions and millions. Where would the government start? Who could believe such a thing?

The sea of tin shacks lying lazily in the flats, surrounded by gentle white hills, sandy hills dotted with scrub, gave us (all of us, parents and children alike) such a fantastic sense of security we could not conceive of its ever ceasing to exist. Thus, convinced of the inviolability offered by our tremendous numbers, the size of our settlement, the belief that our dwelling places, our homes, and our burial places were sacred, we laughed at the absurdity of the rumour.

'The afterbirths of our children are deep in this ground. So are the foreskins of our boys and the bleached bones of our long dead,' Grandfather Mxube, the location elder, told Mama one day, when they were discussing, once again, this very same question of forced removals. Blouvlei was going nowhere, he said. 'Going nowhere,' he reiterated, right fist beating hard against palm of the other hand.

How his words reassured me. This was home, they said. Home. Always had been. Always would be. HOME.

After a while, the whole move rumour thing became more of a joke than anything else. Our parents laughed at the absurdity of the rumour of the removal of Africans, all Africans, to a common area set aside only for them. A corral.

But the government was not laughing. The government never showed its smiling teeth when dealing with any matter in connection with Africans.

to replicate to copy
scenario sequence of events
to refute to deny
unpalatable (fig.) unpleasant
paraffin oil for heat or light
grimy ['graɪmi] thick
to bare your teeth to show your teeth

ordeal very unpleasant experience
harness (normally): *Geschirr* (here): hard and monotonous job
tap *Wasserhahn*
incredulous not willing to believe
splotch large spot
uproariously noisily
to stain to leave a mark that is difficult to remove
to wind, wound, wound *wickeln*
peplum a kind of decoration with many folds – It is attached to the waist.
flats (plural) area of low, flat land
to dot to spread thinly over an area
scrub small bushes
inviolability *Unantastbarkeit*

to reiterate (formal) to repeat

The year rolled on. I forgot the rumour. Or it paled … like the memory of a nightmare in the bold, unlying, evidence-inducing sun of day. The rumour paled, in time, it was all but forgotten. Forgotten, I dare say, by everybody, including Tat' uNonjayikhali, who had brought it to the location, in the first place. If such was true.

Then one day, the rumour, all grown and bearded, armed with the stamp of the government, returned. It was not smiling. Like its authors, it had learnt to bury its sense of humour when dealing with the African problem.

The day was a Sunday. Sunday afternoon, I still remember. Tata, Mama, Khaya and I had been to church. Upon return, as usual, I helped Mama cook. The family sat down to the highlight of the week, the special Sunday lunch: meat and rice. With potatoes, carrots and cabbage. Sunday. The only day of the week we ever saw meat … and vegetable, instead of *umngqusho* or *stamp-enstoot*, as our broken-corn-with-bean meal was sometimes called. As usual, my brother had escaped as soon as we'd finished eating. I washed the dishes and while the grownups, dozing, chatted, made good my escape.

Up the hill and down the other side, and there I found my friends, who were overjoyed to see me. They'd been waiting forever for my appearance. My brother and I were among a small group of children in Blouvlei cursed with parents who not only went to church but had the hardened hearts to insist on their children going too. Not content with that form of torture, my parents put other impediments between us and carefree play: homework and the setting sun. Mama and Tata seemed to have no idea whatsoever that the Sunday sun was stingy as a young widow with a dozen little children to feed. So even as we played, now and then I threw anxious glances at the vicinity of my home. It was no accident that my friends and I chose to play on yonder side of the hill. If we played on the side nearer home, Mama seemed to think I was begging to be called home for the most insignificant reasons. She would come out of the house, stand by the door, and holler in her loudest voice, calling me back home so that I could do my homework, make her tea or, indeed, for no reason at all except that the sun was setting.

Within minutes of my joining my friends, the play my arrival had interrupted resumed. Dress skirts stuffed in bloomers to avoid their getting soiled or tearing, we ran up and down the hill, chasing galloping goats and squealing pigs, chasing stubborn, bleating sheep. We picked wild berries from the thorny *intlokotshane* bushes and scratchy-leafed *ibhosisi* vines, built sand castles, played hide and seek among overgrown evergreen thickets. We were completely absorbed in our play; giving it our best because, with the sun going home, our friends feared Mama's voice would soon be calling me home, hauling me there long before the group was ready for the ordeal of separation. Khaya, because he was a boy, didn't suffer from restrictions as I did.

to pale (here): to slowly be forgotten
evidence-inducing causing you to believe the truth of s.th.
cabbage *Kohl*
to make good your escape to successfully escape
to be cursed with s.th. to be affected by s.th. bad
impediment (formal) obstacle, hinderness
stingy unwilling to spend or give
widow *Witwe*
vicinity surrounding area
yonder side other side
to resume to start again
bloomers (coll.) long, loose trousers
to soil to make dirty
to squeal *quietschen*
stubborn *stur*
to bleat *blöken*
intlokotshane (Xhosa) *searsia discolor*
ibhosisi (Xhosa) purple gorse, a plant with edible berries
thicket group of bushes growing close together
to haul to drag, to draw
restriction *Beschränkung*

deafening extremely loud
roar loud, deep sound
to persist in doing s.th. to continue to do s.th. in spite of difficulties
to sprout to suddenly flow out
serpent (literary) snake
capping eyes protecting the eyes from the sun
to strike dumb to cause to momentarily not be able to speak
to smite, smote, smote (literary) to greatly affect
to plummet to fall suddenly
to recoil *zurückschrecken*
to throw up *sich erbrechen*
to emit to send out
harum-scarum (old-fashioned) wildly and carelessly
to steal away to leave secretly
to loath to do s.th. to do s.th. unwillingly
to gasp to take quick, deep breaths
sprint short period of running
blot spot
to disintegrate (fig.) to break apart
wobbly shaky

Suddenly, a deafening roar overhead stopped us in our tracks. All sense of play fled, heads jerked up, eyes pulled to the furiously bleeding sky.

An aeroplane. Flying so low, my friends and I could see the people in it. See their pink-pink skins and the colours of the clothes they wore ... see too the dark glasses hiding their coloured eyes.

The phenomenon was that unusual, we forgot the ritual:

Eropleyni!
'Zundiphathel' iorenji!
'Zundiphathel' ipesika!

Don't ask me why we persisted in asking the aeroplanes for these goodies when the silly things were either deaf or stingier than Ntshangase. Not one of us had ever been rewarded for all our efforts. On this day, however, the manner of its appearance, so close to the ground, so close to us, put this wonder on the same level as the burning bush, the water-sprouting rock and talking serpents of the Bible. It completely stole our tongues. Indeed, the phenomenon was so unusual, the noise so loud, that it hauled even the adults out of the houses and jolted those drinking beer outside onto their feet, heads upturned, hands capping eyes, open-mouthed staring skyward.

Then, where a moment before, we'd been struck dumb, now a new concern smote us and restored our voices.

'*Uza kuwa! Uza kuwa*!' Wide-eyed with fear, we cried out. So did some of the grownups, especially the mothers. But through it all, our eyes stayed glued to the very sight that sent our hearts plummeting to our stomachs. Even as we recoiled from the horror, we felt compelled to watch ... to look on ... witness: Why was the man bending forward, out of the door or window of the aeroplane? 'He's going to fall!' we screamed. 'He will fall!'

But the man did not fall out. Instead, the aeroplane threw up. It emitted a big, fluttering white cloud.

'*Bhasopha! Bhasopha!*' Harum-scarum, we scattered, running as fast as our legs could carry us. 'Watch out! Watch out!' we hollered, fleeing for the safety of our homes, the same from which we'd but so lately stolen away, the same to which we were so loath to return, just moments before. Even as we ran for safety, the frightened voices of our mothers rang out, calling us children home.

Gasping more from fright than the unexpected sprint, we cleared the danger zone. Eyes once more turned to sky. Despite the noise still ringing in our ears, the aeroplane was already a small blot way over there. The cloud it had left behind was even then still disintegrating. Even as we looked, the cloud revealed itself as thin, flat birds, learning to fly. Wobbly, most did not make it, and came drifting down to earth. As some fluttered gently off and away, most spiralled downward and ever downward until, carried by the soft and playful waves and currents of the air, they'd danced their way to the very sand on which we'd been playing. Soon, the sand was carpeted with the flat birds that could not fly ... or had lost their inborn fearfulness to come nest-ing on the dun-colored surface that was dimpled, pitted and pimpled with our footsteps, moats and castles. There they lay, as silent as the plane that had brought them had been noisy.

In little clusters in front of our homes, children and parents huddled together as against a foe. Our eyes raked the sky. But whether the tiny black speck on the far horizon was our plane or a large bird returning home for the night, we couldn't say.

Meanwhile, the strange birds the plane had birthed lay there, all over the place, right in front of our eyes. A few brave souls, mostly boys, ventured forth. Cautiously, they approached the birds. Here and there, some of the birds fluttered and hopped at their approach and made as though they would take off ... but instead hovered a heartbeat or two into the air, just above the ground, and then fluttering still, fluttering, settled back on the sand, a few centimetres or so from where they had been before.

Greatly encouraged by the realization that all the birds wanted was a place of rest, that they meant us no harm, a few more from our numbers stepped out of the safety of our homes.

'It's only paper!' shouted Lumko, one of the bigger boys. 'Look! Look!' he said, holding up several loose leaflets. 'Look! It's paper, that's all!' In a frenzy, willy-nilly, he grabbed an armful more of the papers.

At that, we all scrambled back to our abandoned playfield and scooped up armfuls of the 'birds', now that we knew they would not bite, would not strangle or knife us.

'*Saphani, sibone! Saphani, sibone*! Bring that here and let us see! Here, let us see!' screamed some of the parents. A trace of fear still laced their voices.

But even as the parents called the children to bring them the silent birds the plane had dropped, the demeanour of the older children abruptly sobered. For long moments, they stared at the paper. Looked at it ... pushed their faces right close to it, earnestly examining it as though it were the prettiest face in all of Blouvlei. Their action made the rest of us nervous – what was the matter now? What, about the paper, was so mesmerizing?

I looked at the paper in my hand. Writing. In big letters. Spelling errors. Whoever wrote this, can't have gone far in school, I thought. Why, even I, only in Standard Three, would know how to write all the words written here. And I would spell all of them correctly too. Corrected, this is what the papers said:

YONK' IBLOUVLEI IYAFUDUSWA. ISIWA ENYANGA. KULE NYANGA IZAYO - 1 JULAYI. ABAZICELELAYO BAYA KUNCEDISWA NGELORI.

The message was simple and direct:

ALL BLOUVLEI WILL BE RELOCATED – MOVED TO NYANGA. NEXT MONTH – 1 JULY. FOR THOSE REQUESTING IT, THERE WILL BE LORRIES TO HELP WITH THE MOVE.

dun greyish-brown
to dimple to make a hollow space appear on a surface
to pit to make holes on a surface
to pimple (here): to form small mounds
moat *Wassergraben*
foe *Feind*
to rake to search carefully
speck small spot
to venture forth to go somewhere in spite of danger
to make (here): to appear
frenzy agitated activity
willy-nilly without much thought
to scramble to move quickly using your hands
to scoop up to lift up with a quick movement
to lace (here): to be a part of s.th.
demeanour behavior
to sober to become serious
mesmerizing fascinating
Standard Three fifth grade

A shock wave split my body. It was true, then? Tat'uNonjayikhali's story was happening? I would be lying if I said the fulfilment of Tat'uNonjayikhali's words thrilled me. Or that the thought of a new adventure filled me with excitement and anticipation.

Although I did not ask myself why this should be so, instantly, I was assaulted by a vague disquiet. Now that it seemed more real than ever before that we might leave this place that I had not thought of as one that was beloved to me, Blouvlei suddenly seemed very important and dear to me. For the first time, the reality that it was my whole world, the only place I had ever known ... had ever called home, hit me. Swift on the heels of that realization, came a bleak sadness. At the prospect of losing it, of no longer owning it.

A hush fell on the playground. All play had come to an unceremonious halt once again. Zombies stood where we had played. Stood staring at their hands. Then, as suddenly as we'd been stilled, a veritable stampede broke out, every child, pamphlet in hand, racing home. Racing there with a new urgency now.

'Mama!' I cried out. 'Mama! Mama! Mama!' I hollered, hand high up in the air. Hand holding the paper with the lethal words, I galloped all the way home.

Mama was waiting for me at the door, alarm written all over her face.

'What's the matter?' she asked. 'What are these things the aeroplane dropped?

'Look!' I whispered, my heart in my mouth. 'Look, here they are.'

She snatched one of the pamphlets from my hand. Her eyes, unaccustomed to reading scoured it for a full minute before she turned around and, going back inside the house, said:

'*He, tata kaMandisa, kha ujonge eli phepha*. Hey, father of Mandisa, why don't you take a look at this paper.' Her voice was low with disbelief. 'I told you there were things that plane was dropping off. Look, now,' she said, 'd'you see, what it was bringing us?'

'What?' The caterpillars above his eyes chased the thick forest of his hair, dangerously narrowing the tiny strip of forehead.

'Here,' and she handed him the leaflet.

'*Tyhini*!' exclaimed Tata, after a glance at it. '*Tyhini*!' again, he shouted, 'what are these Boers saying, now? What terrible thing is this that they are saying?'

My parents, who never lost opportunity for praising my brother and me for a good deed, that day, not once did they thank me for bringing them that note. However, sensing a turbulence in them far greater than my little disappointment, I did not dwell on the oversight. Indeed, it was not until days later that the fact hit me. That, in the mad scramble, I'd been given no praise.

'Where do they say they're taking us?' Mama asked.

'*I-iish*!' Tata said, 'They're playing children's marbles, we're not going anywhere.' But the deep furrow that cleaved his brow, gainsaid the words of his mouth. My apprehension grew.

disquiet anxiety
on the heels following
bleak depressing
veritable real
lethal (fig.) deadly
to scour (fig.) to read through carefully and slowly
caterpillar *Raupe*
strip long, narrow piece of s.th.
to dwell on s.th. to think or talk about s.th. that others want to forget
oversight any unintentional error
furrow deep line
to cleave to split
to gainsay *nicht entsprechen*

Just then, the clangorous sound of stout wood striking hollow metal rang out.

Like bees smoked out of their hive, the fathers and mothers of Blouvlei, the grandfathers and grandmothers too, every grownup in the location, poured out of the houses.

NKQO-NKQO!
NKQO NKQO-NKQO!
NKQO NKQO-NKQO!

Fast and furious, wood pounded on empty paraffin tins, Blouvlei's summonses to a meeting filled the late afternoon air. Then, into the clamorous air, came the high and piercing voices of unknown women ululating, accompanying the hollering gongs.

Yeye-e-ee-lee-e! Ye-yee-ee-eele-ee! It has drowned! It has drowned!
Ye-ee-yee-lee! Ifun' amadoda-aa! It has drowned! It needs men!

The distress signal, trilling, a call to all residents of Blouvlei, reinforced the tin-pounding rallying cry to the gathering place, the open field near the dam.

Our parents swarmed to the meeting-place. There was no spring to their step, their shoulders were hunched and rounded as their suddenly too-long arms dangled limp and useless at their sides.

With Mama and Tata gone to the meeting, my anxiety soon subsided, displaced by more pleasurable undertakings. Even though the sun cast long shadows, telling me I should go indoors, Mama was not there to see whether I was in or out. She was not there to call me home. So, finding myself thus freed, I once more lost myself to the urgency of evening play.

The sun dipped beyond the hills and sank, painting the far sky in fiery reds, blinding yellows and searing vermillions. In the afterglow, the hastily convened meeting sat.

As our play took place not far from the dam, now and then we would hear raised voices or even a shout. Even though we were engrossed in our games, we could not escape the anger of our parents, at war with the papers the aeroplane had dropped. Indeed, their wrath invaded the spaces where we hid, lost in the world of play. By and large, however, we kept a little off from the meeting as we did not want to remind our parents that we had not gone indoors.

Imperceptibly, peach turned to plum, another marker of the unusualness of the proceedings. With no streets and no street lighting therefore, Blouvlei knew well enough to conduct its business by the benevolence of the sun. This day, however, there was no thought of adjournment, to say nothing of cancellation. Instead, the meeting was soon held by candlelight. Scattered at random, several candles held in arms pushed up to the sky, gave pale and ghostly light to the strange goings-on. But as the pitch of night thickened, their etiolated light became more and more inadequate and ineffectual.

'Here, *Kwedini*!' Tat'uMavuthengatshi hailed Sakhele, who was passing by.

clangorous loud and ringing
stout solidly built
hollow *hohl*
hive *Bienenstock*
furious wildly
to pound to hit hard many times
summons call to appear at a certain time and place
clamorous noisy
piercing sharp
to ululate (literary) to howl
distress signal message asking for help
to reinforce to give added support
rallying cry call to assemble for s.th.
to subside to lessen
to cast, cast, cast *werfen*
fiery bright like fire
searing burning
vermillion bright red
convened (formal) called together
to be engrossed in s.th. to be completely involved in s.th.
wrath great anger
imperceptibly (formal) in a manner hardly noticeable
peach *Pfirsich*
plum *Pflaume*
benevolence goodness, kindness
adjournment (formal) official end of a meeting
cancellation decision to stop s.th. already arranged
at random *zufällig*
pitch degree, amount
etiolated (formal) lacking force and energy
to hail to greet

to growl to say angrily
full-blown (here): large
ablaze burning
relieved of not subject to

'Take this,' he said, giving him a key.' It opens the shed next to the shop. Go get us some wood, my boy,' he growled. 'Hurry!'

Soon, a full-blown fire was ablaze and, by its flickering light, the meeting carried on till very late that night. Relieved of parental supervision, we children were in paradise. That day, we chased fire flies and bats till late into the night.

Although no one knew this that Sunday, that was to be the first of a month of meetings, sometimes as many as three or four in a single day.

When that meeting was finally over, Tata and Mama called us in. They were both in a bad mood, which made Khaya whisper, 'The meeting can't have gone well.'

Tata's grumbling soon confirmed those words.

to spit, spat, spat out (here): to say aggressively

'Questions! Questions and more questions, all night long!' he spat out, clearly displeased.

'*Ja*!' Mama agreed. 'There sure was no lack of questions,' she said. 'But who had the answers?'

downright quite
out and out completely

'You're right there,' Tata said. 'Those were downright uncooperative and stubborn. They out and out refused to make an appearance.'

'Perhaps, tomorrow, they will come,' Mama said.

They talked about the removals all night, till I fell asleep.

The next day, our parents sent representations to the government. The government refused to receive the delegation.

to take to doing s.th. to begin doing s.th. by habit
to forgo to decide not to do s.th. you'd like to do
to supplement *ergänzen*
peanuts (coll.) an insignificant amount of money

For weeks, following that first meeting, Tata took to coming home early, forgoing all overtime work. That was a tremendous sacrifice, indeed, for his wage at the Cape Town Docks was not high and he supplemented it by working overtime. Mama often said that Tata's real wages came from the overtime and his job gave him but peanuts. But now, like everybody else, he had to attend the meetings and so couldn't take any overtime work.

feeble (here): ineffective

Meeting after meeting was called. But after several such intense meetings with indecisive resolutions and feeble outcomes, our parents appealed for help to Mr Stanford and Mrs Ballinger and the other white men and women who had been the official Native Representatives in the parliament to which they themselves had no access.

access *Zugang*
to no avail with no success

But even that was all to no avail. The government would not listen to anyone's appeals. The government had long made up its mind. Long, long ago. On the issue of black removals. Sure, once or twice, there were postponements. Instead of July, we moved in September. In the final analysis, however, move we did. As the government had said we would. All appeals and delegations had failed.

postponement delay, arrangement for s.th. to happen later

'Mandisa! Khaya! Mandisa! *Vukani*! *Vukani*! Wake Up – Wake Up!'

Deep in sleep, I felt someone shake me roughly by the shoulders.

Fire! The house was on fire!

I leapt out of bed, to run for the door. Shack fires were common in Blouvlei.

Hands grabbed me. Strong arms enfolded me to the not too familiar, tobacco-smelling chest of my father.

Tata? Tata, hugging me? I knew the situation was far worse than a burning house. Something terrible had happened.

Then, it came to me: I was either dead or dying. Why else would my stern, never-demonstrative father be hugging me? Tata was no dog that romped around with puppies.

'Mandisa,' Tata said, still shaking me by the shoulders. I was fully awake now and saw that Mama and Khaya were in the house. Their movements were not frantic. There was no fire. There couldn't possibly be. But then, what was the problem? my foggy brain asked.

'*Abelungu bayazidiliz' izindlu zethu.* Whites are pulling down our houses.' Tata said the words gently, with no hint of emotion whatsoever.

I looked at Mama.

'We have to hurry and pack up everything,' Mama said.' Throw away anything for which you have no use!' She, herself, was bent over a cardboard box, already half full with dishes.

It was long before sunrise on the first day of September. Tata, who left for work at half-past four, had raised the alarm and Blouvlei awoke to find itself under siege.

'Come and see,' Tata said, then taking Khaya and me by the hand, he lead us out of the house.

Outside, the air was hushed, a steady drizzle beating on the still-black sand. In the grey half-light of a cloudy winter's foredawn, foreign shapes loomed in the near distance. Menacing.

As soon as my eyes accustomed themselves to the poor light, they broke my windpipe, robbing me of breath. An army of invasion: a fleet of police. Vans, bulldozers and army trucks surrounded the location. Completely. In its entire vastness, Blouvlei was surrounded and contained.

As though enacting a long-rehearsed macabre dance, out of each of the army and police vehicles and bulldozers sprang uniform-clad white men. Hundreds of them. In a cloud of pink fleshed faces peeping from beneath heavy helmets, beefy hands sprouting from camouflage uniform, the white men set upon the tin shacks like unruly children destroying a colony of anthills.

Eyes peeled back wide, in horror, I watched. *Abelungu* men charged. Tin walls were torn down with the inhabitants of the shacks asleep inside some. Shacks came tumbling down, revealing Primus stoves alight, pots of mealie-meal porridge madly bubbling away in others.

Some of Blouvlei's more stubborn residents chained themselves to the doors of their homes. But the door frames were pulled down just the same. Pulled down with those poor desperate souls chained right onto them.

Grandpa Mxube, who lived up near the top of the hill, broke an arm in one such scuffle. To the day he died, more than a decade later, he never fully recovered the use of that arm.

The pitiless, ruthless attack of the government people jolted Blouvlei into action. Our parents scurried to take more realistic, more

never-demonstrative never showing affection
to romp around to play or run about joyfully
foggy (fig.) *nebelig*
to raise the alarm *Alarm geben*
under siege *unter Belagerung*
drizzle light rain
to loom to appear in a threatening manner
menacing threatening
windpipe *Luftröhre*
to enact to perform
uniform-clad wearing a uniform
camouflage *Tarn-*
peeled back wide wide open
to charge to attack
to tumble to fall suddenly
alight burning
to bubble *blubbern*
scuffle short, violent fight
ruthless *rücksichtslos*
to scurry to run with short, quick steps

aggressive, action. Defeat looked them squarely in the eye and they hurried to salvage what building material they could (not new when first used to build our Blouvlei homes and now rust-riddled and rotting), bits and pieces off their shacks, their homes. Their homes that, even as they fended off the attack, the army and the police and the university students volunteering for public service were snapping off like toys.

rust-riddled full of rust
to fend off to fight back
to snap off to break off suddenly

In the mad scurry and hustle of that day, somehow, Mama prevailed on Tata and a few other men and got them to help move Sis' Lulu and her things.

to prevail on s.o. to do s.th. to persuade s.o. to do s.th.

'If each family takes some of her things, by night we'll have most of them in Nyanga,' was how she persuaded them. She knew that if she asked even Tata to shoulder the full responsibility of moving Lulu, he would never agree to it … no one person would.

Hastily, to beat the eager demolishers and salvage what little they could of their shacks, our parents pulled down the houses themselves. With eyes bright with suppressed tears, our parents pulled down their homes, put the rusty nails in newspapers and wrapped the packets, using old *doeks* or pinafores; packed cardboard, zinc, poles and planks; strapped them into long unwieldy bundles, and carried them on their shoulders and on their heads.

demolisher person who knocks down buildings
pinafore loose dress with no sleeves
plank wooden board
to strap to fasten
unwieldy *sperrig*

Like *imfecane* fleeing Shaka more than a century ago, our parents trekked. Dejected and dispirited, but determined to build anew, they made the long journey through the Flats. From Retreat to Nyanga, going by way of back roads and by-roads, footpaths, barely-there, grass-overgrown dirt tracks, past the endless acres of farms taming the sandy Flats, where no trains or buses ran. Past Klip, Busy-Corner, and other outlying settlements of Heathfield; past the farms that feed Diep River, Steurhof, Plumstead, Wittebomme, Wynberg and environs, they trod. In their hundreds. They trekked. Onto the sheep and maize farms of Ottery and past the chicken farms of Lansdowne, they plodded. A long line of wearied humanity: children, women and men, following their noses, going to a place they had never seen before, where they knew not what awaited them. They trekked. Leaving their lives flattened to nothing behind them. Government vehicles hounding them, bayonets prodding their backs; confused, bedraggled and spent, at last their eyes beheld the wilderness – the barren land the government had designated to be their new home.

dejected without hope
Retreat … Wynberg, etc. all towns in the Flats, south-west South Africa
to tame (here): to make useful
environs surrounding area
to tread, trod, trodden to walk
to plod to walk with heavy steps
to hound to harass
to prod *stoßen*
bedraggled wet and dirty
spent exhausted
barren *unfruchtbar*

We got here, and everything and everybody changed, especially Mama. In Guguletu, the new houses changed us. People believed they'd been bettered, and strove hard to live up to that perception. In their wood and zinc and cardboard houses with wooden windows, they'd needed no curtains or carpets or fancy, store-bought furniture. In the brand-new brick houses of the townships, with their glass windows, concrete floors, bare walls and hungry rooms, new needs were born. But how to satisfy these needs? The wages of fathers had certainly not been augmented. Soon, all our mothers, who had been there every afternoon to welcome us when we returned from school,

to strive, strove, striven to attempt
perception way of seeing s.th.
fancy decorative
brick *Backstein*
to augment (formal) to increase

were no longer there. They were working in white women's homes. Tired, every day when they returned. Tired and angry.

In time we did not remember coming back from school to mothers waiting with smiles.

10.05 pm – Wednesday 25 August 1993

It was getting late. Very late. Still, of the three men in the house, only Lunga was home. Not my husband, Dwadwa, Father-of-Siziwe. But about him, I was not that worried. He works in the Docks in Cape Town and it is not unusual for him to be late. But where was Mxolisi? Not for the first time, I asked myself what it was that made him so different from the other two children. How many times had I not spoken to him about his gadding about? About his being the eldest and therefore the one who had to set a good example for the others? Why was he so consistent in being disobedient?

Siziwe had a pot of *mngqusho* (samp) simmering when I came. I was rested now. As rested as I could get with all that had happened to me earlier that evening. I waited, hoping that Mxolisi and Dwadwa would come so we could all eat together. Hoping, though, that Mxolisi would be the first to make an appearance. I was sick and tired of hearing Dwadwa's mouth on the subject of Mxolisi's long foot that wrote itself on all the streets and corners of Guguletu ... day and night. What had made Mxolisi stop confiding in me? And when had that wall of silence sprung between us? I couldn't remember. He used to tell me everything ... and then, one day I woke up to find I knew almost nothing about his activities or his friends.

To take my mind off the worry about my son, I sorted out some of the washing and soaked whites and fast colours. That meant I'd have less work when I did the laundry, come Saturday. But it also meant I'd have to wake up half an hour earlier the next morning. I didn't mind that. Besides, anything was miles better than the frantic feeling that enfolded me. Indeed, I'd do the laundry now, if it would help me escape the overwhelming anxiety. But I knew I couldn't do that, though. Just a fanciful thought. I'd wake up with not one article up on the line – Guguletu thieves took even face cloths left on the line at night. Next, I took out clothes waiting to be ironed and started on those. That would keep me going ... till my husband came.

Dwadwa returned with a large packet under his arm. Meat. Spleen. He'd had no trouble walking home from Netreg, the train station nearest this part of Guguletu, less than ten minutes away from the house. Yes, there were police vans lying in wait at the station, when he got off the train. But the police were in the cars, not bothering anybody. Yes, he had also seen three or four more vans while walking home. And all those Saracens at the Police Station, inside the yard as well as outside.

to gad about to go about searching for pleasure

samp stamped mealies cooked with beans

to simmer to cook just under the boiling point

to confide in s.o. to disclose private matters to s.o. you trust

fast colour colour not likely to come out in the wash

to enfold (fig.) to cover

fanciful imagined

face cloth (BE) washcloth (AE)

spleen *Milz*

botheration (old-fashioned, BE) things that annoy

poor man's liver i.e. spleen

to boast (here): to speak in proud terms

offal *Innereien*

to season to add spices

to dish up (coll.) to serve food

to send s.o. on a wild goose chase to ask s.o. to search for s.th. that can't be found

Long-bowel i.e. big stomach

snout (fig.) mouth of an animal

to scowl to look at s.o. in an angry way

abomination s.th. disgusting

account report

'You don't know what a botheration I had getting here,' I said. Then narrated my story to him.

I was glad I had delayed dishing up. This *mngqusho* business, everyday, can be boring. I skinned the 'poor man's liver', grateful that Dwadwa was such a good provider. Not many in Guguletu could boast of eating meat more than once a week, on Sunday. Indeed, there were some who did not have even that. But we had meat two or three times during the week. Mostly offal. But still, meat. Now, I seasoned and fried the spleen. Just as I would liver – keeping it a minute or two longer on the stove, because it is thicker.

Everything was ready now. Still, I delayed dishing up. Just a little longer. Hoping against hope that the boy would come. Now and then I took a peek out of the kitchen window or went to the back door to listen for voices. However, each time, the same stubborn silence greeted my investigation. A sure sign that Lunga was still alone, or with his books – which comes to the same thing.

'Mother-of-Lunga,' Dwadwa said grumpily on my return this time. 'You're humming these tuneless songs of yours instead of giving us our food because, once more, this Long-Foot of yours is not home?'

'Siziwe, go and see whether both boys are in the *hokkie*,' I said.

'Don't waste the child's time,' Dwadwa retorted. 'You know full well Mxolisi is not here. Don't send the poor girl on a wild goose chase.'

'Why d'you say that?'

'You think if Long-bowel were here, he'd have kept his snout from the meat this long?' Dwadwa scowled. 'You know his throat is a magnet, where meat is concerned.'

I took myself to the kitchen. Dwadwa's portrayal of Mxolisi was accurate enough. But the boy's greed, his love of meat, all this did not concern me right now. What did, and did so with painful urgency, were his whereabouts.

I dished up and we ate in silence. I could hardly swallow a single spoonful of that food. The thought of Mxolisi about on a night such as this was too upsetting for words. It unsettled me all right.

As I got ready for bed, heavy was my heart with the knowledge that horror and abomination had taken place a stone's throw away from my home. Not just because of the violence. For years ... many, many years, we have lived with violence. This was nothing new to us. What was new was that this time, the victim was white. A white person killed in Guguletu, a black township. Killed, from all accounts, for no reason at all. Killed, in fact, while doing good ... helping the people of the township. But then again, even that was not totally new, was it?

Hayi, ilishwa, eMonti!
Hayi, ilishwa, eMonti!
Hayi, ilishwa, eMonti, eMonti, eMonti!

But that was so long ago, that misfortune in East London. So long, long ago. In a far-away town I had never seen.

Nearer home. In 1960 we saw how little difference it made to black people that some whites were sympathetic to their cause. Three young nurses, new in the country, heard of the atrocities the police and army were inflicting on the African people in Langa. No doubt, thinking the presence of outsiders might act as a deterrent, they came to bear witness. Near the Flats, where 'bachelors' were housed, a group of African men, bearing sticks and God only knows what else, came upon them. And beat them. Three defenceless, unarmed women. Beaten by a troop of men. One suffered a broken jaw. Another, several deep cuts at the back of her head. The third, a sprinter, twisted an ankle. As soon as those poor women were discharged from hospital, they left the country. Back to Belgium.

The night is quiet, punctuated now and then by the sound of gun fire. Nothing unusual about that these days, not in Guguletu. At last, Dwadwa asks, 'Where is this boy?'

'Which boy?' I know perfectly well he means Mxolisi.

Dwadwa harrumphs and says not a word more. But the question he has asked and which I've dodged answering hangs between us as thick as a curtain.

'I don't know whether he's come in or not,' I venture at last, uneasy with the pregnant silence.

'Mmmh-mmhh,' Dwadwa clears his throat. That lets me know he is about to tell me something he believes is important. He wants me to pay attention. I tense, an invisible hand squishing everything inside my stomach.

'Be careful,' says my husband in the dark, for we've already blown the candle out. 'This child, always vagabonding in the middle of the night ... I tell you, Mother of Siziwe, mark my words, he will bring you a big trouble one day.' With that, he turns and faces the wall, giving me his stiff back.

I do not like Mxolisi's gallivanting up and down the township like a sow that's littered during a drought, any more than Dwadwa does. I do not like the secretiveness that has crept into his manner, of late. But here I find myself defending him,' All the children are like that, these days.'

In a shot, Dwadwa sits up as though a snake is writhing beneath him. Then, he appears to change his mind and remains silent ... deep in thought. A minute or so later, he sighs, goes back under the blankets and says,' Hey, Mother of Siziwe, do you hear yourself? Do you hear what you're saying?'

I remain silent. I do not know how to respond to his question.

'Let me tell you something, wife of mine,' says he quietly. Very quietly. 'That is not the answer of a wise mother.'

I am stung to retort, 'What do you think I should do? He is no small boy, you know?'

atrocity cruel and violent act
to inflict to make s.o. suffer s.th. unpleasant
deterrent s.th. that makes it likely that s.th. won't happen
to bear, bore, borne witness to be present and able to report
bachelor unmarried man
sprinter a person who can run very fast
ankle *Fußgelenk*
to discharge to allow to leave
to punctuate to interrupt several times
to harrumph to make the noise of clearing the throat
to dodge (coll.) to avoid
to venture to say in spite of possible criticism
pregnant (here): full of meaning
to squish (coll.) to press together
to vagabond to wander about aimlessly
to gallivant (old-fashioned, coll.) to go from place to place enjoying yourself
sow *Sau*
to litter to give birth
to writhe [raɪð] to twist
to sting, stung, stung (here): to incite, to provoke

to dog to trouble, to plague

rife widespread

Hottentots race of short, yellowish-brown skinned people who formerly occupied the area near the Cape of Good Hope

Bushmen native Africans who were originally hunters

dullard (old-fashioned) stupid person

ordeal difficult situation

Standard 6 8th grade

the likes of her (coll.) for s.o. like her

'You are still his mother.'

'And you?' The minute the words were out of my mouth, I regretted them. Dwadwa is good to my children . . . to all three children. It is not his fault that Mxolisi is so disobedient. He does not treat him any differently from the other two. The boys can accuse him of being overly strict, stingy, or anything else, but in all honesty, they cannot say that he treats them in any way different from how he treats his own child, Siziwe. After my outburst, we fell into an uneasy silence.

I could not bring myself to apologize. I could only imagine what was going on in his mind. But where was Mxolisi? What was he doing wherever he was? Why had he not come home? Why did he stay out so late, despite the numerous talking-to's we had given him? These questions dogged me all night, and they raced through my mind as I lay wide-eyed with sleeplessness.

When I was in school, by the year's end one had not yet learnt the names of all the children in the class. That's how rife overcrowding was in our schools, how bad the education of the African child was even way back then. This is what happened one year during the annual visit of the school inspectors:

'Who were the taller, the Hottentots or the Bushmen?' asked our teacher, standing behind the school inspector, sitting at the teacher's table.

Our hands flew up, even Mehlo, the class dullard, had his hands up.

'Yes?' said Miss Mabanga, pointing to one of the pupils.

'The Hottentots!' came the answer.

The inspector left the classroom and we all breathed a sigh of relief that the ordeal was over.

How clever of the teacher to show us the answer, raising her arms up in the air as she said the word Hottentots and lowering the arms on Bushmen.

With the passage of time, our schools only grew worse. In 1976, students rose in revolt and, before long, Bantu Education had completely collapsed. It had become education in name only.

My son, Mxolisi, is twenty. Yet he is still in Standard 6. Standard 6! As though he were twelve or thirteen years old. But then, he is not alone, neither is he the oldest student in his class. Twenty. And still in Standard 6. And I am not saying he is the brightest pupil in his class either.

Boycotts, strikes and indifference have plagued the schools in the last two decades. Our children have paid the price.

And your daughter, did she not go to school? Couldn't she see all the signs telling her this is a place where only black people live? Add to that, where was her natural sense of unease? Did she not feel awkward, a fish out of water, here? That should have been a warning to her ... a warning to stay out. Telling her the place was not for her. It was not safe for the likes of her. Oh, why did she not stay out? Why? Why did she not keep off?

Lying in bed, contemplating the events of the day, as much as I understood them, I was amazed at how an ordinary day can turn topsy-turvy with no warning at all.

I'd had no nightmare, no premonition, no foreboding the night before. No prescience that morning. No foresight whatsoever throughout that day ... a Wednesday. In fact, until Madam's unexpected return, all was well with my little world. Until she came and dragged me out of the kitchen and to the train station to get my bus home, driving as though the devil himself were after her. Yes, till then, it had been an ordinary day – ordinary, in the context of our lives that have become quite complex and far from ordinary.

topsy-turvy (coll.) in a state of confusion
premonition foreboding
prescience [ˈpresiəns] (formal) foreknowledge

Look now. Look what the children have done! Poor, poor child. The one who is dead. Poor child. And her parents. I feel for her parents. For the parents of this poor child, killed by our children. My heart sorrows for them. For her mother.

The havoc our children are visiting upon our homes has made hell-holes of these houses in which they live with the adults who brought them into this world. Intolerable. The children, in their new-found wisdom and glory, have decided that all parents carry sawdust where their brains used to be. In this new world of confusion compounded, the children are aided and abetted by adults we call leaders. Leaders of the community. Women and men we all look up to ... or should. People whose word and deed we emulate ... follow without question.

to sorrow to feel grief
havoc destruction, ruin
compounded made worse
to abet to assist or encourage, especially in wrongdoing
to emulate (formal) to try to equal or do better

'Make the country ungovernable!' So said the leaders. I don't know about the government now. Whether or not it is coping with the task of ruling the country, I cannot say. But I do know that we, parents, have become toothless dogs whose bark no one heeds.

to cope with s.th. to deal successfully with a difficulty

How did it all start? How did it begin? Where were we when the problem first cut tooth? When it first appeared in our midst?

to cut tooth (fig.) to first appear

The answer to that is very easy. What is not, are the whys and wherefores behind it. But even that, yes, even that we can answer.

First, our children stoned cars. We cheered them on. The cars were not our cars, they were not the cars of our neighbours or our friends, they were the cars of white people.

Hayi, ilishwa, eMonti!
Hayi, ilishwa, eMonti!
Hayi, ilishwa! EMonti, eMonti, eMonti!

Bamtshis' uSista! EMonti!
Bamtshis' uSista! EMonti!
Bamtshis' uSista! EMonti, eMonti, eMonti!
Oh, what abominable misfortune – in East London!
They burnt a nun – in East London!

abominable wretched, miserable

I was very young when the teachers made us sing that song. Seems so long ago now. I can't remember how we heard about the event that inspired it, though. Now we have radio and television, but how did news travel back then? Travel such distances too? East London is a good one thousand kilometres away from Cape Town.

I think I know how we must have heard. In all probability, the news came to us via some maid or other type of servant, people employed in white homes. They would have been told by their employers. It would have been an event of which the *mlungu* woman or the *mlungu* man would have felt compelled to inform her or his servant. See what those natives (I believe that was the term then) have gone and done? Just see what they have done! Murdering a poor, defenceless woman, a woman of God. And what was she trying to do? Help them, for crying out aloud.

for crying out aloud *Verdammt noch mal!*

But, in our school, we sang the song of the nun who was killed by black people, Africans, in far-away East London. Sang the song when not one of the teachers had taken the trouble of explaining to us that the people of East London should not have done that.

AmaBhulu, azizinja! Today's youth have been singing a different song. Whites are dogs! Not a new thought, by any means. We had said that all along. As far back as I can remember. Someone would come back from work fuming: *amaBhulu azizinja*, because of some unfairness they believed had been meted out to them that day. A slap. A kick. Deduction from wages. A deduction, neither discussed nor explained. Unless, a gruff – YOU ALWAYS LATE! or YOU BROKE MY PLATE! or YOU NOT VERY NICE TO MY MOTHER! qualifies as explanation. So, yes, our children grew up in our homes, where we called white people dogs as a matter of idiom … heart-felt idiom, I can tell you. Based on bitter experience.

to fume to be very angry about s.th.
to mete out to give s.o. a punishment
gruff rough and unfriendly
idiom (formal) (here): special expression for a particular situation

AmaBhulu, azizinja! they sang. And went and burnt down their schools. That's uncalled for, a few of us mumbled beneath our breath. Well beneath. Even so, we were quickly reprimanded. There was a war on. Besides, those ramshackle, barren things were no schools. No learning took place there.

But swiftly, our children graduated from stoning cars, white people's cars. They graduated from that and from burning buildings. Unoccupied buildings. Public buildings. Now, they started stoning black people's cars. And burning black people's houses.

uncalled for unnecessary
to reprimand (formal) *rügen*
ramshackle poorly built and not kept in repair
barren (here): lacking equipment
to graduate from s.th. (ironic) to move up from s.th.

We reasoned that those black people to whom such a thing happened deserved what they got. The children were punishing them for one or another misdeed. Or, indeed, some misdeeds. They had collaborated with the repressive apartheid government. *Iimpimpi*, informers, we labelled the whole miserable lot. People on whom the students' righteous and wrathful acts fell. They deserved all they got. And then, some more. *Iimpimpi*, we called them. We called them that, without tangible reason on our part. Had the students, our children, not told us that? By burning their cars? Why would they single them out for such treatment if it were not for their guilt? We saw no paral-

wrathful full of hate
tangible real, substantive

lel between the actions of the children and the witchdoctor's smelling out of a *mthakathi,* a witch.

Our children made our homes the target of their wrath and visited untold devastation on them. A few of us gasped. Privately. Safely. In the comforting isolation of our homes. What were we so afraid of? Why didn't we ask those questions buzzing in our heads? Loud in our hearts? Demanding our attention. Demanding answers. From us. From our parents, our children, our leaders ... the one and the same? Why didn't we ask those questions. Ask them out loud?

Oh, what faith we had in the integrity of the court of public opinion. The majority of us, believing ourselves safe and sound, wearing the thin shield of our innocence, wondered how our erstwhile friends had fooled us for so long. Of course, they were sell-outs. Wasn't that what the students said? Wasn't that why they had burnt their houses down?

The Young Lions! We praised them. Praised our children. Down with all *iimpimpi*! We echoed the slogans their mouths spewed, the slogans that had become their gospel.

The Young Lions. From near and far, admiration fell on their already swollen heads. They had tackled the much-feared enemy, the big gogga that had for so long trampled on their parents and on the parents of those parents. And theirs before them.

Our children fast descended into barbarism. With impunity, they broke with old tradition and crossed the boundary between that which separates human beings from beasts. Humaneness, *ubuntu,* took flight. It had been sorely violated. It went and buried itself where none of us would easily find it again.

Then, a man was stoned. A black man from Guguletu. A man – not a car. He was stoned and kicked and punched and knifed. Senseless. Punched blind, he reeled, fumbling his way. The children put a garland around his neck, an old, worn tyre. Then, into the tyre they poured some liquid. The fumes hit the man's nostrils. He gagged.

A hiss and a flash. WH-H-HOO-OO-OSHH!

In a flaming heap, the man fell to the ground.

Cheers rose from the crowd. The children drew nearer and nearer. Nearer to the figure writhing on the ground. Grotesque, smouldering magnet. The spectators were positively mesmerized, dazzled by the brilliance of their handiwork. Drunk with power.

Click-click! Would you believe human beings have the capacity to stand still long enough to take aim and shoot such a horrific, marrow-chilling scene? Take pictures? Instead of setting the poor person out of his misery? Click-click! went the cameramen – several from various newspapers – from all around Cape Town. The beautiful city of Cape Town. Click-Click! They jostled each other for better positions, a better angle.

THE NECKLACE. A new phrase was coined. Verb: To necklace. Necklacing. Necklaces. Necklaced. A new phrase was born. Shiny

- **to visit** (here): to bring about
- **devastation** destruction
- **faith** *Vertrauen*
- **sell-out** a person who betrays the people he or she is supposed to support
- **to spew** to spit out
- **gospel** Bible
- **to tackle** to challenge
- **with impunity** without fear of punishment
- **to take flight** (fig.) to vanish
- **sorely** very much
- **to violate** to abuse, to treat without respect
- **to punch** to hit with the fist
- **to reel** to walk with unsteady steps
- **to fumble your way** to use your hands to find your way
- **garland** *Girlande*
- **fumes** (plural) smoke
- **nostril** *Nasenloch*
- **to gag** to struggle for breath
- **to smoulder** to burn slowly without a flame
- **marrow-chilling** (fig.) causing an extreme sense of horror
- **to jostle** to push roughly
- **to coin** (fig.) *prägen*

brand new – necklace. More deadly than gun. The necklace. That is what we chose to call our guillotine. Necklace. What an innocent-sounding noun. Who could imagine its new meaning? Just as we kept on calling, insisted on calling, the people who did the necklacing 'children,' 'students,' 'comrades', we called a barbaric act the necklace, protecting our ears from a reality too gruesome to hear; clothing satanic deeds with innocent apparel.

Not many of our leaders came out and actually condemned the deed. Indeed, there were those who actually applauded the method, the innovative manner of killing a human being, of doing away with those with whom one was in disagreement. They said it would lead us to freedom. However, to this day, I have never heard it said that even one of the oppressors was necklaced. I had not known that it was our own people who stood in the way of the freedom we all said we desired.

Meanwhile, soon others were similarly garlanded. All those singled out for this form of execution, were thus adorned with the quick, flaming and caressing colours. Without benefit of trial, with neither judge nor jury. No due process. No recourse to defence or appeal. Human beings were summarily murdered – No, necklaced. Quite different that is to saying someone has been murdered or killed. Necklaced. Is it more palatable?

The mighty police appeared impotent. They did nothing about the necklacing, or did so little as to make no difference. Justice was on holiday. Or busy with more deserving matters: terrorists who, at the instigation of foreign meddlers, especially communists, were planning to overthrow the government. And, of course, always there were the pass offences.

A war was going on, the children said. They were fighting the apartheid government.

gruesome horrid, marrow-chilling
apparel (fig.) clothing
oppressor *Unterdrücker, -in*
to adorn to decorate
to caress to touch gently
benefit of (here): the legal right of
jury *Geschworene*
due process (law) a trial that is fairly conducted according to the legal code
recourse *Zugang*
appeal taking a legal decision to a higher court in order to try to overturn the decision of a lower court
summarily without delay
palatable acceptable
impotent unable to act
instigation urging
meddler person who interferes in matters that don't concern him/her
pass offence crime of not having the right pass (identity card)

Chapter Six

4 am – Thursday 26 August 1993

The shiny green arms of the alarm clock next to the bed say it is half-past-three. Long before my wake-up time. But I'm wide-eyed up. I'll call it up although Lord only knows if I ever was down. This night just past, Dwadwa and I finally fell into an exhausted, nerve-racked and sullen silence. It wasn't long thereafter, and I heard him snore. Typical.

I blew the candle out and watched the dying glow of the taper. When it finally breathed its last, it seemed to give birth to a thickening in the air. In the dark, the smell of burning wax wafted slowly till it hit the bed. Imagining its aerial travel, in the gloom, I stared at shapes cavorting through the room, my fantasy working overtime.

I guess some time between then and now I must have caught some sleep. From the way I feel, however, numbness more than sleep is what must have come over me – eventually. My eyes smart as though I'd spent the night cooking over an open fire in a windowless hut – using wood that I'd left out in the rain. The muscles supporting the neck tell me I've been standing on my head throughout the night. By the pale light of the moon, the room is cast in the thin gloom of almost-there light.

What woke me up? Even the birds have not yet begun their morning chirping and twittering. In the foggy recesses of my mind, there is a hazy groping, a reaching, a searching for something that flits and slips further and away, always just out of my grasp. What woke me up? Dream or something real? What? What?

In the flannel petticoat in which I'd slept I sit as though carved in stone, my legs dangling down the side of the bed. Behind me, Dwadwa's breathing is steady and soft ... calm as a new-born babe's. Some people's cool! I am not one of those people. All night long I fretted, tossed and turned in my half-sleep, half-worried-out-of-my-mind state. Not my husband. His capacity for sleep is truly amazing. He says all that loading and off-loading of cargo onto and from the ships saps every ounce of his strength. As soon as he flops into bed, closes his eyes, he is immediately snatched into the sea of unknowing. I work as hard. But does that give me this huge appetite for sleep?

A sound hits my ears. Not loud, but still noise where, but a short moment before, deathlike silence reigned. The sound is muffled, but there. Suddenly, I knew.

That sound! That is what woke me up. The same sound. Yes, yes, that's it. I could swear it is the sound of a car door being shut. Carefully. Very, very carefully. Stealthily?

Now I'm all ears. Waiting for another surreptitious, ever so slight clash ... muffled ... a car door closing. Will there be another, I wonder.

nerve-racked completely stressed
sullen bad-tempered
taper *Docht*
to waft to drift
to cavort to dance around
numbness inability to feel anything
to smart to feel a sharp pain
is cast in the thin gloom of ... (here): is filled with the thin gloom of
to chirp *zwitschern*
recess deep part
hazy vague
to grope to try to find with your hands
to flit to move lightly and quickly
to carve to cut out pieces of wood or stone to make a shape
to fret to worry
to toss and turn to keep moving about in bed
to sap to gradually destroy
to flop to lie down in a heavy way
to reign [reɪn] to dominate
muffled dim, suppressed
stealthily done quietly and secretly
surreptitious done secretly so no-one will notice

car-hijacking stealing a car with violent threats
to turn nasty (coll.) to have unpleasant results
to strain to make a great effort to do s.th.
lest for fear that
to creak *quietschen*
inevitable unavoidable
eerie strange
fraught with filled with
to wag (here): to move rapidly in talking
to suffocate to make it difficult to breathe
lull quiet period
thunder-clap loud sound of thunder
onslaught violent attack
hail *Hagel*
clamorous noisy
torch (BE) *Taschenlampe*
rap knock
knuckle *Fingerknöchel*
to wield to hold as a weapon
to detest to hate
drawers underpants
anathema (formal) s.th. detested
rider additional comment
to clamber to climb with difficulty
to vacate to leave empty
to whimper to cry softly
to pat to touch gently several times

Mxolisi? By car? Thoughts of car-hijacking flood my mind. Heaven forbid! And those can turn nasty. But Mxolisi is not a bad boy. Not at all a bad boy. Just a young person taken up with this business of politics. As all the students have been these past twenty years or so.

Why, only two weeks ago, did he not risk his life saving a girl from a group of men who wanted to rape her?

I strain my ears, hoping to catch the slightest sound. Silence. In my mind's eye, however, I see people approach the house. There, they climb over the low fence, avoiding the gate lest it creaks. I wait for the inevitable footfall. Who are they and what do they want? Could it be Mxolisi? Did he ever come home last night?

The only answer to my frantic questions is an eerie silence that blankets the pre-dawn air, pushing the walls of the house inward ... inward ... and ever inward. This is no longer the silence of before whatever noise hit my ear. This silence is fraught with all manner of possibility – bubbling with dark, shadowy happenings that force our eyes to scream and tear our ears. Happenings that will loosen some tongues, set them wagging for years to come, while others it will still ... still as effectively as the tongues of *izithunzela*.

My heart is a witchdoctor's drum. The silence is suffocating. Scary. The lull between the thunder-clap and the onslaught of hail.

GQWAA! GQWAA-GQWAA! BANG! CLANG-BANG! On door. On window. On wall. At once, the whole yard is alive and clamorous. Back and front. Torches shine through the bedroom window, accompanied by loud, unruly raps – knuckles and sticks wielded with enthusiasm from the sound of it. I hear the same noise coming from the direction of the other rooms. The house is completely surrounded. More than the noise, however, it is the simultaneous nature of its occurrence, the intensity of the onslaught, that freezes the marrow in my bones.

Dwadwa leaps out of bed. He is naked as the day he was born. My husband does not believe in pyjamas. He detests underwear, calling the short pair of pants he is forced to wear beneath his long pants 'women's drawers'. If truth be known, the whole concept of clothing is anathema to his nature. 'If God had wanted human beings clothed, he'd have given them fur or some other kind of cover as He did with animals,' is his constant rider whenever the subject comes up. If it were not for the fact that in his job he often has to strip to the waist, I'm sure he would not bother wearing underpants.

Even as Dwadwa grabs his pants, which he'd thrown over a chair the previous night, and kicks his legs into them, Siziwe suddenly comes charging into the room. Next thing I know, there she is clambering right into the bed, into the space vacated by her father but a moment before. She is whimpering and shaking like a leaf blown about by a fierce south-easter gale.

I put my hand over her mouth, shake my head at her while, with my other hand, I pat her on the back. Pat her as though I were putting a little baby to sleep.

There is a fresh barrage from outside. Loud, gruff voices demand, 'Open up! Open up!' There is angry thudding and banging against the back door, as though someone were butting his shoulder against it with all his might. Pushing against it. Forcing the door open. Breaking in by force.

Years ago, there would have been no question in my mind that this was a police raid. However, with things what they are these days, what they have become, who can be sure? It is not unheard of that *skollies*, hooligans, common criminals or comrades come disguised as police. And, at times, it is hard to know which is worse. To be fried alive is a terrible thing and little solace can come from the knowledge that one dies at the hands of one's own group, fighting for everybody's freedom?

'Who's that?' Dwadwa, who by now has his pants and a shirt on, calls out in the dark. At the sound of his voice, the commotion stops.

'Police! Open up!'

Is it the police? ... At this time? A new fear stabs my heart. Mxolisi! Did he return last night? Has something happened to my child? In the back of my mind I know that the police wouldn't come like this, in the middle of the night, to tell us about something happening to Mxolisi.

'Coming!' my husband shouts back, in answer to the resumption of the clangorous raps, which are, if anything, more ferocious this time.

I reach for the box of matches under my pillow, strike a match, and light the candle. That is when I realize that I should put on a dress ... that I am not dressed to have strange men's eyes rake over my body.

In the frail and reluctant light of the candle, no one speaks. No one has words to say. However, there are questions galore. Questions. Frightful, frightening questions chase each other. In our eyes. Wide with fear and apprehension. But there are no answers there. Not in any of the eloquent eyes. Only questions.

Dwadwa turns on his heel and leaves the room. A second later, I hear him unbolt the kitchen door. Suddenly, there is a loud crash.

'What d'you think you're doing?' I hear Dwadwa's angry shout. 'Don't you see that I'm opening the door? Why do you break my door?' he bellows.

C-R-R-AA-A-CK! The sound of wood connecting with bone.

'Uhh-huh!'

Footsteps. A horde of feet, marching, trampling over the wooden floor of the kitchen. Bold and angry footsteps enter the dining-room.

'They're going to kill us! Mama, they're going to kill us!' The nearer the footsteps come, the louder Siziwe screams. Her eyes are wild with fear.

'Sshh!' I say, bending over the bed and scooping her into my arms. 'Sshhh!' I wag a stern finger at her then put it on my pouted lips.

barrage large attack
to thud to hit with a low, dull sound
to butt to push hard
raid short, surprise attack
solace comfort
resumption (formal) act of beginning again
clangorous with a crashing and ringing sound
ferocious very aggressive
frail weak
reluctant hesitating
galore (coll.) in large amounts
apprehension anxiety
heel *Ferse*
to unbolt *entriegeln*
crack sudden, loud noise
horde vast crowd
to scoop (here): to quickly lift
to wag to move to the left and right
pouted lips lips pushed out

to scrape to rub against a rough surface
beam *Strahl*
to dart to move quickly in a certain direction
to illumine, illuminate (formal) to shine light on s.th.
upsets its tummy (coll.: [stomach]) (fig.) makes the candle feel bad
molten liquid
to scald [skɔ:ld] to burn your skin with a hot liquid
stinging causing a sharp pain
sniff inhaling sharply
glitter bright light with little flashes
brass *Messing*
epaulette [ˈepəlet] decoration on the shoulder of a uniform
bumbling behaving in a confused way
to brandish to hold in an aggressive way
skittering moving quickly and lightly
to plunge s.th. into darkness to suddenly make everything dark
save for (formal) except for

Clutching the blanket tightly around her, she nods. Several times rapidly, her head goes up and down. Her eyes are wider than the Sahara.

'We said open up an hour ago!' The voice booms as though coming through a loudspeaker; my heart stops; the walls of the house shiver. There is no answer from Dwadwa.

'Why did you take such a long time? What'ah you trying to hide?' Thunk! The sound of a boot connecting but is quickly followed by the scraping of the floor as a chair or some other heavy object overturns.

Through the slightly open door, agitated beams dart back and forth, illumining the pitch black of the dining-room; flashes of lightning spearing an inky night. I want to scream, but there is a frog at the back of my throat.

I snatch the candlestick. The movement is abrupt and unplanned; it frightens the candle, upsets its tummy and it erupts, spewing molten lava which scalds the back of my hand. Fighting back the stinging tears, I bite my lower lip. Siziwe's sharp intake of breath sounds like a sniff. I peer at her. Make my eyes hard, a sign that tells her Don't Move! Then, holding the candlestick high, I make my way to the front room.

An army of policemen has taken the dining-room over. I say policemen, for even in the erratic and unevenly flashing light the glimmer and glitter of brass epaulettes is unmistakable. Enough of the men are in police uniform, although just as many are in plain clothes. What a relief to see that our visitors are, indeed, the law.

However, swift on the steps of that relief came apprehension. Yes, these were police, but ... what did that mean? The police are no security to us in Guguletu – swift comes the correction as I remember people killed by the police ... including children. Mzamo. Zazi. The police even killed important people like Biko. Even important white people, sometimes. That's what people say. Although we do not know the names of those white people, but we know that they too were killed.

Alarm tasted bitter in my mouth. What did the police want? And why so many of them? What did they want? And why this pre-dawn raid on our house?

The police were everywhere; but where was Dwadwa? In the forest of blue-clad legs, bumbling bodies and flashing torches, he seemed to have disappeared.

Meanwhile, my entrance seemed to have signalled an open invitation to the bedroom, the room I had just left. Unceremoniously shoving me to the side, three or four of the men rushed in, brandishing their torches.

I turned to follow them.

Another pushed past me, sending the candlestick skittering on the floor, plunging the room into darkness – complete darkness save for the flashing light of the torches.

Without thinking, I fell down on all fours, meaning to retrieve the candlestick. A hopeless task since the fall had snuffed the candle out. The sudden dark, thicker than before I'd lit the candle. Just then, two sounds hit my ears: a loud crash from the backyard. Instantly, I knew that someone had broken the *hokkie* door down. And Siziwe's scream.

I forgot why I was on the floor, hands blindly groping around in the shimmer-filled, splintered dark, hands dodging angry raps of torches ... searching. In one second flat, I reach the bed.

Siziwe is no longer here. Even with the faint and flickering light of the restless beams, I see that the bed is bare. Nevertheless, I grope all over the bed.

All the while, an unholy din dyes the air. Boots hammer the floor, boots kick at what furniture there is in the house, sending things crashing against walls, colliding with each other and clattering onto floor. Planks creak and groan. Walls reverberate while the very air grows thick and warm.

A large, unfriendly hand grabs my neck, stapling flesh and garment. As a pin lifted by a magnet, I am snatched from the bed. Only to be dumped on the floor. The same hand (or its brother or cousin) clasps itself to my shoulder and hauls me up ... drags me bumpity-bump along the floor. Out of the bedroom, through the dining-room and into the kitchen. Mercifully, this room is now all lit up. Enough torches in steady hands beam here. A whole *klomp* of policemen line the room, doing nothing except hold their torches high.

My eyes dart about, searching for the girl. However, the search is disrupted as one of the men asks:

'Where is he?' The voice is raised and angry. It is a hideous voice, quite startling. There is something not human about it. And one look at his face and you know he robbed some poor bull frog of his ... and an ox for his neck and eyes.

'Where is he?' bullfrog-face snarls at me. Only, the snarl is not at all successful – it is a cross between a growl and a bray. The voice comes straight from a donkey.

'Where is who?' I ask, putting my arm across my face to shield my eyes from the light of the torch trained hard on them.

'This boy of yours?'

'Which one?'

'*Wat is die jong se naam, jy*?' He addresses himself to one of the African policemen there.

'UMxolisi, Mama,' the African policeman, gives the answer directly to me.

'Where is he?' Donkey Voice glares at me.

'I don't know,' I reply, truthfully.

Quick as a wink, I feel the sting of his beefy hand. My face is on fire. Even so, lying on the floor, I wonder – Where did that come from? What amazing swiftness from someone of such girth! Crazy, the thoughts that assail one ... crazy and incongruous at a moment like this.

to retrieve (formal) to get back
to snuff out to put out
splintered (here): mixed with thin rays of light
to dodge to avoid by moving suddenly
unholy *unheilig*
din loud, unpleasant sound
to dye to colour
to clatter to make a rattling sound
to reverberate to shake because of a loud noise
to staple *heften*
bumpity-bump (coll.) up and down along a surface
klomp (Afrikaans) bunch
hideous disgusting
bull frog *Ochsenfrosch*
snarl an angry manner of speaking
growl *knurren*
bray sound a donkey makes
to shield to protect
to train to aim
Wat is die jong se naam, jy? (Afrikaans) You, what is the boy's name?
to glare to stare
quick as a wink very quickly
such girth having a large waist
incongruous (here): strange

to elongate to lengthen
to feint (fig.) to make a mock attack to confuse your opponent
to frolic to move about in a happy way
vantage position
nightie (coll.) nightdress

On the walls and ceiling of the unlit room, the unsteady, flickering torch beams paint thin, elongated, ghost-pale figures. The figures feint and dance and gaily frolic.

As I get used to the light from this vantage, I see that Dwadwa and the children are here . . . the two younger children. Of course, Mxolisi is still God only knows where. Absurdly, that is when I realize that I am lying in that pool of light with nothing on but the flannel petticoat, thin with wear, that doubles as nightie by night.

meticulous *gründlich*
lining *Futter*
rafter *Dachsparren*
to dismantle to take apart
plank narrow, long board
from scratch from the very start

Had the police been searching for a needle, they could not have been more meticulous. They practically pulled the house apart; tore mattress, pillows, the doors off wardrobes and the lining off coats hanging in those wardrobes. They looked in beds, they looked under beds, and they took the ceiling down and peered between the rafters. They pulled the floor boards up. They knocked a wall down. Outside in the backyard, they simply dismantled the boys' *hokkie*. They tore the planks off, breaking each and every one of them. Breaking them so that we would never be able to put them together again. That *hokkie* would have to be built up from scratch. Starting with getting new planks, new cardboard, and a lot of nails besides.

When they were quite satisfied Mxolisi was not in the house, not in the *hokkie*, not in the garden, they beat up Lunga although we told them over and over again that he was not Mxolisi . . . not the boy they were looking for. They beat up Lunga even though we told them his name was Lunga and not Mxolisi. They beat him up because, as they said, he should have known his brother's whereabouts.

brother's keeper cf. Genesis 4:9
uproariously loudly
kind'affer (S. African English) kind of a

'You must be your brother's keeper, *ma' an!*' said one, laughing uproariously. 'Otherwise, what kind'affer brother you are, hey?'

'We are tired of this *andaz', andaz'* of you people,' another threw in, as they left. At last.

to hurtle to throw with force

Now they were gone. The police were gone. Gone to wherever they had come from. We could not. No, not us. We could never go back to who we were before they had come. We could never go back to that time or place. Nothing would ever be the same for us. We had been hurtled headlong into the eye of a raging storm.

Chapter Seven

From the beginning, this child has been nothing but trouble. But you have to understand my son. Understand the people among whom he has lived all his life. Nothing my son does surprises me any more. Not after that first unbelievable shock, his implanting himself inside me; unreasonably and totally destroying the me I was. The me I would have become.

to implant (here): to become fixed inside the womb and grow

Troubles come thick as the hairs of a well-fed dog, my people say. In 1973, they certainly did for me. Fifteen. I was only fifteen. But that is the year my son was born. January 4th. And all I had feared at the beginning of the previous year was the monster of a teacher I was getting, strict Mr Vazi.

I was thirteen, almost fourteen, January 1972. About to start the final class of Primary School. I was going into Standard Six and, come year's end, would sit for external examinations. A not insignificant step, as Mama reminded me daily: Gone is the time for playing.

Standard Six eighth grade
external from the central school board

Mama had high hopes for me ... for both of us, my brother and me. Our parents believed that education would free us from the slavery that was their lot as uneducated labourers.

lot fate

Yes, we had our plans. But the year had its plans too; unbeknown to us, of course.

Looking back, I don't even know where to start. Where to lay a finger and say, this is where things began to unravel for me.

to unravel (fig.) to fall apart

But, of one thing I am certain: 1972 definitely delivered more than I had bargained for. However, things began going all awry from the previous February 1971, when my moon time first appeared. That was bad luck number one. As that upside-down year limped to an end, even the long summer holidays promised little reprieve from the ennui brought by Mama's constant worry that I would get pregnant. Not that I'd given her any reason to think like that. But everything about me seemed to upset her these days.

more than I had bargained for more than I had ever expected
awry [əˈraɪ] completely wrong
moon time *Monatsregel*
to limp *hinken*
reprieve *Schonfrist*
ennui [ɒnˈwiː] (literary) boredom

Then, my best friend and I had a fall out. On the first day of the year, too. New Year's Day, 1972. Bad luck number two.

fall out quarrel

We had gone to the beach, as was customary then. Teenagers converged at the beach during what we called the 'Big Days', the public holidays over the Christmas season. That day I discovered that Nono had a huge secret from me. She was my brother's girl friend. I felt such a fool. The two had been seeing each other for months. Nono coming over to my home, pretending she was coming to see me. Khaya, my stupid brother, just happening to be there. Oh, for weeks thereafter I would not speak to her. As far as I was concerned, she had betrayed me in the worst possible way ... with my brother. So, for a while, I was a loner because, of my school friends, Nono was the only one who lived close by.

to converge to get together

halcyon [ˈhælsiən] (literary) happy and peaceful

fancy idea

feeble weak

to yearn for s.th. *sich nach etwas sehnen*

errand short trip to perform a certain task

chesty having a large chest

to whirl around to quickly turn around

to brace yourself to prepare yourself for a difficult task

to heave to lift s.th. heavy

bustling moving about busily

to shoo (here): to shout

gum-boot dance dance with rubber boots that originated with African miners in South Africa

braggart (old-fashioned) a person who boasts loudly about himself/herself

thwack short, loud sound

to sling, slung, slung (here): to place on s.th. where it hangs loosely

CNA a chain of stores in South Africa that sells books, magazines, stationary, CDs, DVDs, Software, PC hardware, etc.

horse-racing card card for placing bets

One day, Mama sent me to Claremont, the white suburb where we did grocery shopping. Imagine my surprise and delight when I ran into a former classmate from the halcyon Blouvlei days. This was a rather rare experience, one often accompanied by promises of staying in touch forever thereafter, 'Now that we've found each other again.' However, with no phones or money with which to take the occasional bus trip and visit one another, maintaining ties could not and did not happen. In what was a fond fancy, a feeble attempt to hide our embarrassment at yearning for the impossible, we'd say to each other on such occasions, 'Come and visit me!' We'd say that, not really expecting what we were asking for to happen ... Not believing it would. And the answer, equally simple and easy and impossible, 'Soon,' never failed to come. 'Soon!' or 'Sure!'

Stella and I had shared a desk since Sub-Standard A, the first year of school, until, with the forced removals, we were separated. I was half-way through my errands, walking along the Main Road, when I heard a voice hail me from behind. Time simply fell away. I was flung back into then and there ... to that warm and familiar place ... to that other time, that had been so much sweeter. That voice – at once chesty and robust – as though the owner suffered from a perpetual cold but had lungs the size of an elephant's – that voice that reminded one of an organ ... never a pure note to it but far from frail.

I whirled around and there three-four metres behind me, on the other side of the street, legs bent out backward at knee as though bracing herself to heave a mighty weight upward, there she was.

Excitedly, we waved at each other in between gaps made by passing cars and bustling pedestrians. At once, Stella indicated by wave of hand, shooing me to stay put, that she would cross over to my side of the street. How long had it been since I'd last seen her? A year? More? My heart doing the gum-boot dance, I waited.

At last, there she was, right beside me. We hugged and kissed, unashamed tears streaming down our cheeks. Then we stepped back, the better to see. We held each other at arm's length. We were both a lot taller and carried a lot more flesh on the bone than we remembered each other. Acknowledging the tremendous changes that had taken place in our bodies, we smiled knowingly.

The way a braggart of a boy would show off, Stella hooked thumb at shoulder, digging beneath the blouse, and pulled: *thwack!*

My mouth fell open. 'You wear a bra?'

Her brows shot upward. 'Of course,' she said, lips slowly spreading sideways, chasing the ears.

Arms slung carelessly around each other's shoulders, we strolled to a CNA bookshop to get Mama's horse-racing card. This was my last errand and Stella had already finished whatever business had brought her to Claremont. On our way back the way we had come, now going to the buses, Stella suddenly stopped, looked at me eyes widened comically and whispered, 'Let's go over there.' She was pointing away from the direction of the bus terminus.

My brows shot up, this time.

'You know how nosy these *toppies* are,' she answered my unvoiced question.

Although we had always felt that adults were meddlesome, I didn't recall our ever actually fleeing from them in the old days unless, busy at play, we were dodging being called home. Why would she be avoiding grownups now?

'Whatever for?' I asked. 'Just come!'

Not waiting for my response, Stella lead the way up Station Road and toward Saint Saviour's Anglican Church behind the shopping area. I followed her and we walked up the road and into the church gardens.

As soon as we'd found a seat, my friend fished out a small packet of cigarettes and a box of matches from her bra.

'Don't be such a baby,' she said to my involuntary gasp of astonishment.

'You smoke?' The silly question slipped past my lips. I felt such a clot. Why is it that a mouth doesn't come furnished with a lid or zip? Lips can be so inadequate. This was one of those times I knew mine would certainly have done with a more secure guard.

Stella blew smoke right into my face. I guess that was a fitting answer to a dumb question.

I moved back; sliding along the bench till I was a foot or so away from her.

She did not attempt to close the gap my moving away had created. The cigarette smoke curled up, forming a hazy screen in front of her face, making her eyes squint and cry. She looked so grown up, all of a sudden.

'D'you know that Toptop has a stomach?' she asked.

'No, she doesn't!' I moved back, closer to her again. 'You're pulling my leg!' I gave my friend a hard, searching look. Toptop was our age. How could she be expecting a baby?

But Stella nodded several times slowly. 'Yes, she does,' she said, again blowing out smoke. Then she answered a question I had not even thought of asking.

'My boyfriend taught me,' and pulled hard on the cigarette.

Stella stayed near many of the people from Blouvlei. The families that had got into concrete houses from the word go, formed a little cluster, an enclave within the township. They even called that part of Guguletu Blouvlei.

The litany of disasters was endless. Nomabhelu, another ex-Blouvlei girl, had been married off to a man old enough to be her father, Stella said. And on and on and on. None of the news I was getting was cheering. Stella didn't seem to have anything to tell me that was funny, happy, or carefree. Problem after problem, that's all she talked about. And I was worse off. I had no news to give her … nothing that, in light of her startling revelations, seemed at all important.

toppie (slang, Afrikaans) dad
meddlesome always interfering
involuntary unintentional
clot (coll., BE) ass, fool
to furnish to supply
lid *Deckel*
zip (BE) *Reißverschluss*
hazy *dunstig*
to squint to partly close the eyes
to pull s.o.'s leg (coll.) to tell s.o. s.th. that is not true
litany (formal) series of events
revelation s.th. revealed that is surprising

imminent soon to happen
subdued unusually quiet
bout short period
withered dried up, shrunken
stump *Stumpf*
to croak *krächzen*
nogal (Afrikaans) moreover
to bare to show
to lurk to be hidden
venom (fig.) poison as produced by a spider or snake
addled (old-fashioned) confused
to swear, swore, sworn (here): *schwören*
funeral [ˈfjuːnərəl] *Begräbnis*

We were both quiet as we walked back to the Main Road and toward the buses. I suppose we both were a little sad at the imminent parting. I know I was somewhat subdued from all these things I had heard.

Suddenly, Stella stopped walking and cried out, 'Oh, I nearly forgot!' A bout of coughing forced a pause before she continued. 'Did I tell you that Sis' Lulu passed away?' A look of sadness passed over her face. Very briefly. One second, it was there, the next, gone. Had I imagined it?

My stomach plunged to my knees. I dropped the bag of groceries I was carrying, for my arms had died while the fingers of my hands changed to withered stumps, totally without feeling.

'Wha-aat?' I heard an unfamiliar voice croak.

'Ja,' Stella shrugged. 'Last month. She and one of the twins. The one called Guguletu, *nogal*.' Incongruously, she smiled. That is, I saw her lips stretch sideways, baring her teeth. But as for her eyes, whatever lurked there, however briefly, horrified me. The furthest thing from a smile I'd ever seen. Since then, I have ever only seen such once or twice. Those eyes burned with an intense and urgent hate. A murderous venom.

However, the next moment, the eyes returned themselves to their former look. Gone, the fierce loathing. And while somewhere in the deep recesses of my addled brain I feebly groped for understanding, Stella added:

'You do remember, she had twins?' Brows raised, eyes widened in question, she asked.

All I could do is shake my head. Not that I meant that I did not remember. Indeed, I remembered only too well. The twins, nicknamed Guguletu and Blouvlei, because people swore one was born in Blouvlei and the other in Guguletu. Of course, that's an exaggeration, they were hours old when they came to Guguletu. Still, it's a way of remembering, I suppose, how they had to run to obey the law as soon as they were born. Guguletu and Blouvlei. And now little Guguletu and his mother were no more.

Later, when I told Mama about Sis' Lulu, she said, 'God! we've been so dispersed, so divided and scattered in this place, we hear of such sad news months and months after the event and after the person's been long buried.' She stopped and looked at me ... but her eyes said she was looking far away.

'She was so young. Poor Lulu; she shook her head. 'Wonder what will happen to the children now.' Mama's voice had aged. It had become her mother, Makhulu's voice: thin, uncertain, distant and unfocused.

Hearing bad news always makes me stupid. It's as though my mind refuses to take in certain matters that it finds unbearable. It was only days later that I asked myself how Sis' Lulu and her baby were buried. This time of year, I knew, *Bhut'* Willie was away at sea. Who had seen to their funeral? Could mother and son have been buried without him? If so, what did that mean? Had he been told of the deaths? How? Would he return one day to find he no longer had a wife? Find one of his three boys also dead? Half his family was gone?

I really meant to visit Stella. That would show Nono I didn't need her. But, strangely, it was that meeting that put Nono and me together again. For when I saw her near the bathrooms, where hers and ours and those of the two neighbours between us converge, I couldn't help blurting out:

'Know what? I saw Stella in Claremont, yesterday.' And that was the beginning of the end of our silly quarrel. Which was tremendous good luck, for me, as things turned out. A new boy arrived from the village of Cala. Handsome as spring weather, and as popular. But it was me China chose for a girlfriend. I, who had never before had a boy interested in her in her whole long life. Bliss was my name.

Only trouble, boyfriends were forbidden. Mama would kill me if she found out. I wasn't even sure that Khaya wouldn't tell Mama if he knew. Nono was my only ally. Dear, darling Nono. And I sure needed an ally. Mama had become quite unreasonable. Ever since my moon time came. With the coming of the red monthly visitors, Mama went berserk, I swear.

'Never let a boy come anywhere near you. Do you hear me?' She said, 'You will have a stomach if you do.'

For months, thereafter, I went around avoiding touching, even hands, with any boy. Including my own brother. It was Nono who explained what Mama meant. Mama who used words so much, one would have thought she could have done a better job explaining this whole business to me.

But that was not her way of doing things. Not as far as my being in danger was concerned. She seemed to think each time I left the house, I could only return with a stomach. To the disgrace of the entire Chizama clan; not just our family. Besides, she was a secretary of the Mothers' Union at our church. With such a high office, she didn't want anyone to say she had raised a rotten potato. By all means, Mama made sure her potato stayed unspoilt.

'Come, lie down, here,' she said the first time.

Puzzled, I looked at her and at the white towel to which she pointed. Why had she spread a clean towel on the floor? I wondered.

'Take off your bloomers and lie down on the towel.' Mama never used the word panties. Bloomers was her word. Always. She had explained to me that was what they were called when they first appeared in her village. Bloomers. So, in her mind, bloomers they stayed. Forever.

There was a struggle, brief and feeble on my part. However, when Mama wanted something done, it got done. And in the manner she wanted it done. That was the beginning of many a trial, for me. Mama's making sure I remained 'whole' or 'unspoilt' as she said.

to blurt out to suddenly say without thinking

bliss extreme happiness

ally [ˈælaɪ] *Verbündete(r)*

red monthly visitor (coll.) period

berserk uncontrollably angry

disgrace *Schande*

Mother's Union international Christian organisation that supports families

unspoilt *unverdorben*

trial (here): unpleasant experience

'God put mothers on earth, to ensure the health of their daughters,' I heard often, whenever I attempted to resist the practice. Each time she looked, she'd wash her hands thereafter. But I was the one who felt dirty. But then, who could I tell the terrible secret to? My best friend, Nono? I'd rather have died first.

During the March ten-day school holidays, bad luck number three fell upon us all. We closed school on Friday. When we woke up, Sunday morning, Ribba was dead. She attended our school and was only two-three years older than Nono and me.

She died during a botched back-yard abortion. The only kind available then. Even then, pretty scarce, difficult to procure, and, needless to say, illegal.

botched done badly
abortion *Abtreibung*
to procure (formal) to obtain

The monthly examinations changed to once a month and every time I was late coming home. No matter where I'd been or with whom. Next, Mama took out the hems of my skirts and dresses. She didn't want me running around asking for trouble, she said. Besides, I was no longer a child. I was grown, a woman.

to take out the hem (*Saum*) (here): to make longer

Manono, Nono's mother, let her wear pants, short skirts, and anything else she wanted. I was sure she did not inspect Nono. Of course, I didn't ask my friend about that. How could I do that without letting her know Mama did that to me? I would die, I was sure, if anyone ever got to know that about me.

China did, though. From our first meeting, he knew. He guessed from my blurting out, 'Mama will know!' and refusing even to sit next to him, in the bush, where we were meeting. Although I loved him with all my heart.

Fortunately, he was a very sensible and sensitive boy. Respected me. Respected and feared his father. Therefore, he had no intention of getting me or himself into that kind of trouble. We spent any time we could squeeze together, kissing and having 'play sex.' No penetration. Mama had warned me never to sleep with a boy as a wife does with her husband. With Nono and China's help, I eventually worked out what that meant. And, with China's complete agreement and support, stayed away from it.

I don't know what got Mama to suspect something was going on between Khaya and Nono. She began to find fault with Nono and her frequent visits. But, above all, with her going into Khaya's *hokkie* even without me being there. Khaya, a year older, was Mama's darling. It killed her that he was in the same class as Nono and me.

to find fault with s.o. to look for mistakes that s.o. makes

Mama's increasing dislike of Nono could hardly escape notice, for Mama mumbled what amounted to obscenities about the girl, whenever Nono came by.

to amount to to be the same as s.th.
obscenity vulgar expression

'Look at those short things she is wearing. Tell me, just tell me, is she not asking for trouble? What does her mother think, letting her go out of the house naked? Oh, she is selling herself, that's for sure. She is selling herself. Do we not all know that a hoe is bought when its shiny sharpness is seen?'

hoe *Hacke*

Nono told her mother about Mama's remarks. Manono came to complain to Mama, who feigned shock and surprise that Nono had taken offence at anything she might have said ... to her or about her.

'*Mmelwane*,' a much surprised Mama said. 'Can we no longer tease our children? Has it come to that?'

But Manono was no born-yesterday chicken. A few choice words were exchanged. By the time she left, she and her good neighbour had papered over things a bit.

But, 'I don't care what they think or say,' Mama fumed as soon as Manono left. 'And the less you or Khaya see of that she-dog, the better,' she said. 'I don't like her ... and never will.'

Imagine Mama's chagrin, her bitter disappointment and anger, when, two short months later, in the second week of the June holidays, a tight-lipped Manono came to tell Mama that Nono was pregnant, and Khaya was responsible. An already far from pretty situation turned uglier. Naturally, in her anger and disappointment, Manono cursed Khaya. More, she cursed his whole clan.

Mama retaliated by forbidding me to talk to Nono.

'I will kill you with my bare hands if I catch you talking to that she-dog!' she said, putting all the blame on Nono.

'Nono should have taken better care of herself,' she said. 'It is the girl's responsibility, as far as I'm concerned, to see that certain boundaries are not crossed.'

Instead of blaming Khaya, Mama said, 'Manono should look in the mirror and ask herself what it was she had failed to do for such a thing to happen to her daughter.'

Not that she made much sense to me, but Mama seemed to be of the opinion that Manono was even more to blame for Nono's pregnancy than Nono herself. Khaya, she pointed out, could not be blamed. 'What do you expect from a boy if you go and spread yourself beneath him?'

I was lucky that way. As I've already said, China was careful and all we did was play sex, with him never going higher than a little above mid-thigh. As I had so often heard Mama grumble, 'A good girl does not sleep with a boy in the manner of a wife with her husband.' And I was a good girl.

Naturally, I was terribly sorry for Nono in her situation. Moreover, her getting pregnant got me back into a grave I had managed to escape. Mama went back to demanding to see me. When I'd come to realize that the event was going to be routine, I'd flatly refused. Not scolding nor threat of beating would move me. Not even threat of putting me out of the house would make me budge. Eventually, Mama had given up, telling me, '*Isala kutyelwa sibona ngolophu!* – She who refuses advice will learn through burn marks!'

But now, with Nono pregnant, Mama resumed her demands and told me up front, 'If you don't want me to see you, I'm calling your

to feign [feɪn] (formal) to pretend
to take offence to feel insulted
chagrin (formal) annoyance
to retaliate to repay an injury in kind
thigh *Oberschenkel*
to scold *ausschimpfen*
to budge (fig.) to change your opinion
to resume to begin again after stopping
up front frankly

untoward improper
encounter meeting
stand-off situation where an agreement is not possible
to derange to drive mad
to plead to ask in a serious way, to appeal earnestly
to no avail useless
to banish *verbannen*
cock *Hahn*
to crow *krähen*
ridge raised strip
to brand (here): to cause marks
welt raised mark on the skin produced by a blow
to stir to move slightly
rondavel (Afrikaans) round, grass hut with a pointed top

fathers to come and do it themselves. I will not be responsible for anything untoward happening to you.'

'Nothing is going to happen to me, Mama,' I said. Not for the first time, I was deeply grateful China didn't demand or expect that I split myself wide open for him in our secret encounters.

The stand-off between Mama and me lasted less than a week. I fully expected Mama to act on her threat at the weekend. But, of course, I also hoped against hope that she wouldn't call my uncles to come and inspect me. I also knew that if she did, they would certainly give me some kind of option, a way out in their eyes. I could hear one of them clear his throat and say:

'Mmh-mhh! Our daughter, ehh ... our sister, your mother here, has called us to our home because of her love for you. She only wants to do what is good for you ... good and right and proper. Fitting. Now, are you going to force us to do this, or will you let your mother do what she must do, what all mothers should do?'

But I had not realized how completely Nono's pregnancy had deranged Mama. Come Friday, didn't she come up with something I had totally not foreseen?

'Mandisa, get your school books and uniform ready. On Sunday, I'm taking you to Gungululu.'

I cried and pleaded with her. I promised to be good, do all the housework, do it even before she asked me to; never miss school; do all my laundry as well as my brother's. I would do hers too, I said. And Tata's, when he came back from sea.

But all was to no avail. Nothing I said or did would change my mother's mind.

I was so desperate not to be sent away, banished to the village, where one never saw meat until a cow or another beast died, I even brought the hated white towel out myself, spread it on the floor and urged Mama to see me ... see that I was still a whole girl, complete and untouched.

But, nothing helped. Mama had lost all reason. She felt that the only way I could escape getting pregnant was if she went and hid me in the village, 'where children still know how to behave.' She would not trust even her own eyes, she said.

Two months to my fourteenth birthday, Mama took me, by train, to the hard place of her birth and growing up, the village of Gungululu, where children were named according to the spaces between the years of rain. Fourteen, almost. Banished to a far-away desert. To go and stay with her mother, Makhulu, someone I had not set eyes on in all my life. Someone who had never seen me before.

Gungululu – September 1972

First cocks had not yet crowed. The ridges of the grass mat on which I lay branded welts to my side. Not a mouse stirred, the rondavel was dead, dead quiet; a mirror to the eerie quiet pressing the walls inward till they threatened to collapse on me. Outside, I knew at this time of day, lay the heavy still darkness that precedes dawn, muffling all life as petulant night held its breath before it gathered itself up for inevitable flight at the assault of dawn. On my back, in the dark, I lay wide-eyed staring at the ceiling - at the dizzying rafters radiating from pillar to wall, dividing the thatch above me into twelve neat sections. I had counted them, soon after my arrival here, during those sleepless nights, three months ago. Three long months ago.

Swifter than a blink, my mind sped to Cape Town. To a special someone there. Was he up? I wondered. China. The dear face swam before my eyes. Fleeing the all-too-familiar pain, I kicked the blankets off, got up, left the hut and went around to the back.

I was just reaching for the door, on my way back, when Makhulu's voice hailed:

'*Sowuvukile? Unjan' ukuvuya, nivala?*'

'*Ewe*, Makhulu,' I answered. That yes would suffice for both questions, I reckoned. I was up and sure was glad the school holidays had come. Finally.

The last day of the third quarter of the year. My first quarter at a new school, hundreds of kilometres from home. My mind turned to the last school closing. June. And the events surrounding it. Events it hemmed. So remote they seemed now. Their consequences, however, were my daily bread. Bitter as gall. They were the reason for my being where I was: Gungululu Village, my mother's girlhood home.

I remembered my fervent promises to Mama. But those promises of good behaviour fell on deaf ears. Thinking about it, even now, made me so angry, my eyes smarted. I had given Mama no reason for concern, but had that stopped her from pursuing '... the only solution I can see.'? She banished me to this remote village of the Transkei, where I thought I would die. The by-product of Mama's caution, separation from China, was unbearable.

China. I was certain that were it not for him ... and, to a lesser extent, Makhulu, the end of the school semester would not have found me alive. Dear, dear China.

But it was Makhulu, Mama's mother, whose daily ministrations, especially in the beginning, had helped keep me not only sane ... but bodily alive. She made sure I ate, in a roundabout way finding out my preferences and making sure to cook those even when, as I found out later, she didn't particularly care for the dish herself. When I returned from school, I could bet on her saying, '*Kalok' umam' akho akakho apha,*' as she planked a bowl of *umvubo* or some other titbit on the kitchen table even as I changed from the black gym dress and white shirt to my day clothes. But I saw through her guise. If Mama's absence were the only reason for her caring so much, her kind acts would surely have worn off soon after Mama left. However, Makhulu's kindness, her gentle ways, could not stop that other hunger. The gnawing question in the mind of the abandoned child, the banished child, the forsaken child. Since the day I watched as Mama walked

eerie strange, weird
to precede (formal) to happen before
to muffle to make quieter by covering
petulant ['petjulənt] irritable, bad-tempered
pillar metal, stone, or wooden post to support the roof
thatch dried grass or reeds for making the roof
to suffice (formal) to be enough
to hem *säumen*
remote far away
gall *Galle*
fervent passionate
to smart to feel a sharp pain
Transkei a former African enclave
by-product *Nebenprodukt*
ministrations (plural) act of helping and taking care of s.o.
sane having a normal, healthy mind
to plank to place heavily
umvubo a traditional Xhosa meal, consisting of maize meal, water, and sour milk
titbit (BE) small amount of food
guise [gaɪz] behavior that masks the true motive
to wear off (here): to eventually cease
gnawing (here): constantly causing anxiety

heron *Reiher*
brand (here): type
to brew (here): to prepare
to discount (here): to ignore
wholly (formal) completely

away … watched her dry-eyed, still as a heron fishing by the riverside, I had never again been alone. Mama left. A stranger walked into the place in my heart she had left unoccupied: grief, sharp as a new razor.

But here I was. I had survived the first three months. Three to go. Then I'd be done with Primary School. What then? What special brand of torture was Mama brewing back in Cape Town? As far as I could see, we had two choices: Cape Town, where I could attend one of the two high schools in the area. Cheaper, as I would be living at home. Or, I would be sent to boarding school. I prayed it would be the latter. But of late, God had been less than inattentive to my prayers; so although I had not come to discount Him completely, I thought it best not to depend on Him wholly. Look where that had got me in the past.

detour [ˈdiːtʊə] *Umweg*
wearisome making you feel tired
tedious [ˈtiːdiəs] boring
lead [led] *Blei*
to tread, trod, trod to walk along
wont (old-fashioned) habit

Three weeks before school closed, on my way from school, I had stopped for mail at the village shop, where the whole region, some twenty or so villages, got its mail. *Baas* Setheni, a white man, and his wife ran the shop. No letter from China. Leaving the shop, the detour I'd made suddenly wearisome, tedious and long, my feet lead, I trod homeward. Mocking me, was Makhulu's letter in my hand. What did she need with a letter?

As was her wont, Makhulu was sitting on her grass mat on the floor, doing some mending, when I got home. She sat with her back against the wall, and her legs, stretched out in front of her, were loosely wrapped in her black skirt so that only the feet peeped from beneath the loose floral pinafore she wore on top.

pleasantries a few friendly remarks

'Where is it from?' she asked when, following the exchanging of greetings and a few pleasantries, I told her she had a letter. She didn't look up.

'East London.'

'East London?' she stopped. Stopped the sewing and looked up. 'East London!' she repeated. However, this time, her words were more exclamation than question.

exclamation strong emotional statement

'Yes, Makhulu,' I said. 'It is from East London.'

deluge [ˈdeljuːdʒ] flood

'Hurry and get every living thing inside,' she said quietly. 'It's not rain but a deluge that'll fall upon us, if that letter's from Funiwe!' In the same unhurried voice, Makhulu continued. Sewing still in her hands, she had not resumed the mending but sat there, looking at me as though she couldn't quite believe what I said. Auntie Funiwe is Mama's younger sister. Her only sister. Malume, their brother, is the middle child.

'What are you waiting for?' Makhulu asked suddenly. 'Open it and read it for me!'

'What?' midway through the letter, she interrupted my reading. 'Read me that again,' she said. 'Read over that again.'

I did.

Again and again, Makhulu made me stop and go over some detail.

'*Bulisa kuBhuti lowo. Yithi ndiyamkhumbula, kumnandi ke kuba siza kubonana kungekudala*. Greetings to older brother. Tell him I miss him and am glad we will see each other before long.' I had come to the end of the letter. At long last.

The mending carelessly thrust to her side – for once, she had not folded it neatly and put it back into the sewing-bag – Makhulu sat still, her jaw dropped so that her mouth hung open as her eyes stared blindly into the distance.

'*He, Mntan'omntan'am*, Hey, Child of My Child,' Makhulu said solemnly. Her voice a bare whisper, she continued, without looking at me, standing there at her feet. 'Where does it say, this letter, that it is coming from Funiwe?' she asked, eyes still focused on some distant object only she could see.

I showed her the name, knowing full well the squiggles on the page meant nothing at all to her. Makhulu scrunched her face. Eyes narrowed to a slit, she peered at the point where my finger lay. It would not have mattered two hoots whether I had showed her to the salutation, body, or ending of the letter. But the way she poured over those letters made me a little uneasy. As though she could really divine the mystery they held.

I thought she was satisfied for, nodding her head, she harrumphed and made as though she were about to resume her mending. But as I turned around to go to the bowl waiting for me on the table at the top of the hut, once more, Makhulu's voice arrested me to the spot.

'You said, did you not, *Mzukulwana*, that the letter comes from Funiwe herself?'

'That's right, Makhulu.'

'And it says she is going to have a baby?' 'Yes, Makhulu.'

There was a pause, but I remained where I was, for I sensed that she was not done with her questions. I was right. Although, what came next were not really questions but observations, musings.

'*SesikaLizbethi waseBhayibhileni, ndifung' uBaw' ekobandayo*! It's Biblical Elizabeth's story all over again, by my father's bones in the cold earth!' There followed some mumbled comments I couldn't catch before she went on in a more audible manner, her voice once more raised:

'Funiwe? The same who got married even before you were born? Funiwe? Expecting a baby?' Then, in a calmer voice, she turned to me and, addressing me more directly, said, 'Does she say she's had the baby or she's still expecting it?'

'Makhulu,' I answered, 'Auntie Funiwe says she's coming here to have the baby.'

'Here?' she asked and quickly added, 'When does she say she's coming?'

'She doesn't say exactly when ... only as soon as schools close. But yes, she's coming to have the baby here.'

'Schools? Schools?' Makhulu asked, brow furrowed. 'What has she got to do with schools? When did she become a teacher?'

to thrust to push suddenly in a certain direction

squiggle handwriting with twists and curls

to scrunch to squeeze together

slit thin opening

two hoots (coll.) at all

salutation greeting at the beginning of a letter

to divine (formal) to guess

to harrumph (coll.) to clear your throat

musings thoughts after contemplating

Elizabeth Cf. Luke 1: 5-80 – Mother of John the Baptist, who gave birth to her son late in life

audible loud enough to be heard

brow (literary) forehead

to furrow (here): to pull together and make lines

She made me go over that letter four more times. Then, when she finally accepted what it said, when she allowed herself to believe the news, her shoulders sagged as a long soft sigh escaped through her immobile lips. Hands lay open and limp on her thighs. Her eyes closed. Only to open an invisible tap inside. Great blobs of silent tears coursed down her trembly cheeks and washed over the finely wrinkled face. I stood there, unable to move, filled with fear lest I disturb the wordless thanksgiving, so heartfelt.

Many moments later, Makhulu brought herself back. Wiping her face with the back of her hand, she tried to smile. But that just brought a fresh waterfall. Quickly, she bent forward and reached toward her toes, grabbed the hem of her pinafore, turned it over and brought it to her face.

That night, as I lay dozing off at that time between warm woozy wakefulness and complete collapse of consciousness, the final plunge into oblivion, a bell rang ... deep in the inner recesses of my mind: BOO-OING! Triggered by something Makhulu had said earlier.

Yes! I would ask Auntie Funiwe. I would ask to go and do my high school studies in East London. Stay with her. I could help with the baby too. She would need help. Anyone who had a baby couldn't help it ... they always needed help. They were such a load of work, babies were.

The very next day, I sent off a letter to China, outlining my strategy.

Every day thereafter, sometimes several times a day, Makhulu would make me read the letter to her. Whether she didn't or couldn't bring herself to totally believe the good news or bouts of doubts assailed her at moments, I couldn't say. But her behaviour increased my curiosity about this aunt of mine, whom I had never seen. The aunt who was married seven months before I was born. The aunt I had determined would be my salvation. Escape from Mama. Escape into a better arrangement, nearness to China. He must apply to the boarding schools in the Ciskei, I'd told him in the letter.

New life injected itself into Makhulu's being. She hummed ceaselessly as she went about her chores. Old daily tasks were done with the speed of lightning. New ones were found and attacked with ferocious enthusiasm: let's air the blankets! Are the visitors' sheets clean? Have all the pots been scoured till they shine? Sinda! Smear the floors with cow dung to clean and freshen them. Auntie was arriving in two days. I began to fear that the excitement would kill Makhulu long before she arrived. I had not seen her this excited in the three months of my stay in Gungululu. She was a woman possessed. I shared Makhulu's enthusiasm for Auntie Funiwe's advent. I shared it because, for the first time since my bitter banishment, the serrated knife that ceaselessly tore at the tender flesh of my heart took a pause. I dared not hope, though. I had been too badly scarred by the move. I was too

to sag to hang down
immobile motionless
limp loose
tap *Wasserhahn*
blob large drop
wrinkled with many folds

woozy (coll.) dazed, confused
plunge drop
oblivion state of having forgotten everything
to trigger *auslösen*

bout (here): short period

salvation *Rettung*
Ciskei a former African enclave in South Africa
inject itself (fig.) flowed into

ferocious aggressive
to scour to clean by rubbing hard
dung *Mist (Dünger)*

possessed under the influence of a powerful force
advent coming
serrated with a series of sharp points along the edge
tender soft, delicate
to scar to cause a scar/scars (*Narbe*)

scared to hope ... I couldn't afford to have anything as precious as that be dashed. Once again.

Now, wide-eyed, I lay on the bed, blankets flung to my feet, eyes wide with excitement. What did China think of my plan? Surely, he'd got my letter by now. And would Auntie Funiwe take me up on my proposal? Oh, Dear God, would she? And when, exactly, would she come?

Stirrings outside. The animals, awake at last. To the gaggling of geese, who seemed always to wake up arguing querulously, sheep baah'ed and cows lowed. From behind the homestead, the trees were alive. Birds twittered and chirruped. A lone owl to-hoot-hooted and I imagined him circling lazily before gliding on one wing to his diurnal haunt. Through gaps in the curtain peeped jagged pieces of an angrily red mist risen high up above the still-black mountain peaks. Dawn had broken.

Not one child was in uniform. The teachers had told us the previous day to come in our house dresses. There was to be a big clean-up for the closing. Looking at the motley gaggle all around me, I could have sworn there were more children than usual. Had the numbers swelled and multiplied? Then again I thought that might be the result of the day dresses we were wearing. Whatever it was, on one thing though, I'm certain: school was anything but ordinary that day. Even classes stopped early, with lunch break. Thereafter, assembly was called.

In the courtyard, the hard clearing sheltered from the forever howling southeaster by the huddle of rondavels, our classrooms, we waited with barely concealed impatience. Eager and noisy. Unable to stand still or keep quiet. Again I was struck by how little resemblance there was between the rabble I found myself in and the neat rows of spindly-legged girls in black gyms and white shirts and boys in grey flannels and black blazers usually assembled there on normal school days. A slight, brief hush fell as the five teachers came and stood in front of us on a raised platform made from desks. The first six classes: A and B; One and Two; Three and Four shared a teacher and only Standards Five and Six had teachers all to themselves.

We quietened down some. The teachers were about to give out the results of the end-of-term test we'd just written.

Class by class, starting from the little ones, the Sub Standards A's and B's and going right up to Standard Six, the teachers called out the names and class positions of their pupils. After the Sub Standards came Standard One. Then, Standard Two. Then, Three. At fourteen, I was in Standard Six. And, at long last, our turn came. Mrs Songca stepped out of the line of teachers and called out:

'Sidney Sokuyeka!' My heart turned to a ragged-edged block of ice that tore at something inside me till it bled. I had not expected to gain first position, for although I had done exceedingly well in my old school, I'd been a little lost, if not downright bewildered, on com-

precious valuable
to dash (here): to destroy

to gaggle to make a loud noise
querously in a very irritable way
to low to moo
homestead house with land
owl *Eule*
diurnal daytime
haunt place always returned to
jagged with rough, pointed edges
mist fog

motley assorted, dissimilar
gaggle group of noisy people

to shelter to protect
huddle objects close together

rabble mob
spindly-legged with long and thin legs

downright quite
bewildered confused

ing to Upper Gungululu Primary School, back in early July. All these months, it had not occurred to me that I could come last. But once the thought planted itself in my brain, it fastened itself there like a sore tooth. I could not shake it off though I told myself it could not be. There were hopeless cases, real duds, who could never, ever, get better marks than me or anyone for that matter. But still, the doubt stayed. How badly had I done? There were thirty-three of us in the class. I'd never in my life brought up the rear. Would this be the first time? Suddenly, my mouth went dry. I swallowed, but nothing went down. Again I swallowed. As though to make quite sure. Again, my throat remained stubbornly parched.

dud (coll.) a person who is a failure

to bring up the rear (fig.) to be the last in a race

parched very dry

Just then, the teacher called out:

'Mandisa Ntloko ... Number Two!' A loud raucous burst of air escaped from my mouth. Till then, I had not realized that I held my breath. Waiting. Fearing I might be the tail. What would Makhulu have said to that? And China? God, I would have been so embarrassed. China was such a good student. Almost as good as I had been, back at my old school, my real school, Vuyani Primary School in Guguletu.

raucous loud and rough

After the cleaning and final announcements, we were dismissed. On the way home, I soon outran my group, left them behind. Twenty of us made the daily trip to and from the valley to the school, high up the ridges walling the village in. Not for me, today, the dillying and dallying of my school mates and fellow travellers.

to dismiss to allow to go

dillying and dallying taking your time doing s.th.

My feet swift and light, my heart sang for I was quite pleased with the test results. I knew that Makhulu would be pleased. So would China. And to me then, China was who mattered most.

The thought of China lent me wings. However, much more than the ten days off school or even the good examinations results made my heart sing. My Auntie Funiwe, Mama's only sister, was coming. As soon as schools close, the letter had said.

to lend, lent, lent (here): to provide for a short time

Half-way home, I stopped at the village shop. To get Makhulu her Extra Strong's, the triple X mints she called her snuff. Also to check the mail.

snuff *Schnupftabak*

Two letters. The maize-coloured envelope, one of them. Trying hard not to show my impatience and excitement, I snatched the letters from *Baas* Setheni's hand, spun around and was at the door when a voice stopped me. Could this already be the reply to my letter to him last week? The letter about next year's plans?

'The Extra Strongs!' *Baas* Setheni shouted, a hard bang on the counter, telling me he'd put them there.

Leaving the shop, Makhulu's mints gripped tightly in one hand, I raced downhill. The fast walkers ahead, clearly visible. The hum or buzz of voices too near for my liking. Especially with China's letter burning a hole over my heart.

If it had not been for his letters, I don't know how I could have got over the months of banishment. Not that Makhulu was not kindness itself. But there was a lump in my throat each time I thought of how Mama had plucked me from Guguletu, in Cape Town, and come and dumped me in this remote village. Far away from everything and everyone dear to me. Not that, as I have already said, I was ill-treated or anything like that. The school was not bad either. I could have forgiven Mama all those things. Except China. Her taking me from Guguletu meant that I was separated from China. Even the pleasure of a good examinations result was marred by the anger that I still felt. It would have served Mama right had I failed the test. Served her right for taking me away from school, from my beloved teachers, and from all my friends. And China.

Tall, handsome China. Small slanted eyes. Short hair, never combed but always resembled peppercorns carelessly strewn about. A decided mix of uncomplementary features that, somehow, managed to end up with the most pleasing outcome. And such a good sportsman. So popular with both students and teachers. How I missed him.

However, as of now, my heart sang, my feet were swift and light, barely touching ground as I galloped towards the cluster of rondavels that, for the last three months, I'd called home. To be honest, though, I was not so much hurrying home as I was hurrying away from the other children.

I reached the hillock beyond which lay Makhulu's homestead. My back against a gum tree, I sat and took out the letter. Carefully, I down-tapped the letter, making sure the top end of the envelope was clear. Then, slowly, I tore it open. Slowly. Carefully.

Four pages. Folded in three equal parts. Always meticulous.

The unfolded pages lay open. The familiar scrawl. A never-ending source of amazement. China, so handsome, so elegant. How did he end up with such a handwriting? As though one had dipped a fly in an inkwell, fished it out, and let it crawl all over the page as the fancy took it.

Nights in the village are total, pitch black and impenetrable, unless there is a full moon. Auntie arrived on a moonless night. In the unmitigated darkness outside, before she came into the rondavel in which Makhulu, already in bed, awaited her, I sensed more than saw that she was at least as large as Mama. Once she was inside, by the dim light of a candle, she appeared to have a milky-coffee complexion where her sister is the colour of the berry of isipingo, a blue-tinged black. However, because of the time of day and conditions of light, this was all rather vague, more an impression than firm opinion.

The next morning, when I brought coffee into Makhulu's bedroom, where Auntie had spent the night with her mother, I was too shy to out and out look at her, examine her better, see if my impressions of the previous night were borne out by the light of morning. What if she caught me staring at her? Wouldn't she think I was rude? However, the eye being what it is, so difficult to keep in check, twice I

lump *Klumpen*
to mar to spoil
slanted eyes *Schlitzaugen*
peppercorn *Pfefferkorn*
to strew, strewed, strewn to scatter
uncomplementary not fitting together
hillock small hill
gum tree a eucalyptus tree
to down-tap to hit gently downwards
scrawl careless writing
inkwell *Tintenfass*
fancy momentary desire
impenetrable cannot be seen through
unmitigated complete, absolute
berry of isipingo black berry found in eastern South Africa
blue-tinged with a slight blue colour
to bear, bore, borne out (BE) to confirm

stole a glance at her; twice I found her staring at me, a puzzled frown splitting her forehead.

How sharp her eye to have discerned what the experienced one of Makhulu's had failed to see in the more than two months of my stay in Gungululu. Although, upon further reflection, perhaps all Auntie Funiwe did was help peel back the veil of love that occluded the bitter truth from Makhulu's vision.

'Is this child of Kukwana's well?' she asked Makhulu as I left the hut. Kukwana is Mama's girlhood name.

'Why do you ask?' I heard Makhulu ask, for Auntie's words had stopped me just outside the hut, ears against the closed door. My heart-beat quickened. Why were their voices guarded, cautious?

'When did you say her mother brought her here?'

'June,' Makhulu answered.

'Three months ago!' Auntie's voice was slightly raised now. It sounded as though she were alarmed. A pause followed. Fearing discovery. I stepped back and quickly walked away from the door. But not before I had heard Auntie ask, 'Has she been ... ?' Been what? My mind groped for the rest of that question.

Been what? What was it that so concerned Auntie? Her voice had been truly laced with apprehension.

'How do you think I should know about such a thing?' Makhulu's voice, now querulous, reached me where I had stopped, just outside the kitchen.

They both sounded angry now, their voices strident. Neither seemed bothered any more that I might overhear their discussion. Did this mean what they were talking about was not serious? Not something they needed to hide from my ears? Had I made a mistake, earlier, thinking otherwise?

Relieved, I tiptoed back. From the sound of their voices, they had not moved from where I had left them ... on Makhulu's bed. 'Mama!' Auntie's voice said she was agitated. 'What are you telling me? Have you not seen ... ?'

'Seen what?' sharp came Makhulu's irate answer. 'You know girls these days no longer use rags. What am I supposed to see?'

Silence.

How long did I stand there, my feet turned to lead? Makhulu's words had laid bare an awful fact that I had ignored. How had I not realized that in all the time I had been in Gungululu I had not once seen my periods?

Oh, the gruelling interrogation. The frantic and futile denials. Eventually, sobbing hysterically, I broke down.

'Yes, Makhulu,' I choked, 'I do have a boyfriend.'

Even so, I clung to the truth. NO NO NO! How could Makhulu and Auntie think I could have so misbehaved. I had done nothing wrong, I told them. Ferociously, I defended my innocence, despite the evidence that pointed so clearly and unambiguously to my guilt.

to discern to detect, to recognize
reflection careful thought
to peel back (fig.) to remove a covering
veil [veɪl] *Schleier*
to occlude to cover or block
guarded careful so no-one can hear what you are saying
laced (here): filled
apprehension anxiety
querulous annoyed
strident [ˈstraɪdnt] aggressive
irate very angry
rag (here): anything used to soak up menstrual blood
to lay bare (formal) to uncover, to reveal
gruelling harsh, exhausting, severe
interrogation questioning
futile useless
denial *leugnen*
to choke to speak with difficulty because of being unable to breathe properly
to cling, clung, clung to s.th. (fig.) to hold tightly to s.th.
ferociously in a very aggressive manner
unambiguously in a clear manner

'You have to believe me!' I screamed. 'Makhulu, and you, Auntie, you must believe me when I say I have done nothing shameful.'

'Yes, Child of My Child,' Makhulu answered, her voice heavy with sadness, 'but you have to be completely honest with us about this matter.'

Honest? But that is what I had been all along. Honest. I look at Makhulu, make my eyes look at hers. Long moments of silence follow. What's the point? I think to myself. They already believe the worst about me. They all do. At last, I heard myself resume the discussion.

No, I told them, Mama had not told me how to be with a boy. She had told me never to be with one. Never. Yes. Yes, the boy concerned had known what to do, how to keep me safe. No. No, not once. He had never gone inside me but always played outside, between the thighs. Yes. Yes, he respected me. He did. Neither he nor I wanted to do anything to disgrace our families. His father was a lay preacher in the church.

lay preacher *Laienprediger*

Both Auntie and Makhulu wanted to know who this boy was. His name.

'China,' I said.

'China?' Makhulu asked, her brow creased. 'From which family is he?' She did not recall such a name, she said. Whose child was this China?

to crease to make a line in the skin

'Makhulu, China does not live here,' I explained, lifting my eyes in amazement at the realization that they thought I had a boyfriend here in the village.

'He lives in Cape Town,' I said.

If I had said China was *impundulu*, the firebird, Makhulu and Auntie could not have been more shocked.

'D'you see what I was telling you?' Makhulu turned to Auntie Funiwe. 'This child has been indoors every time she was not at school or in church. I've known her whereabouts each moment she's been here with me. And nights?' here Makhulu raised her voice. 'Nights, why, she sleeps the sleep of the dead!' There was a pause. As though both women were going over what had just been said, neither uttered a word. Then, once more, Makhulu spoke.

to utter to speak

'So, I kept thinking my old eyes were deceiving me ... playing tricks on me ... that it couldn't be.'

to deceive to mislead

Again, she paused before adding:

'Remember now ... remember that her Mama brought her here saying she was whole. She told me herself that she had been seeing this child. So what was I to think?'

'I see,' answered Auntie Funiwe. 'I see,' she repeated as if to herself.

'I told myself to wait and see,' Makhulu went on. 'With time, you know that if you have kneaded, the dough will certainly rise. I knew that, sooner or later, therefore, everything would become clear ... obvious.'

to knead [ni:d] *kneten*
dough *Teig*

'I see,' Auntie Funiwe said again. Her voice said she was as puzzled or as confused as ever.

midwife *Hebamme*
parchment (formerly) skin of a sheep used for writing
tentative uncertain, cautious
tumult (formal) violent agitation
hired rented
to slump to sink or fall heavily and suddenly
torrent violent stream
to gush to pour out suddenly
unchecked not prevented from continuing
to wail to make a long cry of grief
to keen (old-fashioned) to lament
to rejoice (formal) to express great happiness
numb unable to feel anything
to drain to cause to become empty
virgin *Jungfrau*
solace comfort

And it is after that discussion between Makhulu and Auntie Funiwe that Makhulu sent for the village midwife, an old, toothless woman with dry, wrinkled parchment for skin. Wise eyes. A walking bag full of the smell of snuff. The old woman who came and looked at me the way Mama had done. She looked and saw that what I said, that I had done no shameful thing, was true. But she saw something else ... something I did not know – did not understand. Even when she put what she saw into words, I still did not know what it was she was saying.

The old woman said, '*Utakelwe*! She has been jumped into!'

If I live to be a hundred, I will never forget those days. The first days following the old woman's one-word sentence: *Utakelwe*.

Following the words of the midwife, the very next day, Malume went to town to go and send a telegram calling Mama back to the village. That day, too, the baby inside me announced his existence. Out of the blue, there in my belly, was the small, tentative movement of a mouse awakening from deep sleep. Slowly, gradually, the stirring quickened to a tumult. Equally bewildering, were the answering feelings inside my heart. A strong feeling I could not identify ... too scared to give it a name. But I was warm, all over. And, from myself, I couldn't hide the wide, wide smile in my heart.

Two days later, Mama arrived in a hired car; the driver, a man I did not know.

In silence she received the news. Eyes staring unseeingly, she sat slumped against Makhulu's shoulders, listening as though the words meant little, if anything at all, to her.

Then, the flood came. A torrent of tears gushing unchecked down her cheeks. Then followed the wailing. Mama keened as though announcing the death of a beloved, honoured relative.

'What will the church people say?' Mama wailed. 'What are they to think of me?' The shame to the family would surely kill her, she said.

Auntie Funiwe reminded her that this was a sad accident and that the family had nothing to be ashamed of.' This child has not disgraced the name of the family.'

'Oh, you don't know anything,' Mama continued her wailing. 'My enemies are going to rejoice. They're going to laugh at me now.'

'What do you care for such small-minded, mean people?' Auntie asked. 'Let them laugh, their turn'll come,' she said. 'Ours now is to look after this child,' she nodded my way. 'We must support and protect her now. How do you think she must be feeling?'

Feeling? I was numb, beyond feeling. Mama's coming, her reaction, had drained the last ounce of feeling from me. Fear. Shame. Anger. All these and more mingled together to form one strong thinning liquid that replaced my blood. A corpse would have more feeling than I had right then, I was sure. Like Mama, the fact that the midwife had confirmed that I was a virgin was little solace. I was pregnant, wasn't

I? What was to become of me now? What good was that precious virginity under these changed circumstances? I wished I would just die. Right then and there. I was so ashamed. So scared. My whole world had simply collapsed and was no more.

However, despite all Auntie's solicitations and Makhulu's advice and admonition, Mama would not be consoled. Neither would she be moved. Not by word or by deed, not once did she indicate that she considered me an innocent victim and therefore someone worthy of her sympathy.

How had this happened? How could a 'tadpole' from China's 'life water' make its way up and inside me without me feeling a thing? How could it have entered me like that?

Auntie Funiwe. So much store had I put on her coming. Made great plans, banking on her benevolence. But, the very next morning following her arrival, not only did those grand plans unravel but my very life came to an abrupt halt. The life I had known. The life I had envisaged. Everything I had ever known had been bulldozed, extinguished, pulverized. Everything was no more. Not as it had been or had seemed to be ... or was about to be ... such a short while ago. Only days ago.'

solicitation request for support, plea
admonition (formal) warning
to console to comfort

tadpole (fig.) *Kaulquappe,* i.e. sperm
to put store on s.th. to consider s.th. as important for the success of a plan
to bank on s.th. to rely on s.th.
benevolence kindness, generosity
to envisage to imagine what might happen in the future
to extinguish (fig.) to destroy
to pulverize (fig.) to crush into a powder

Chapter Eight

Three children have come from my womb. Three claim me as mother. Three. But now, since your daughter's unfortunate death, I have been called mother to so many more: Mother of the beast. Mother of the serpent. The puff-adder's mother. There are those who even go as far as calling me Satan's mother.

I know. With a mother's pierced heart, I know. All these names refer to but one of my children. He who was first upon my nipple. He who came unbid; bringing a harvest of shame to my father's house. Bitter tears to a mother's proud heart.

The journey back to Cape Town was strained, awkward and agonising, most of the time. It was filled with uneasy silences as the hired car rattled along the long, deserted dusty by-roads. We were avoiding the main roads and thoroughfares, the driver said, because of fear of harassment from the Traffic Cops, 'Who will stop a car driven by a black man as a matter of course.'

The driver, sure-handed on the wheel, was a taciturn man, quite content to hum along with the tune crackling from the car radio. Making the speech about the Traffic Cops was the most animated I'd seen him. Once the strategy of which roads to take and why had been decided upon, I rarely heard a word from him except, 'Thank you!' when Mama gave him something to eat or, 'Excuse me!' when Nature called and he had to stop the car by the side of the road and lean close to it or go into a nearby thicket.

'Look at that!'

The shout woke me up. With a start, I saw that I must have dozed off.

'D'you see that!'

What was all this screaming about? Without appearing too interested, I looked out the window. Nothing. Cows bent lazily over the grass. Hundreds of them ... but still ... cows were nothing over which to get all excited.

'Can you believe that all these cattle belong to one Boer? We have been driving, for over an hour, through ONE farm? The man owns half the Transkei, doesn't he?'

Surprise, surprise, surprise! The man of little words had suddenly become quite loquacious. On and on he ranted, Mama supplying the occasional 'Mmhh-mh!' The driver (whose name I didn't get to know throughout the trip, Mama referring to him as *Mntuwenkosi*, Man of the Lord, which means nothing) went on about how the Boers arrived in the country, long ago, with not one animal between them.

'Stole them from us. STOLE everything from us. Where do you get to buy a farm such as this one ... for a copper bangle?'

'*Mmmhh-mh! Mmhh-mmmhhh!*'

puff-adder large, extremely poisonous snake found in Africa *(Bitis arietans)*
pierced with a small hole made with a sharp instrument
nipple *Brustwarze*
unbid not asked
strained tense
agonising causing great suffering
thoroughfare main road
as a matter of course routinely
taciturn (formal) tending not to say much
to crackle to make a series of slight, sharp noises
when Nature called when it was necessary to urinate or defecate
to lean to rest against s.th. for support
thicket group of bushes
Boer [bɔː] (Afrikaans) a person of Dutch origin
the Transkei former African enclave in South Africa
loquacious (formal) talkative
to rant to speak in an angry way
bangle gold, silver, etc. ring worn around the wrist

Bumpity-bump-bump-bump went the long, cavernous car; the driver's thin frame hunched over the wheel. Mama huddled against the opposite door, and I sat somewhere behind them but in such a way that I wasn't so much behind the driver that I was kitty corner to Mama, and thus in her direct line of vision should she turn around. At the same time, I had no wish to be directly behind her. That would be too close, certainly for my comfort. I might have been wrong, but I sensed that Mama too had no wish for my nearness. Although the music was not low, the silence between the three people in the car was louder. It nearly drowned the music. It hung over us thick and palpable. It enveloped us, each in a separate cocoon of terrible, unbearable unease.

Whenever Mama broke that heavy and brooding wordlessness, it was with a haunted voice, a voice that said to the world at large that she had suffered some unimaginable pain. If she'd lost her husband and both her parents in one train crash, I doubt her face could have been longer, or her eyes more waterlogged. Her jaw set, now and then I would hear her grind her teeth. I tell you, that return trip was twice as long as I remembered the torturous journey out. And I had believed that one arduous, trying, and hard. Terrible. Compared to this one, it had been a slice of watermelon on a hot summer's day.

In Cape Town, the situation grew worse. If before packing me off to Gungululu Mama had been strict, following my return her restrictions bordered on the ludicrous. I was a prisoner in my home. Mama forbade me even to go to the toilet except during the period between the real dark that comes hours after sunset and the heavier dark that precedes dawn – she actually forced me to use a chamber pot during the day. That concerned she was about the neighbours and their wagging tongues. Like a brooding hen her nest, Mama guarded me that first week following my premature return. She didn't even go to work, must have taken a two-week vacation, I reckoned afterwards. Those long, interminable days. Torture. Meals were silent, uneasy affairs. But even had I not lost my appetite I'd have found it difficult to eat.

We arrived in Cape Town in the early morning, on Saturday, a week to the day since the old village woman, Madlomo, had told Makhulu, '*Utakelwe*!' We arrived to find that in Mama's absence, Nono had had her baby. What incensed Mama was to be told that the child had already been named. Named, with no consultation whatsoever with Khaya's parents. Named, furthermore, Nobulumko, Mother of Wisdom, which Mama saw as a dig at Khaya's family; implying that we had dealt with Nono's family in manner sly and underhanded, clever or wise in the unsavoury meaning of the word.

I'd spent that first day fearing the look on Tata's face while itching to see China. To get word of my arrival to him, at least. Let him know how things stood. When Tata returned from work, that afternoon, he went about the house as though there was no one in my bedroom; as though I had not come back from the village. That whole day, I was

bumpity-bump ... sound of going over bumps
cavernous very large
frame (here): body
kitty corner opposite but at an angle
palpable very noticeable
cocoon *Kokon*
brooding (literary) constantly thinking sad thoughts
haunted obsessed, worried
waterlogged full of water
to grind to rub together
torturous causing great pain
arduous strenuous, harsh
trying upsetting, annoying
to border on to be close to
ludicrous absurd
chamber pot *Nachttopf*
brooding sitting on an egg that will hatch
premature before the expected time
interminable seemingly endless
to incense to make s.o. very angry
dig sarcastic remark
to imply *unterstellen*
sly *gerissen*
underhanded dishonest
unsavoury offensive, insulting
to itch (coll.) to want very much

to confine to keep in a closed space
forlorn miserable
Master Lock ™ a manufacturer of especially strong padlocks (*Vorhängeschloss*) and combination locks
notwithstanding (formal) in spite of
pitch volume
to blare away to make a loud, unpleasant sound
confines (plural, formal) limit, boundary
vivid seemingly real
point-blank directly, bluntly
to bunch to press together

confined to that one room in the house. Not allowed even to help Mama around the house, I sat forlorn in a corner of the room, where I'd sat since coming home. I sat there, too ashamed to lie on the bed although every bone in my body ached from the long car journey. I feared looking as though I enjoyed or took the slightest advantage of the unfortunate situation I found myself in. Oh, if only China could come. But I knew that was totally out of the question. I also knew I couldn't go to see him. I could go nowhere, in fact. Not with Mama's eyes stronger than a Master Lock. The next day, a Sunday, she didn't even go to church. However, despite Mama, despite her weird actions, I continued to hope that by some miracle, China would come. Hadn't he heard? Notwithstanding Mama's precautions, I believed he would know I was back, that somehow he had heard. That powerful is the location telegraph, and that strong was my belief in it. Besides, our walls are nylon thin; visitors from outside the townships often request their hosts to lower the volume of the radio so that conversation can proceed at normal pitch of voice only to be informed that the radio blaring away is the neighbour's.

But China did not come. Not on Saturday. Not on Sunday. Not for the seven days of that whole week, including Sunday, our second back in Cape Town. Again, Mama stayed away from church.

Tata continued to ignore my presence completely. I helped in the illusion, for as soon as it was time for him to come back from work, I made myself pretty scarce, went back to the confines of my bedroom. This seemed to suit him fine. Not once did I hear him inquire about me or my whereabouts.

Locked in by day, there wasn't even the chance I might catch sight of China at the back of his house. By night, the window stayed stubbornly quiet, undisturbed, the so-well remembered scratch of nail on glass did not come. It was so clear in my mind, so vivid, that I often imagined I heard it ... and it woke me up from deepest sleep. Why, not just once I got up from bed and went to the window, believing I'd heard it ... only to be mocked, laughed at, by the empty and sightless window. Worse still, when the light was on, my own stupid face stared back at me.

The restrictions meant that I did not get to see China till I'd been back in Cape Town for more than a fortnight. Mama told me point-blank to have nothing to do with him until my fathers had gone to see his people regarding payment of damages for what he had done to me. I didn't see the logic behind Mama's words.

'Shouldn't he know?'

'Oh, he will know, all right!' I knew she meant when men from my family took me to China's home to present the case before them.

'Isn't it better that I tell him?' I didn't add the word 'before.'

'Why?' asked Mama, brows bunched.

'This has happened to him as much as it has happened to me,' I said.

'What, exactly, has happened to that dog?' Mama spat out.

I shrugged my shoulders and, with the numbness of the anaesthetized, went back to what I'd been doing, sweeping the floor. For, if she didn't want me going out and about, Mama insisted on my stirring myself within the confines of the house.

'You need the exercise,' she said. 'It's good for someone in your condition.' Till the baby was born, Mama never once used the word 'pregnant.' I understood that, even at that late hour, we both still wished the 'condition' away.

Late, one sleepless night, I scribbled a note to China. How I would get it to him was unclear but I decided it was better to be on the ready. This way, whenever the opportunity presented itself, I would be prepared. The chance never came. Not that whole long week of Mama's self-imposed confinement.

Finally, however, Mama had to go back to work.

'Remember, now,' she said, 'do not get in touch with this boy.' She had told me many times over that it would be unwise and dangerous to meet China before the case had been brought before his family. He might think up all sorts of excuses, try to wriggle out of assuming responsibility. He had to be taken by surprise, according to Mama.

As soon as I was sure that she was gone, I went to the dining-room window, looking out to the street. Standing between the heavy inner curtain and the thin and transparent lace curtains on the outside, I could see the passers-by without being seen by them.

I waited. But Mama had left so late, the school children had already passed. Thus it was not till the afternoon that my golden opportunity came.

Jean and Joan, eight-year old twin daughters of a neighbour, came up the street. No one else with them.

I tapped on the window pane. Beckoned. A finger on my lips. As one, their eyes widened in surprise. Because they did not know I was around? Or because they had not expected to see me?

I opened the door before they came to it.

Their eyes widened even more on seeing me, the whole of me, the now obviously pregnant me.

'Please, take this to China,' I said and gave the note to Joan, who seemed to take the situation more in her stride than her sister.

'When did you come back?' she asked, arm extended.

'Last week.'

'Oh!' Came from both.

'Don't give that to anyone but him,' I said, pointing at the letter.

'That's right!' Again, it was Joan who answered. Jean had lost her tongue. I didn't blame her. What had they heard? I wondered.

'Oh, wait,' I called out as they turned for the door. I went back to the bedroom. On my return, Jean was standing just inside the door while Joan had chosen to wait out on the stoep, midway between the door and the gate. So it was to Jean that I gave the twenty cents.

'Get yourselves *vetkoek* or sweets.'

to spit, spat, spat out (here): to say angrily
to anaesthetize *betäuben*
to stir yourself to move about
on the ready ready for action
self-imposed (here): forced
to wriggle out of s.th. (coll.) to try to avoid responsibility for s.th.
lace *Spitze*
window pane *Fensterscheibe*
to beckon to make a signal with your hand for s.o. to come
to take s.th. in your stride to deal with s.th. difficult with little worry

'Thank you! Thank you!' they said, in perfect harmony although more than a metre must have divided them.

They had just disappeared from sight and I was still standing where they'd left me, wondering whether they had found him when someone burst into the house through the back door. Was it my brother, Khaya?

'Mandisa!'

That grating voice. Unmistakable.

'Mandisa!' China shouted from the kitchen. Shouted, even before I saw him ... or, he saw me.

'I'm here,' I said. 'Come right in.' I had mentioned in the letter that I was by myself.

Long, hurried strides blundered towards the dining-room, where I was.

Hearing his footsteps nearing, my heart gave a violent lurch and a flood of warmth bathed me. He is here! Here! Then, as suddenly, a cold cloying shyness came over me. Suddenly, I remembered how different I looked – I would look to him.

China bolted into the room. I had risen from my seat, ready for a greeting ... a hug ... a kiss?

No greeting came. First, I had waited for his, expected him to greet me. When that didn't come, my own greeting froze in my throat.

At the sight: China's face, a mask carved from the hardest wood, the greeting that had sprung to heart at hearing his footstep, died in my throat.

My heart sank. This was a difficulty I had not anticipated. Belatedly, Mama's words came to my mind. Had she been right, all along? Did I have something to fear from China? Was my trust in him misplaced? Could he turn against me? But how? Why?

I spoke first. Told him everything. Which, in the stony silence of this new China, was brief indeed. Even as I spoke, I could see resistance in his granite face. I could see he didn't want to hear a thing about his being a father-to-be. With the advantage of more than a week, I had forgotten how bewildering, how frightening, the idea had been to me at first. I was still grappling with it as it were, myself. Reeling. At odd moments, I found I actually slipped into fantasy; persuaded myself it was all a terrible mistake. And that I would wake up and find that it had all been a nightmare.

'No!' China snarled after I finally stopped talking, explaining the situation we were in.

'No,' he said, his voice low, barely above a whisper. The well-remembered, beloved eyes, mere slits at best of times, were narrowed till they looked as though they were closed. Yet, incredibly, from those almost imperceptible slits darted thin but deadly tongues of fire.

'Mandisa,' China hissed, voice now raised and forceful. Jaws clenched tight, he told me in no uncertain terms: 'Go and find whoever did this to you.'

grating harsh, rough
stride *Schritt*
to blunder to move in an awkward way
lurch sudden, unsteady movement
cloying excessive, oversweet
to bolt to move suddenly
belatedly happening late
to grapple with s.th. to try to find a solution to a problem
to reel to feel shocked
to snarl to speak in an angry way
imperceptible hardly noticeable
to clench to press together
in no uncertain terms *eindeutig*

A cold hand clutched my little heart ... and ... squeezed.

'China,' with a voice suddenly gone hoarse, I called his name.

'China,' again, I said, 'let me explain. Please ... please, let me explain.'

'Explain to your heart, Mandisa! Explain to your heart, not me!' roared China, turning away from me so that he now faced the door.

Aghast, I looked at his rigid back. What was he saying? How could he say that? What did he mean? Why had he turned away from me? Was he leaving? How could he? But China wasn't quite done.

'You know as well as I do that I had nothing to do with whatever it is you are carrying in your belly!' he threw over his shoulder.

My legs buckled beneath me. An involuntary gasp escaped as I lunged forward, grabbing the back of a chair for support. But the awkwardness and suddenness of my movement sent the chair skittering across the floor while I staggered drunkenly and almost fell flat on my distended belly.

The commotion startled China. He turned fully around and stood once more facing me; although not narrowing the gap he had created between us by one jot.

His words had winded me with a force more than that of a physical blow. When I'd found my feet again, I stood where he had left me, struck speechless by them and the vehemence with which they'd been said. For a full minute neither of us spoke.

'China,' irritation now wrestled with fear. I had to make him see ... understand. 'It's ... it's not like that, at all. I can explain everything. Give me ... ' But he did not let me finish what I was going to say to him. My words seemed to have unbottled him.

'I am going to boarding school the following year,' he said, his voice flat, with neither gladness nor sorrow in it. With no trace of sadness or regret.

I opened my eyes wide. Not in surprise. But I would not let him see my tears. I opened my eyes wide, spreading the tears plumping them, burning the widened space between my lids.

'Mandisa,' China said. I could see that he had difficulty reading my reaction. When he saw that I remained silent, still, he continued.

'The teachers have helped me get a scholarship. They think I am bright, I deserve to get a higher education. And Father has been wonderfully cooperative ... I have his complete support.'

I could not believe his insensitivity. Did China really think I had wanted to leave school, have a baby, become his wife . . . or anybody's wife, for that matter? Did he think I had not had plans for continuing with my education?

I stood there, my feet weighed a ton. I stood there, and a heavy stone came and lodged itself inside my heart. While he was busy explaining his plans and his difficulties, I saw another side to the boy I had so adored and not that long ago. China was vain. Self-centred. And weak. He was a low-down heartless cur.

hoarse *heiser*
aghast horrified
to buckle to bend
gasp quick, deep breath
to lunge to make a sudden movement forward
awkwardness clumsiness, uncoordination
to skitter to move lightly and quickly
to stagger to walk with unsteady steps as if about the fall
distended (formal) swollen
by one jot not even a bit
to wind to make it difficult for s.o. to breathe
vehemence intensity of feeling
to unbottle s.o.(coll.) to cause s.o. to release suppressed feelings
to plump to make softer and rounder
to lodge to implant
vain *eingebildet*
low-down (coll.) mean
cur (old-fashioned) dog

pent-up not released
to well up to rise to the surface and flow
ear drum *Trommelfell*
incensed very angry
huffing and puffing breathing heavily
to saunter to walk in a slow and relaxed way
to carry s.th. off to succeed in doing s.th. difficult
betrayal *Verrat*
turgid swollen
nectar sugary fluid of a plant
plump soft and full
aloe [ˈæləʊ] tropical plant whose leaves contain a lot of water
dreaded greatly feared
faded with the colour no longer bright
demeanour appearance and behavior
preliminary introductory
due expecting

All the pent-up disappointment and bewilderment and fear of the past ten days welled up, all rolled together into a massive wave of anger. A terrible roar threatened to burst my ear drums.

'Why, you!' I had not meant to, but I heard my voice scream. China's small slanted eyes popped out. They grew so wide, it was the funniest thing ever. I would have laughed, had I not been so incensed.

I strode forward, toward him, arms outstretched.

He took one long jump backward, grabbed the door handle, opened the door and stepped out.

Huffing and puffing, I stood in the middle of the dining-room, looking at him. Suddenly, I made for the door he had left open. China leapt for the gate, reaching it with maddening ease. He stood just inside the gate. Stood there as though he were at a loss what to do next, how to proceed. For a few seconds, we regarded each other ... no love in those eyes, looking at me. Right then, I could have killed him had it been possible ... and not illegal, something one would go to jail for. That was not an option I entertained. I was in enough trouble without going looking for more.

'Don't you ever,' I hissed, then stopped, then continued.

'Don't you ever dare set foot in this house again!' Without one word more, I turned around and sauntered away. Difficult as it was, in my condition, I did my best to carry it off. Without a single backward glance, I walked off. Leaving the door open as he had left it. If the knowledge of my pregnancy had been bitter, China's betrayal was the thick turgid nectar of the plump aloe leaf.

The dreaded day arrived. Already six months gone, I was taken to China's home.

It was not exactly a march. I walked ahead by a metre or two. The three men, my uncles, followed in a loose cluster; the two, Father's brothers: Middle Father and Little Father, smoking their pipes while Malume, Uncle-Who-is-Mother's-Brother, walked with both hands plunged deep into his trouser pockets.

Down the short road, to China's home. We were awaited.

Three young men, in their thirties, at a guess. And an older gentleman, grey-haired and wearing a suit. Faded. But still, a suit. In Guguletu. On a Saturday. That, and some indefinable quality, something about him, but what? I couldn't quite lay my finger on, set the grey-haired gentleman apart. He looked learned. His whole demeanour made him stand out from the rest. During the preliminary small talk, the how are you's and where have you come from's, he kept his silence. Looking from one to the other of those who spoke, a finger massaging the side of his nose, now and then.

'Why do you bring her here, when she looks as though she is due any day now?' One of the younger men chosen to negotiate the case for China's side, asked, once the reason for our being there was stated. It had to be stated, although we had sent word, which is why the four men were there ... why they awaited us.

This was something my group had anticipated. One of my uncles explained the peculiarities of my situation: the late detection; being away from Mama; and then, the bombshell, my relative innocence.

'You say she is wha-aat?'

'She has not been entered,' explained Malume. 'She is still whole.'

'Who can attest to that?' growled the older of the four, the gentleman. This was the first time I'd heard his voice, a deep-set bass. Low but thunderous.

'The women have seen her. They say she is whole,' Middle Father spoke up in his no-nonsense voice.

'But, how far gone is she?' the older gentleman asked, his voice lowered. The finger, once more busy at the side of his nose, his eyes on stalks.

Back and forth. Back and forth, the argument went. In the end, the be-suited man told my fathers:

'We will send word, soon. The clan's going to meet over this, first. You shall see us, when we are ready to answer you.'

On the way back, the discussion of the small group centred on the fact that we had not been dealt the most terrible blow. China's people had not out and out said they were not responsible. The words (hated by the family of the 'damaged' young woman): 'We will see from the child,' had not been uttered. Words that cast doubt on the behaviour of the girl, that said the young man concerned might not be the only one implicated. No, China's people had spared me that, at least. Although they'd been far from enthusiastic in assuming responsibility: they had not said they would not only pay damages but would take me for a wife - go up the whole arm and not stop at the hand – *benyuke nengalo*. So that was a little disappointing to my uncles. My disappointment was not catching even a glimpse of China. Some residual doubt lingered in me that, were he to get a second chance, see me again, surely, he would change his tune ... especially, now that he had had time to think the whole thing over ... adjust to the unexpected. So, even as we trod our weary way back home, how I regretted those hasty words: Don't you ever dare set foot in this house again.

I was eight months pregnant, big as a balloon, the next time I saw China. At the Priest's office. Father Mark Savage had taken the matter into his hands. He was a white man and a priest. Therefore he did not have to convince China or his father or anybody else of his truth. It was a naked truth. Clothed only in the two things he was: White. A man of God. In straightforward and blunt language, he said, 'My son, you will marry this girl. You were baptised. You are a Christian. A Christian can only do what is right.' What was right, under the circumstances, was that the father of the child I was carrying marry me.

All that remained, thereafter, were the formalities. The *lobola*, foremost. Hastily, new-wife dresses had to be sewn. And all the other paraphernalia I would need in my new life.

bombshell (coll.) an unexpected and surprising event

to attest to s.th. to prove s.th.

to growl to speak in an angry manner

to deal s.o. a blow (formal) to take an action that has a terrible effect on s.o.

to cast doubt *in Zweifel ziehen*

concerned *betroffen*

to be implicated to be responsible for s.th. bad

to spare *verschonen*

residual remaining

to linger to continue

tune (coll.) opinion

to baptise *taufen*

paraphernalia all kinds of personal articles or equipment

China, too, needed to change his status. No boy can take a wife. He had to go and get himself circumcised. So, off to the bush he went. For a whole month, at least. We would get married as soon as possible after he returned.

divine according to God
predictable *vorhersehbar*
to demean to try to lower a person's character
to set (here): to determine
afoot being planned
to flout to defy, to ignore
savageness ferocity, fierceness
to ooze to flow slowly
areole the ring of skin around the nipple light
tug pull
all-infusing filling all parts
light-headedness feeling faint
grudge feeling of anger because of s.th bad that s.o. did to you
to ablate to surgically remove
sprig *Zweig*

Nature follows a divine order. Predictable. Each day, the sun's rays pierce dark night and bleed a new day into being. There is no stopping that, no hindering it, no slowing it down. While the two clans argued, fought, blamed and demeaned each other, my time came. As it was meant to be, set the day the seed that would be this stubborn child pierced my womb. Without my say-so, without any invitation or encouragement from me or anyone else, for that matter. While the negotiations regarding his parents' union were still afoot, all over the place, he came. Waiting on no one's readiness or convenience, flouting both legal and religious convention, he came.

On the fourth day of January in 1973, my son was born. Eight pounds four ounces, he weighed. Throughout the pregnancy, I had had mixed feelings about him: anger, sometimes; joy sometimes. On the whole, though, I think anger was uppermost. His actual arrival didn't improve things. The terrible pain that tore me apart with the savageness of the jaws of a shark, killing all feeling below my hips, thighs dead numb while my centre was blazing, a hot raging fire tearing through it, told me I hated this child ... hated him or her with a venom too fierce ever to die.

The minute I put his puckered, fumbling lips against my breast, guided my oozing areole into that hungrily sucking mouth, felt the strong tug of his jaw, I forgave him.

Forgive? Perhaps, that's not the right word. What had he ever done to me that I should think I had to forgive him? Accept. Welcome. No, even those do not say what it was I felt at that incredible moment of oneness. All I know, all I felt, was this all-infusing, light-headedness that came over me. My heart melted, all pain forgot, all disappointment and bitterness, all grudges, everything negative, ablated. Joy, pure and simple ... I think that comes closest to describing what I felt.

And I named him Hlumelo, for even though I would be lying if I said his birth had been a cause for celebration, something that brought me pride, still I saw and thought and felt, that from him good things might come. Especially, the children, my grandchildren. Hlumelo, Sprig. Unexpected and unasked for, nonetheless in full existence now. He had to be acknowledged.

And at first it did seem as though good things would come, for it wasn't long before Tata had a change of heart. '*Ngawuthi ndigone lento yakho,*' he said one day. 'Let me hug this thing of yours.' And that was the beginning of the end. Henceforth the baby was his first stop on his return from work.

More than a whole month after my baby's birth, a grim-faced Tata said, 'You hear, then, Mandisa, my daughter.' His eyes were glued to his feet.

I remained silent. Stunned. I couldn't believe my ears. Tata had been the more supportive of the two. Once he had got over his shock. Or outrage.

'Unfortunately, daughter,' he stopped, looked at me as though he thought I would say something. But I kept my peace. Then, talking around my silence, he went on, picking up from where he'd left off – '... we are ruled by laws. We live our lives through advice, consultation and allowing or bowing down to the voice of the majority. Never can I trust my eye above the eyes of the many, who are my family, my clan.'

He looked up then. Looked at me, his eyes bright with unshed tears. There was appeal in those eyes. Only days before, we had gone over the whole affair. This marriage to China. The negotiations had been tardy, to put it mildly. I had told Tata and Mama then where I stood. And Tata had supported me. To Mama's chagrin. Mama just didn't understand.

Late February. Hlumelo (or Michael as Mama insisted on calling my baby) was almost two months old. By this time, I no longer wanted to marry China. As I said to Mama then, the whole reason for marrying China no longer stood ... was no longer valid.

'I've had the baby now,' I pointed out. 'So what's the point of marrying China?'

'He is the father of your child, is he not?' Mama retorted.

'Yes.'

'So, why are we arguing? Why, now, when his people are beginning to see reason?'

'Mama,' I said, 'we were supposed to get married so that the child would not be born out of wedlock. So that I would not be an unwed mother, bring disgrace upon the family.'

She said nothing. Just looked at me as though I were something smelly the cat had dragged in. But I was not deterred.

'Well, that has already happened,' I said and, pointing to the bedroom, added, 'There's Hlumelo lying on the bed, inside there.'

Mama's eyes following my hand. Then, she pulled her eyes back and looked at Tata. When she saw that he was not going to say anything, she said:

'It would still be the best thing to do.'

'Why?' China and his people had annoyed me greatly. He had turned out to be a lily-livered, spineless dog, who shunned his responsibilities. That had certainly cured me of any notion of love for him.

Looking at Tata, Mama said, 'Is this the last child she will ever bring to this house?' She paused, turned her eyes to me, eyebrows raised to the ceiling, before continuing.

glued (here): fixed
stunned shocked
outrage *Wut*
unshed not having flown out
tardy moving slowly
chagrin disappointment
valid *gültig*
out of wedlock with parents who are not marred
to be deterred to be discouraged
lily-livered (old-fashioned) cowardly
spineless *rückgratlos, charakterlos*
to shun to avoid
to cure *heilen*
notion idea

to dare *herausfordern*
Asssorted Biscuits (fig.) i.e. children with different fathers
to worry (here): to bring forth
phlegm [flem] thick liquid that forms in the nose and throat
to dredge to dig along the bottom of sth.
to dig your heels in to refuse to change your mind
bleak hopeless
the way of all evil a very unpleasant ending
patch small area
nettle *Nessel*
to sprout to suddenly grow
to persist to continue despite difficulties
sting sharp pain
vehemently [ˈviːəməntli] forcefully, intensely
racket loud commotion
impassioned filled with passion, fervent
plea earnest request
to prevaricate (formal) to avoid giving a direct answer
to enrol to register

'Or ... ' again she looked at Tata, daring him, pulling him back into the argument, ' ... are we going to be raising a whole packet of Assorted Biscuits, here?'

Tata coughed ... or worried some phlegm, more imaginary than anything else, deep in his chest. Of course, the cough sounded hollow, as though he were dredging an old, dry, no-longer-in-use well. He shifted his weight from one to the other foot, looked around the room as though he had forgotten which way the door lay.

'Mmhhm-mmhhm-mmhm!' He loosened his shirt collar and scratched the side of his neck. But no word came from his mouth.

I dug my heels in. I wanted to go back to school. We had discussed this and they had agreed. But that was when things looked bleak, as far as my getting married to China went. The negotiations had become ugly. And looked as though they were going the way of all evil.

'Mama, please think about this,' I said fighting back tears. 'What marriage do you think China and I can ever have, if he has to be forced into it? *Asikokuzibophelela nenj' enkangeni oko*? Is that not tying oneself to a dog in a patch of nettles?'

Mama looked at me as though I had suddenly sprouted horns. But I persisted:

'Mama, what do you think the dog does each time he feels the sting?' That started a heated argument, with Mama accusing Tata of siding with me. Which thing, of course, he denied vehemently, while I helped him do so. Now, we were all talking at the same time so that quite a racket resulted.

Finally, after my impassioned plea, Tata spoke.

'There is truth in what the child is saying, Mother of Khaya,' he said.

'If you say so?' At that, Mama remembered she had something on the stove. Went to the kitchen, where she remained until Tata called her back.

'Are we done, here?' he asked her.

'I think you and your daughter have made your decision.'

'And you?' Tata asked.

'I do as I'm told,' Mama said. 'That is what my father taught me.'

'I am not just taking what this child says,' Tata explained. 'But, you have to agree that these people have treated us shabbily. Time and again, they have broken their word. They have lied, prevaricated and accused us of being cheats, liars and worse. More and more I'm beginning not to see the sense of giving my child to such people. Perhaps, she's right and the thing to do is for her to go back to school.'

Over Mama's clear if unstated objections, Tata had agreed to my suggestion. That same week, had given me money and I went and enrolled for evening classes at St Francis Adult Education Centre, in Langa.

But now, here was Tata, himself going back on his word. His brothers, and the whole clan, were opposed to the idea of my going back to school. Not when the Thembu clan, China's people, were ready to make me a wife.

'My hands are tied, my child,' Tata said, seeing my distress. Custom dictated that he listened to the counsel of the clan. I was not his possession but belonged to the whole clan in good and bad times. And decisions affecting my life were not his to make . . . not alone or to the exclusion of what collective wisdom dictated.

distress mental pain, anguish
counsel advice

Hlumelo was two months and three weeks old when we left the only home he had ever known. For the home that vowed to treat us as their very own. China and I finally got married. Not in church. Not in the magistrate's office. But only by mutual agreement between our respective families. Which is to say, his people gave my people *lobola* and were accepted by my people as in-laws; people who had taken the daughter of this clan to be their child.

to vow to earnestly promise
magistrate *Friedensrichter, -in*
mutual *gegenseitig*
in-laws *Schwiegereltern*

There was no ceremony. The arrangements made, a day fixed, my dowry bought. On that day, Mama gave me a bag and said, as casual as you please:

dowry ['daʊri] *Aussteuer*

'I'd take my underwear, at least. And a sweater, if I were you.' I gathered I was allowed to take a few of my personal things with me. Things from the girlhood I was leaving behind. The girlhood I had hardly had time to experience, never mind enjoy.

to gather (here): to assume

Friday. Early evening, a little after dinner-time, Malume came, in a borrowed van. Malume, Tata, Khaya and Dumisani, Malume's friend and the owner and driver of the van, packed the van.

'Don't' forget your bag,' said Mama.

'Yes, Mama.'

As I was leaving, Mama suddenly said, 'Will you let me know when you're going to the clinic?'

Puzzled, I looked at her.

'He needs me,' she said simply. 'He's used to me and I haven't really taught you how to take him about,' she stopped, slowly shook her head, sighed, 'and now, it's too late.'

'I'll let you know,' I said. Poor Mama. She had come not only to accept her Michael but love him too, I now saw. She would miss him.

The men had finished packing the van. I stood in the middle of the dining-room unable to move. The thought that I was leaving had become intolerable. Unbearable. I did not want to do this. But, in this too, it was too late.

'It's getting late,' Mama said, her voice catching. Her words unglued my feet.

As I left, I thought I saw a glint in her eye. Was she crying? But why? To see me go out, baby on my back? Yes, I thought to myself, that must be something to her ... awful. The final admission. I had a baby. All and sundry could see that plain as day. There. I was actually carrying the baby on my back. Mama had accompanied me to the post-natal clinic the few times Hlumelo and I had gone, and each time she had had him on her back.

catching (here): having a similar effect on s.o.
to unglue (here): to loosen
glint sudden flash of light
admission acceptance of a situation
all and sundry (coll.) everyone
post-natal after birth

to suffocation (here): to the point that no air was left
to bring home to s.o. to cause s.o. to fully realize s.th.
turmoil great anxiety and confusion
to abandon to leave behind
aspiration strong desire to achieve s.th.
to troop in to march in
to claim damages *Anspruch auf Schadensersatz erheben*
ululation long cry
squat small and low
to induct to formally introduce
blur (here): vague memory
versed expert in
pertaining to having to do with
curse *Fluch*
to decree to officially declare
stead place
impact effect
remote far away

The two new suitcases, big and packed to suffocation, and two enormous cardboard boxes took up most of the space at the back of the van. Malume was driving and he told me to sit next to him. There was only one other person, sitting on the outside, Tatophakathi, Middle Father.

This would be the first time I would sleep with the baby. Mama had done that from the first day Hlumelo and I returned from the hospital.

Once more, it was brought home to me what turmoil the coming of this child had brought to my life. Were it not for him, of course, I would still be in school. Instead, I was forced into being a wife, forever abandoning my dreams, hopes, aspirations. For ever.

We stood outside the gate at Tooksie's, where China lived with his aunt, Tooksie's mother. A young man I recognized as one of the three present the day we had brought our case came to meet us.

'I've been asked to ask you to please come inside,' he said.

Malume thanked him and we trooped in. As on the day I'd been brought to this same house so my family could claim damages, I led the little party.

As we opened the door, the sharp, piercing sound of a sole *ululant* greeted us. At once, other women picked it up, and soon the trill filled the whole house and spilled out onto the street.

KIII-II-KIIKIIIIKII! HALALAA! HA-AALAA-AALAA!

I imagined surprised doors, left and right and up and down the street, jerked open as curious faces peered, following the ululation.

We were in the front room now, the dining-room, the largest of the four little rooms. Four, including the squat kitchen to the back. Malume took me by the hand and handed me over to a small group of young women, Tooksie among them. These would be the daughters of the clan ... my new sisters, who would induct me into wifehood, into becoming part of this clan. Taking me by the hand, they led me away, to the smaller of the two bedrooms.

'This is what she brings with her. *Nantsi impahla eza nayo*,' I heard Malume say to the gathering from which I was being led away.

The rest of the evening is a blur. Not because of the tears, expected of all brides as otherwise the woman is branded 'a born-knowing,' *umavel' esazi*, who came to her wedding day fully versed in things pertaining to wifehood. A curse to her mother-in-law, certain ruination to her husband, who would have to obey her rather than the other way round, as God long, long ago decreed. The marrow in every bone in my body seemed to have dried up. In its stead, filling the bones till they threatened to crack and split open, boiled all the resentment and anger and hurt and fear I had been experiencing lately. All this activity numbed me. Words were said, directed at me. My ears heard them. But they had little, if any impact on me. It was as though they were being said to another. Or to me at a time remote ... a time still to come ... or one long gone.

Quickly, two of the younger sisters-in-law helped me get out of the clothes I wore while the ones who looked older directed operations. I was then dressed in two flannel petticoats, a blue, still-smelling-of-the-shop German-print dress, coming down to just above the ankles and a black headkerchief with a grey border pulled low down so that it almost hid my eyes. A towel around my waist and another over one shoulder, pinned under the other arm completed my new-wife mode of dress. It was time to be presented to my in-laws … presented to them as a wife, not the girl who had stepped in a little while ago.

'Why,' someone, a man, exclaimed, as we re-entered the dining-room, 'the German-print has swallowed her up.' I had been under so much stress during the pregnancy and after, I had lost a lot of weight. I had not been exactly heavy to start off with and now the German-print dress, tied around the waist, made me a veritable beanpole tied in the middle.

'What are you calling her?' asked someone else even as I was being led to a chair, in a corner of the room, to sit there all by myself. I waited, for I knew the ritual. Someone would bring me a cup of tea and call out a name. I could refuse the tea till a name I liked came up. On the other hand, if my in-laws wanted to be nasty, they could stop at some point and give me no alternative. Then, I'd very well be stuck with an unpalatable name … especially if they did not like me or thought I had refused names they themselves rather fancied.

'*Nohehake*!' said Tooksie's mother, the sister of China's father. A snake slithered down the furrow in my back. *Hehake*, an exclamation of utter surprise at some incredible, unimaginable monstrosity, some hitherto unheard of dreadfulness.

Notwithstanding the turmoil raging inside me, my right hand calmly stretched itself out, accepting the cup of tea. Accepting the mockery of a name with which my in-laws chose to welcome me into their midst.

I had expected the name of wifehood. It was the custom to leave all the things of one's girlhood behind, including the name. But I was taken quite aback when my in-laws gave a new name to my son.

'He already has two names,' I said.

'*Molokazana*,' said Tooksie's mother, 'your family had no right to name our child for us.'

'What name was he given?' China's father wanted to know. But before I could answer him, another man jumped in, 'People seem to think naming a child is child's play. All his life, this person will be known by the given name. And often, his personality will reflect that name.'

'You can say that again,' Tooksie's mother said. 'What are these names? You did say he was given two?'

'I call him Hlumelo but Mama calls him Michael.'

'You? You call him?' China's father asked, eyes widened. 'Are you telling us you named him yourself?'

I nodded.

border *Borte*
veritable real
beanpole (coll.) very thin person
unpalatable very unpleasant
to slither to glide
furrow long, narrow channel
utter complete
hitherto (formal) until now
dreadfulness s.th. causing an awful feeling
to rage *toben*

'Why?'

'There was no one else at the hospital and the nurses wanted a name.'

A long silence followed my revelation. Children are named by grandparents, more often than not. Events around the birth of the child feature a lot regarding what name the child will be given: Mfazwe, was born during a war; Ndlala, during a time of famine; Ndyebo, during a time of plenty; Ntsokolo, strife; Mbalela, drought; even the towns where the father worked as a migrant labourer when the child was born are sometimes used. There are a lot of Capetowns, Funarhenis (Vereeniging), and Rhawutinis (Johannesburg). The history of the tribe, the state of the clan, the hopes the family harbours are other determinants that may go in naming a child.

'Well, *Molokazana,*' again, it was Tooksie's mother who broke the silence. She seemed to be the group's spokesperson.

'We have decided to call him Mxolisi.' A picture of a snot-nosed boy in my class back in Gungululu flashed before my eyes. My head dropped, my eyes smarting. Please, God, don't let me cry. Not now. Mxolisi?

'We hope, though his coming and your coming to us were so fraught with debate and argument, that he will bring the two clans together ... that he will heal the wounds and bring us all some peace,' China's father said.

Mxolisi, he was named that night. Mxolisi, he was baptised, a few weeks later. Mxolisi he became to all, including me, in due course. For some time, however, I'd just called him Bhabha. But eventually, even I would come to call him Mxolisi. He, who would bring peace.

The negotiations preceding my joining China as his wife were stormy, full of recriminations and mud-flinging. Where marriage and marriage negotiations are to bond two families or two clans – these were set on cleaving, sealing our families in a never-dying bond of enmity. Had Father Savage, under whom China's father served as a lay preacher, not insisted that China 'do the right thing as a Christian,' I doubt the marriage negotiations would have started at all. But then, how they dragged on and on and on! And, strangely, it was China's people who, after the baby was born, turned around and now wanted the marriage more than anything else in the world. However, by then, by the time they were hell-bent on it, I no longer was interested in it at all. Only the insistence of my extended family, their pressure on Tata, forced me to go through with it at this point.

On the day of the wedding itself, by the time we eventually went to bed, all my doubts had resurfaced, multiplied a thousand times. The renaming of Hlumelo upset me. Shocked me. It was as though I had lost a child. What joy can there be in a mother's heart even when the dead child is replaced? Hlumelo. Mxolisi? Thank God, no one thought to give him a school or Christian name. When he started school, I would use Mama's Michael, I vowed.

revelation disclosure, uncovering of s.th. hidden
famine time when there is not enough food
strife fighting
drought [draʊt] time of little or no rain
to harbour to cherish, to hold dear
snot-nosed (coll.) arrogant
in due course eventually
recrimination angry statement in the context of mutual accusations
mud-flinging, mudslinging insulting an opponent
to cleave (literary) to split
to seal *siegeln*
enmity hatred
hell-bent on s.th. determined to do s.th. regardless of the results

The snide remarks I'd overheard during my induction (and perhaps overheard is not quite accurate, as these were said loud enough that I should hear them) cropped up at bedtime.

'How could you bring such a miserly dowry,' said my husband. 'I hear the girls' skirts are some cheap material; the doeks of the grandmothers, too small to wrap in any but the most simple style; and only one bottle for the vat of beer?'

'You should talk!' I retorted. 'Your people haven't even finished giving us *lobola*. I shouldn't even be here, lying next to you.' We spent our wedding night with backs to each other.

That was the beginning of a pattern: argument and counter argument formed the basis and backbone of our marriage.

The next morning, like all good *makotis*, I jumped out of bed at four, my day had begun. Half an hour later, took in coffee to Tooksie's parents and China's father, in the two bedrooms. China and I were in one of several *hokkies* in the backyard. Instead of a garden, the backyard had two rows of *hokkies*.

I soon got used to the gruelling routine: last to bed and first to rise. I was perpetually so exhausted I took naps during the day. Naps of sorts. Sitting up, I would pretend I was feeding the baby while both of us were fast asleep. He, in my weary and aching arms. I had come to my wedding thin. In three months, I was skin and bones. When Mama passed by one day, she asked:

'Do they hang you in the rafters when they eat?' And the next time she came, she had a message for me from Tata. 'He said to tell you to mind you don't go out of doors on windy days as you might be blown away.'

We laughed but Mama said, 'Seriously though, Tata is worried. He said to tell you, don't forget you can always come home.'

China got a job working at the Cold Meat Storage in Cape Town. He got in at seven in the morning and knocked off at seven at night. There was a big break, from twelve to four in the afternoon and his *mlungu* said he could sleep at the back of the storage, during that lunch break. But although he needed that sleep, as he left the house at six, China wanted to get out of that place each moment he could.

'Place makes my clothes smell of blood,' he complained.

Thus, China too suffered from lack of sleep. However, when he came back from work, he could take a nap. Actually get into bed or lie on top, close his eyes and snore should he chose. No pretend sleep for him. I was filled with envy.

Before the baby had come, if you'd squeezed a whole bush of aloe and put the juice into a large pail, that pail would not contain half the bitterness in my body. Bitter. For the tadpole that was growing in my stomach when I had kept myself pure. Now, I was bitter for another reason. The fires that had so tortured China and me when we were not supposed to quench them in each other ... now that we were man and wife ... with everything else going wrong between us those treacherous and torturing fires were gone. Dead. I don't know about

snide nasty, unkind

to crop up to appear

doek (Afrikaans) square cloth to cover a woman's head

vat large container for liquids

pattern regular way s.th. happens

gruelling difficult and tiring

nap short sleep

to knock off (coll.) to stop work

to quench to extinguish, to put out

treacherous (here): harmful, dangerous

vicious wicked, foul

to slake (literary) to satisfy

Canaan the promised land of the Israelites

log *Baumstamm*

napkin (old-fashioned, BE) nappy

to take your stomach out (coll.) to get an abortion

to fling, flung, flung (here): to say suddenly

to punch (here): to push quickly through s.th.

to stomp to walk with heavy steps

agape wide open

China. All that tortured me at night, with him lying dead right next to me, on the same, same bed, were the vicious memories of our stolen nights together ... long, long ago, it seemed now. Then, everything I could ever desire, was right there in his eye. All he'd ever thirst for, he found in mine. It was like that between us then. Which is why we could slake the burning thirst in each other's knees.

But now, with all Canaan open before us, we were suddenly struck blind to whatever beauty lay in the other. I was very familiar with China's stiff back.

'Don't breathe on me,' I would snarl, whenever I sensed he wanted to come close. Most nights, I confess, I wanted none of that. Too tired. Just simply too tired. All that work they made me do as a new wife, *umakoti*, just killed me. Soon, we got used to being together like that. Two dead dry logs.

To leave at six, China had to be up at five. Being China, the moment of getting out of bed was always but always postponed till it became inevitable. Usually, to just a quarter of an hour before he had to leave. One morning, I heard Bhabha cry and went back to the *hokkie*. Seeing that it was half-past-five, I woke China up.

'Wake up! Wake up!' I said, patting him on the shoulder.

'Shut up, will you?' barked China, rolling over onto the other side.

'Oh, excuse me,' I said, attending to the crying child. The cold tone of voice must have surprised China. He shook the blankets off his face and growled:

'Do I work for you? What d'you care when I wake up?'

'I thought I was helping.'

'It's too late for that, now,' he said. 'When you could have helped me, you chose not to.' I finished pushing the pin through the baby's napkin and fastened it. Then I looked at him.

'What d'you mean?'

'Look at me!' roared China, finally springing up and out of bed. Beating his bare chest with the thumbs of his balled fists, he screamed, 'Look at the mess I'm in. Just look at me! Not yet twenty and already out of school, doing a job I hate!'

I knew he was talking about our being parents. No. About his being a father and a husband. The dog in the patch of nettles. The dog and I. So soon, though? So soon, he had started feeling his life a waste ... something he would always resent?

'What's that got to do with your being late for work?'

'Don't you see? I wouldn't be working now, doing a stupid job, getting peanuts for it.'

'That's my fault?'

'You could have taken your stomach out!' China flung as he left the *hokkie*, punching his arms through the sleeves of a jacket as he stomped out of the door.

Surprise sprung my jaws wide open. For a full minute they stayed like that. Mouth agape. But no scream came.

All morning, all day, Ribba's face stayed before my eyes. Her throaty chuckle that flashed the uneven but strangely attractive teeth; her carefully careless gait; feet always in shoes; always so beautifully attired. Ribba. Dead, long before she was twenty. Dead, trying to take her stomach out. Each time I thought of what China had said to me that morning, I sucked my teeth. Sucked my teeth in and shook my head. Each time I held my baby in my arms, put him on my breast. And die? For what?

chuckle quiet laughter
gait manner of walking
attired (formal) dressed

If China was fed-up with his lot, I could hardly wait for my period of *ukuhota* or initiation to come to an end. Ordinarily, this event is marked by the arrival of the first child or the end of what was deemed a significant period – usually, a year. Since China and I had put the cart before the horse, I hoped I would get a discount or abbreviated sentence. Six months, perhaps.

My day was longer than China's, who seemed not to notice that fact. When he left, the baby was getting his first feed, the adults had already had their morning-in-bed coffee, and breakfast was waiting in the wings. When China went to bed, Mxolisi drank his last bottle for the day. Between that bottle and the next morning's, I nursed him at least three times. In the course of the day, I seldom put my tired bones down, not a moment's respite. Early morning: coffee – breakfast – schoolchildren and adults – wash the younger children and get them ready for school – dress them up and collect their books, scattered throughout the house and in some of the outside *hokkies* – empty chamber pot now that the adults have left for work – get the children off to school – pick up night clothes strewn all over the place – make up beds – sweep through the house – do laundry, iron yesterday's – attend to the baby – it's time to start supper – the schoolchildren will be back any minute now, get their snack ready – dinner almost ready – there – there, the first adult has come home: make tea – later, everybody's back from the saltmines: feed the tired army – then much later: listen to China whine about his job, about the tiredness of his feet, about how much he doesn't make a week.

Lucky him, he got paid. He had money in his hands, and he had a week, with a beginning and an end. My week was one long round of chores, with no break whatsoever. Sundays were the worst. At least, during the week, I didn't have to serve lunch. Not Sundays. The deacon, my father-in-law, had to come back to a meal's-ready house. This, after the hefty breakfast I had served, had to serve, before they all left for church. And cooking for my father-in-law was no easy matter. The man perpetually reminded me of his prowess as a chef at the Grand Hotel in Muizenberg. Big *abelungus* ate out of his hand, he bragged often.

period of initiation time when you are prepared for full membership
to deem to consider
to put the cart before the horse (saying) to do things in the wrong order
a discount (fig.) a price reduction
abbreviated shortened
sentence punishment determined by a judge
in the wings (fig.) ready
to nurse *stillen*
respite [ˈrespaɪt] short break
strewn scattered
saltmine South Africa is a major producer of salt
to whine to complain
deacon assistant to a priest or minister
hefty large
perpetually constantly
prowess (formal) great skill
Muizenberg suburb of Cape Town with a large beach
abelungus (Xhosa) white people
to brag *angeben*

As the year drew to a close, I began to feel better, to dare to hope. Things had to get better next year. They would get better. Would I not be taking evening classes at St Francis Adult Education Centre?

to draw to a close to come towards the end

When that happened, my in-laws would be forced to share the chores. Besides, my year's initiation would be over. Yes, my heart danced, things would be much easier for me next year. I just knew they would.

Early in December, fearing schools might close before I had registered at St Francis for the following year, I brought up the matter of schooling with China.

'We'll have to talk to Tata about it,' China said. My father had already talked to his father about it. Way back during the marriage negotiations. Why did we need to do more talking?

'Your father agreed I would go back to school.'

'Well then,' said China, 'we'll just let him know, then.'

'*Molokazana*,' my father-in-law said that Friday afternoon. He never did call me by my married-woman name, Nohehake, which Tooksie's whole family used religiously. 'My son mentioned you're thinking of school, next year.'

religiously (here): carefully, exactly

'Yes, Tata,' eyes lowered, I replied.

'Is it not too soon?' My eyes flew right up.

'I mean,' he said quickly, no doubt seeing the look of consternation on my face, 'is the baby not too young still?' I had no intention of waiting for my son to start school before going back to school myself. But how to approach this man, who wielded so much power over my little life?

consternation anxiety, dismay

to wield so much power to have so much power

'Mama will look after him, when I'm in school.' I could hear my heart knock against the rib cage. Painfully. 'And,' I added as an afterthought, 'it wouldn't be every evening.'

'We'll see. Let me think about it, then.'

That year, the baby was too young for his mother to be about at night. I had to understand that babies were fragile. All kinds of evil roamed about at night and I would bring him some of that evil. Did I want to kill their child?

to roam about to wander about

I waited. What else could I do? Mxolisi turned one year. A part of me hated him. Not him ... but what he was ... had been ... the effect he seemed to have on my life. Always negative, always cheating me of something I desperately wanted. I shrunk; because he was.

to shrink, shrunk, shrunken to become smaller

As for killing their child, now, that was a laugh. If I had not scrimped, scratched around for odds and ends, and stretched the scraps my father-in-law brought back from the hotel on the days he was off duty, their child would have starved to death. Why, on occasion, I had to take money or food or both from Mama. And I mean for the baby.

to scrimp to spend as little money as possible

odds and ends all kinds of necessities

scrap (here): small leftover piece of food

'Don't forget to leave me some money for the baby's formula,' I reminded China one morning.

'Have you taken him off the breast?'

'No. Why?'

'You seem to be using up a lot of his SMA. Didn't we just buy him two tins, the other day?'

SMA brand of baby's formula

'Two small tins.'

'Try to give him more breast than bottle,' said my husband, reminding me his father gave him but so much a week.

Mercifully, the interminable year drew to a close. Again I raised the question of my schooling.

This time, money was scarce. My father would give me the money, I said. No, came the reply from my father-in-law. No, they had their pride. How often would I run home each time there was a problem in my new home? Would that not say to my blood family, their *abakhozi*, that my husband and his family could not cope with looking after their new daughter, now their own child? I saw then that the promises my in-laws gave, certainly as far as the matter of my education went, were water to a sieve. Those promises would be postponed, deferred and broken till my dreams were finally forgotten. Till they had died.

Then, one *shushu* day, without warning, without saying good-bye, China just upped and walked right out of my life. These past twenty years, I have not heard a word from him.

In the new year, we had celebrated Mxolisi's second birthday. Two weeks later, his father was gone. Just like that. One Monday, he didn't come back from work. The next morning, everyone looked at me as though I had done something wrong. Or, in some manner I could not fathom, had failed.

'He must have gone to his father,' Tooksie's mother said. Her brother still worked at the grand Grand Hotel out in Muizenberg and came to us at weekends, when he was off duty. On Friday, my father-in-law arrived. He was furious that we had not called to tell him of his son's disappearance.

'*Makoti*, My Child!' shaking his head, his eyes looking anywhere and everywhere except where I stood, he said in a low voice full of despair. 'I thought I could trust you.'

I was stunned. How could it possibly be my fault China had taken himself wherever it was he had gone? But his father was not quite done with me. Not by a long shot.

'I leave you here with my son,' he said. 'And now, I find him gone. He is not here. But you are still here, with your son and you didn't bother letting me know mine was gone.'

'We thought he was with you, Tata,' I said.

'I see.' But I could see that he did not see. That my words made no sense to him at all.

After that, without even having had the cup of tea I had put before him soon after he came, he left. He was going to China's place of work, he said. See if something had happened to him there. Since that was the last known place where he'd gone, that's where he'd start looking.

China had last been seen at his job on Monday. Knocked off at seven, as usual. Then he didn't show up the next day, or the next.

mercifully thankfully
interminable seemingly endless
sieve *Sieb*
to postpose to arrange for a later date
to defer to delay
to fathom to understand
Not by a long shot. not at all

locker *Schließfach*

offence an act against the law

ward *Station*

precaution s.th. done in advance to avoid problems later

to reveal itself *sich zeigen*

distraught extremely anxious and upset

square peg (short, narrow, four-sided piece of wood) **in a round hole** (BE) *fehl am Platz*

sapling young tree

bountiful with a large amount

When he didn't come on Thursday, his boss broke into his locker and found it bare. He hired someone else in his place.

What was so clear to China's boss was far from clear to his family. His face long, my father-in-law told us of his findings and then announced:

'How does that *mlungu* know China ever kept anything in that locker, in the first place?' The search had begun in earnest.

Maybe he had been arrested for a pass offence or something else. His father went to the Police Station. Then, to the hospitals. Phoned each and every one of those that had wards for black people. Took the train and went to those within the vicinity of Cape Town: Groote Schuur. Conradie. Wynberg. Up and down he went, up and down, that whole day. No China. Not a trace of him anywhere. A whole week my father-in-law spent looking for his son. Took off from work to do that. No pay for him that week. Looking for China. Everywhere. Everywhere. But the ground had opened up and swallowed him whole.

Nearly twenty years later, I have not heard from him. Not a word from the father of my first-born child, in almost twenty years. I don't think he ever got over not knowing, till I was full three months pregnant, that he was about to be a father. Going to Gungululu certainly messed things up properly for China and me. Perhaps. For, I can never say for sure. Will never know. Sometimes, though, when I think about it, I say to myself, perhaps if that whole sad situation of our finding ourselves about to be parents, when we had taken all necessary precautions, had revealed itself to both of us at the same time and place, things might have turned out differently. But, as I say, I will never be sure about the truthfulness of that.

Meanwhile, with China gone to only God knows where, I soon found I needed a job. His father was so distraught, he couldn't bear to come to Guguletu any more. He stayed away from his sister's house. Naturally, that meant we stopped seeing the colour of his money too. And soon, it became obvious, although people kept calling me *makoti* that whose *makoti* I was, was a puzzle. A burden.

I took a job. What else? As a domestic servant. Sleep out. That didn't mean I was excused from my *makoti* chores. So I had to get up two hours before dawn. To get myself and the baby ready for work and then give everybody their breakfast before they went to work and I, baby on my back, made my way to my job. But, within the first six months of working, I left Tooksie's house, where I had become a real square peg in a round hole. Which is why, desperate as my situation was, I didn't go back to my home, my girlhood home. Instead, I looked for and found a *hokkie* for rent at the back of someone else's house. A *hokkie* of my own.

Mxolisi grew as though he were a sapling during a summer of bountiful rains. As fast as he shot up physically, other aspects of his development were even more spectacular. At two, he could say things in a way anyone could understand, not just his mama. By that age, he knew more words than children twice his age. He ran the day he learnt to walk. Of course, he never crawled. He was such a marvel child that everyone loved him. Mama and Tata absolutely adored him. More so when, following his losing his father, his other grandfather, China's father, soon also disappeared from our lives.

While I would be lying if I said these developments brought me any regret, still I felt Mxolisi's distress at the abrupt changes in his little world. Certainly, to me, he appeared to miss the old geezer. And for a long time after China's disappearance, he would ask me to do some of the things China did with him, such as kick ball or spin a top for him. Also, he would repeat the word *tata tata tata* to himself during play. Especially when he was all alone while I was busy around our little *hokkie*. In time, however, I found him saying it less and less. But, not once did he ever directly ask me for his father. Not once, until one day when he was three times the age he'd been when he last saw that father. Meanwhile, we did everything together. He went to work with me, and I played with him, when we were home in the evenings and over the weekend. He loved peek-a-boo and, later, hide-and-seek. What fun we had teaching him *imfumba* and *qashi-qashi*! Later still, I learnt a lot of little boys' games. We learnt to kick ball and spin tops together.

to crawl *krabbeln*
marvel wonder
to adore to love deeply
regret *bedauern*
geezer (coll., BE) man
top *Kreisel*
peek-a-boo *guck-guck*

One day, Mxolisi was at the big house at the back of which we lived, where I almost always left him when I went to work or to do grocery shopping. He liked staying there because there were older children who doted on him. The two boys, Zazi and Mzamo, both in their early teens, took him everywhere they went: to the field where the location boys gathered and played soccer, a game of marbles, spun their tops, or just spun yarns about those things of interest to boys that age ... boys knocking at the door of manhood.

On this day, however, the boys had left Mxolisi behind as they did when going to school or somewhere else where his presence would be a nuisance. Recently, that had been happening with increasing frequency and not because of school either. Students were boycotting classes. Again and for the umpteenth time, in the past five or so years.

Suddenly, gun shots rang.

'*Unganyebelezeli, kuza kudlalwa!*' piped Mxolisi's little voice, calling for daring and defiance. To look at him do the war cry of the Comrades, poised in a defiant stance, his tiny fist up in the air, couldn't but send all those who heard him into paroxysms of laughter.

There was nothing unusual about this. Mxolisi, now four years old, could already tell the difference between the *bang!* of a gun firing and the *Gooph!* of a burning skull cracking, the brain exploding.

This day, however, minutes after the onset of the firing, Mzamo, mouth frothing, ran into the house; Zazi, eyes hanging out of their sockets from fear, close on his heels.

Quickly and with the help of their father, they opened the back door, flung out Zazi's jacket, threw it far to the back of the path cut-

to dote on s.o. to treat s.o. with great love
to spin, spun, spun a yarn to make up a fantastic story
nuisance s.th. or s.o. who is annoying
umpteenth (coll.) very many
to pipe to speak in a high voice
daring willingness to do s.th. dangerous
defiance open refusal to obey
poised in a position ready for action
defiant stance position demonstrating defiance
paroxysm [ˈpærəksɪzəm] uncontrollable expression
to froth to produce saliva
socket *Augenhöhle*

ting through the *hokkies* and going to the back fence. The mother then squeezed the boys into the wardrobe and locked it.

'Don't move! Don't breathe!' said the father to the boys.

Everybody went to the back in 'witness' to the fleeing boys.

A few minutes later, the police stormed into the house. Casting caustic glances left and right and into the eyes of those present, they stomped through the house, into the bedroom, into the sitting room, into the kitchen and out onto the backyard.

'Where are they? Where are the boys who ran in here a minute ago?' they barked.

Mute with grief-tinged fear, those at the back of the house pointed reluctantly over the fence.

The police went to the fence, realized that the boys had cleared it and ran out of the yard of the adjacent house.

'We'll get them next time,' they vowed.

One policeman viciously kicked at the lifeless jacket on the ground. Kicked it till it jumped into the air, which filled it up, momentarily ballooning the sleeves. Then, slowly exhaling, the jacket danced its way back down. Slowly came down. Till, finally, it fell limply back onto the ground. And lost all its airy lifelikeness. At which, one of the uniformed men viciously stamped on it and, with both feet, ground it to the the dirt-strewn earth; battering it although it offered no fight, no resistance at all.

Then, epaulettes gleaming under beefy biceps, the three trooped back into the house on their way out.

'Tell them, we'll be back. They will not escape, next time!' the leader, sandy, sparkless eyes narrowed, growled, standing at the front door, glaring at those inside the house.

The last of the three men had one foot out of the door when he suddenly whirled around, stopped short by a small, shrill voice.

'*Naba*!' clear as spring water high up the mountains, rang the voice, once more raised in excitement.

'*Nab'ewodrophini!* Here they are! Here they are, in the wardrobe!' screamed Mxolisi, pointing to the wardrobe. A clever little smile all over his chubby face.

He said those terrible words and, swift as a wink, witnessed their outcome. The boys jumped out and made for the window. But when they hit the back garden the police were waiting, and shot them then and there. He was struck mute by what he saw the police do to the two boys. His beloved friends. After that, he zipped his mouth and would not say one word. Not one word more – for the next two years.

On Saturday, that same week, the two boys were buried. We all feared for Mxolisi who, by nights, thrashed about and screamed in his sleep since that episode. By day, he was a walking zombie; went about wide-eyed, staring into nowhere and never said a word. Stared, not a tear out of those suddenly enormous vacant eyes. Not a tear. Could a

in 'witness' to the fleeing boys. i.e. supposedly witnessing the two boys fleeing – an event that had not really taken place
caustic sarcastic
mute silent
grief-tinged with a small amount of fear
reluctantly unwillingly
adjacent next
viciously brutally
limply lifelessly, loosely
to batter to hit several times
beefy thick
sandy reddish-yellow
sparkless blank
chubby plump and round
wink *Augenzwinkern*
to zip (fig.) to close with a zip (*Reißverschluss*)
to thrash about to move about in an uncontrollable manner
vacant ['veɪkənt] (here): expressionless

child that age grieve? What were those sounds he made that day of the funeral? Sounds that came from deep down his throat? Why, no tears? Why, we all asked, had the child not said a word since?

In the days before the funeral, we waited. In the midst of all that grief, the wailing and the swearing (for there were not a few who said big words of terrible anger against the Boers as a whole and the government in particular), now and then our minds were pulled back to Mxolisi, who had stopped talking. Stopped, once he'd witnessed the children of the words his mouth had uttered.

Then the day of the funeral arrived. Should he or should he not be taken to the grave site? They were his friends, some said. Therefore, he should go to the graveyard and say goodbye to them. If he doesn't get to bid them farewell, he will think he is being punished and blame himself forever after for what's happened, said others. No, said those directly opposed to the latter view. That's exactly what will make him believe he is being punished; taking him there. Spare the child this much, voiced yet another group. He is too young to grasp the meaning of all these events.

Mxolisi would not be left behind. Clutching my hand as though the two were welded, stone-faced, wide-eyed, he sat through the entire service. While tears streamed down the cheeks of many, Mxolisi's eyes had become two deep, bone-dry wells on the plane that was his face; dry as the Namib, his cheeks.

For days, then weeks, we waited for him to come back. Return from wherever he had gone. Clearly, he was not with us. Had not been since that day those two boys were killed. We waited. A whole month went by. Still, not a word from the child's mouth? Had he permanently lost his power of speech?

Mama took him to work with her. Her employer was a resourceful lady; always came through at times of stress. Also, she and Mama had known each other all these years.

'Madam says we must take him to the children's hospital, in Rondebosch East,' Mama came back saying. Her *mlungu* woman had phoned the doctors there and we were to take Mxolisi to the hospital the following week.

I'd asked Khaya to come and see me over the weekend. The *hokkie* had a leaky roof. One Saturday, he came with his daughter, Nobulumko. Mxolisi seemed happy enough to have Nobulumko all to himself while his *Malume* was on the roof. Before his silence, he'd enjoyed playing with her as well as with other children his age. And although she was seven months older, he appeared the older of the two. He bullied and took advantage of the poor thing till, more often than not, I had to step in.

I held my breath. Would he say something to her? Would the words return to his mouth? But although they played, his cousin

to swear *fluchen*

site place

to bid s.o. farewell to say a final goodbye to s.o.

to spare *schonen*

to weld *schweißen*

service *Gottesdienst*

well *Brunnen*

plane *Fläche*

the Namib coastal desert in southern Africa

resourceful good at finding solutions to problems

Rondebosch East suburb of Cape Town

antic funny action
at her fancy (here): whenever she wanted
dumb unable to speak
to scorch away to burn away
sketchy incomplete
host large number
amiss wrong
to heal *heilen*
mphokoqo traditional porridge made with maize meal and sour milk
grace quality of politeness
tentative hesitant

giggling endlessly at some antic or her fancy, I couldn't say, Mxolisi stayed stubbornly dumb throughout the afternoon.

At the Red Cross Children's Hospital the doctors and nurses and social workers were kindness itself. We went there several times. But with all their kind hearts and the many clever things they made Mxolisi do, they could not bring words back to his mouth. They could not plant what the police had scorched away by their violent actions.

They looked into his throat, into his ears, up his nostrils. They made him draw: complete half-drawn pictures, fill out sketchy outlines and make up completely new pictures. They made him imitate the sounds of animals, domestic and wild; watch children's films and a host of other things besides. Why, one doctor even had him put to sleep ... talked to him while the boy was fast asleep. However, in sleep or awake, Mxolisi still said nothing to the doctor.

Finally, they threw their hands up and told us Mxolisi was sick. As though we didn't know that. But, they said, he wasn't sick in his body but sick inside. What inside? His mind? No, not his mind, his heart. He needed time, he would get well one day. We shouldn't push him at all. Ignore his not talking. Just go on as though nothing were amiss. In time, he would surely heal.

Well, that was something new. The child had been silent for months. What time did he need? How many years? Not push him? Not push Mxolisi? A child who'd made up his own mind before he was born? Decided he would be born?

It was quite a pleasant surprise to see Nono. She had gone back to school and was too busy with her studies to be a frequent visitor.

'Thought I should stop by,' she said, finding me stirring a pot of *mphokoqo*.

'What are you burning there? Smells dreadful!' she said. When I told her what I was cooking she had the grace to add:

'Oh, that! Difficult to escape burning, isn't it?'After all that, she wanted some. Then she asked about Mxolisi, who was at the front house, the house at whose back garden our *hokkie* stood. 'He's all right,' I said. 'Except he will not speak. He's become as much good as a baby in that respect.'

'Does he hear?' asked Nono, explaining, 'When you talk to him, does he appear to understand what you're saying?'

'Oh, there's no problem at all as far as that's concerned. He understands, all right. Will do what you ask of him, any time.' I said, going to the door.

'Mxolisi!' I called out. 'Boyboy! Where are you?' The back door of the front house opened and there he was, standing, his hand on the door handle.

'Come over here, there's someone to see you!' At that, he stepped out, closing the door behind him. Then, after several tentative steps, he stopped and looked at me, a question in those eloquent eyes that, now that he'd stopped speaking, seemed to have taken over the function.

'It's Nobulumko's Mama!' His eyes lit up and a huge grin painted itself all over his face. He would be disappointed. Nono had not brought her child along.

But he wasn't. She had brought something that took the sting of his cousin's absence away. A toy car – sleek and long and gleaming black. She wound it for him, put it on the linoleum floor and, purring, it zig-zagged its way thereon, banging and clanging against the legs of chairs as it went along.

Mxolisi clapped his hands in glee, threw himself on the floor, hands darting forward to grab the erratic car. And although she coaxed and provoked and trapped and in many, many ways tried to trick him into uttering a word, or syllable, some discernible semblance of human speech, a cry approaching it, Mxolisi did everything except utter that word or cry or part of a word. In the end, no doubt exhausted by the paces through which she put him, he fell asleep. Car tightly clutched in his fisted hand.

For a while after I'd put him to bed, we talked about him. Finally, however, we fell to talking about other things. About us. The way we were or had been ... when was it? How long ago had it been?

'That last school year? 1972!' said Nono.

'Boy!' I said, 'that was a terrible year, all right. So many of us had to leave school.'

'Three girls.'

'Poor Ribba!'

'That was so sad. Mind you, at the time I thought she was the lucky one.'

'Lucky?' I couldn't believe my ears. The girl had died during or as a result of a botched, back-street abortion.

'Do you remember the terrible anger we faced? Yes, I know it sounds stupid now, but there were days I wished I were dead, I can tell you that.'

'It seems so remote now, doesn't it? Our people say, "Thunder rumbles and roars but then passes away!" and those are very true words, indeed.' All those memories came flooding back. 'What was the absolute worst, for you?' I asked.

'Oh, the fear of discovery, first. And then, the shame once that had happened. The shame and the sense of having let one's parents down horribly, irrevocably.' She paused and, eyebrows raised, looked at me. 'And you? What was the most difficult, for you?'

'Well,' I said, memory again plunging me back all those years. 'Remember now, things were slightly different, for me.'

'I know.'

We both knew that the knowledge, the fact, of my pregnancy had come as a total shock, a bombshell to me. I had not at all known I was pregnant. What is more, at the time, I was a virgin.

'Those were sure difficult times ... hard times,' Nono said.

sleek smooth and shiny
to zig-zag to go in many different directions
glee delight
erratic having no fixed course
to coax to persuade s.o. to do s.th. with kind words
to trap s.o. *jdn in die Falle locken*
discernable noticeable, perceptible
semblance likeness
to put s.o. through his/her paces to test s.o.'s ability
to fall to doing s.th. to begin to do s.th.
irrevocably in a manner that cannot be changed, unalterably

'You can say that again!'

China's father (for although he had little to do with us now that we had moved away from his sister's house, my parents had felt it was only right to tell China's people of the boy's affliction) came up with the idea we take Mxolisi to see a *sangoma*. Six whole months had gone by, and still Mxolisi had not regained his speech. I agreed to the suggestion. I was desperate enough to try anything.

The woman my father-in-law took us to was about my age. She saw us to one of the rooms, made us sit on the floor, our shoes off. Nothing unusual in that, all according to custom.

Out came her goat-skin. Spread it on the floor before her. But instead of the bones I expected her to throw on it, the bones that would tell her who we were and what we'd come to her about, I heard her call for someone to bring her water. Water? What is she going to do with water? Wash us? Make us drink it?

Another woman, much older than our *sangoma*, brought a clear glass of water, gave it to the *sangoma* and left.

She put the glass on the goat-skin. Looked at us, at the three of us, one at a time. Her eyes intent, slow, deliberate. Then, gently, she laid her hand on the mouth of the glass, like a cover, but not quite closing it. Next, she closed her eyes. And only then did she slowly lower her hand till it rested firmly on the glass.

The water in the glass changed colour. Right before my unbelieving eyes.

Mxolisi gasped.

I turned my head to him in surprise. That was the nearest thing to a word he'd uttered in more than two years full. Again, my eyes turned to the woman. Now, the water was working itself up as though, in another minute, it would come to boil. But no, instead, the agitation led to foaming and that spilled over, seeping from beneath the *sangoma*'s palm until it reached the goat skin and settled all around the stem of the glass.

When the water finally calmed down, she opened her eyes. And, slowly nodding her head at the glass, she made low, grunting sounds before she turned those piercing eyes full strength onto the child.

'*Yebo, ngane yami!* Yes, my child,' in Zulu, she said. As one in a trance, eyes focused solely on Mxolisi as though he were the only person in the room with her, voice floating, soft and eerie, disembodied even, she went on:

'For shoulders so tender, so far from fully formed, great is the weight you bear. You hold yourself and you are held ... ' – she paused before saying the word ... 'responsible.' She said the word with a sigh, as though she were a judge sending a young person, a first offender, to the gallows. Sending him there because of some terrible and overwhelming evidence she dared disregard only at her own peril.

affliction (formal) the cause of pain and suffering
sangoma (Xhosa) witch doctor
to regain to get back
intent concentrated
deliberate careful, purposeful
to foam *schäumen*
to seep to slowly flow
palm *Handfläche*
to settle to come to rest
stem *Glasstiel*
to grunt to make a short, low sound in the throat
piercing very bright and searching
trance a dream-like state
disembodied seemingly separated from the body
tender soft
first offender person who has committed a crime for the first time
gallows *Galgen*
to disregard to ignore
at your own peril at your own risk

Then she turned to us. Why the wrath in her eyes? I recoiled because those eyes, now narrowed, were fixed more on me than my father-in-law. And out of them shone boiling anger and … was it pity?

'Mama,' she said, her voice once more her own. 'You must free this your son.'

I said I didn't understand.

'You know what I'm talking about. Go home. Think about your child. Children are very sensitive. They know when we hate them.' After a small pause she shook her head. 'Perhaps, I use a word too strong … but, resentment can be worse than hate.'

It was my turn to gasp. My whole being turned to ice. Tears pricked my eyes. I felt my father-in-law's eyes on me and turned mine his way. His brow was gathered, his eyes wide with unasked questions. But the *sangoma* wasn't done.

'But to come back to why you have come to see me,' she broke our locked eyes, 'this child has seen great evil in his short little life. He needs all the love and understanding he can get.'

She gave us medicine – roots and powders, with instructions as to how to use which. We paid and left. An uneasy silence between us, between China's father and myself. What was Mxolisi thinking? How much of what the *sangoma* had said had made sense to him?

'Will you let me know, Molokazana, of whatever progress the boy makes?'

I said I would and we parted.

A few weeks after the visit to the *sangoma*, Nono and I were in the kitchen part of my one-room *pondok*, preparing a meal while Khaya romped around with the two children.

'So?' said Nono making bedroom eyes at me.

'So, what?'

'When are you giving Mxo, here, a baby sister?'

'You're a one to ask me that,' I said. 'Where's Nobulumko's brother?' At that, she pushed her tummy out, hooked her thumbs under the shoulder bands of her pinafore dress and raised her brows to her *doek*, startled lashes high up, widening the white of the eye till it showed blue. She exaggerated the pout of her mouth till it resembled Donald Duck's beak.

'I see,' I said. That explained something she had said earlier …that she and my brother were getting married. I had wondered how the two sets of parents had agreed to the marriage. Well, my case was slightly different, now, wasn't it? 'Won't that be a little difficult for me?'

'Why?'

'Have you seen China, lately?' We both burst out laughing. Afterwards, some hours later, when I'd forgotten about this little chat, Nono said, 'Seriously, though, it's been … what? over a year since China went missing?'

'Over two years.'

to recoil to draw back in fear

to prick to cause a stinging sensation

to gather to draw together

to romp around to play and run about joyfully

to make bedroom eyes to hint at sexual activity

tummy (coll.) stomach

lashes *Augenwimper*

beak *Schnabel*

'And … ?'

'And what?'

'We must find someone, for you?'

'Who said I need your help?'

'Is there someone I should know about?'

blatant outright, obvious

'I don't know about knowing about him … ' That had been a blatant lie. What is the matter with you, Mandisa? I asked myself. Who are you saving it for? China? D'you still want him? Are you waiting for him? Or, is it your good name you're worried about? Your virginity, perhaps? D'you think you'll ever be that again? Is that what is bothering you? What you're trying to reclaim what you were cheated out of?

stringent strict, exacting
to rent to tear

That is when the words of the *sangoma* hit me. In all the years of being a mother, I had held on to my having become one in spite of stringent precaution. My virginity was rent not by a lover or husband, even. No, but by my son. This fact, an accident, my people called it, had always set me apart … at least in my own mind. I, unlike the likes of Nono or even Ribba, had not been a loose young woman.

inverse the exact opposite
tender spot warm feeling

Only now, the inverse of the equation hit me. Where I had often heard it mentioned that a woman will always have a tender spot for the man to whom she gave her virginity, how could I feel that way towards my son? Indeed, how often had I not wondered whether my feelings towards him would have been different had his coming been otherwise? When he cried, sometimes instead of feeling sorry for him, I felt sorry for myself. As though he had less reason for his tears than I for his being on this earth. Did I hate my son? Stop it! Stop it! Stop it! How could you hate him? Surely, you know full well that was not intentional. Boyboy never set out to ruin you. He just happened. Why, he wasn't even there … not yet Boyboy or Michael or Mxolisi or Hlumelo.

not yet showing not showing outward signs of pregnancy

Although she was not yet showing, a few weeks after our visit to the *sangoma*, Nono and Khaya got married. Nobulumko was the flower girl and Mxolisi, the ring bearer. I used the *sangoma*'s roots and herbs faithfully, but Mxolisi had still not recovered the power of speech. More than a year since I last heard his voice.

squat short and broad
to purse to form into a small, round shape
to bump into s.o./s.th. to hit s.o./s.th. by accident
encounter (here): contact
faggot bundle of sticks or twigs used as fuel

At the wedding, I met Lungile. Not much to look at – but, could the man talk! Short, squat, heavy-set shoulders, neck almost not there. A thick head of hair. Large forehead. And a nose that made me think of the map of Africa. Lips, thick and pursed as though he hid something in his mouth. Throughout the ceremony, he kept bumping into me till I saw that the encounters were deliberate on his part. My heart started pounding. Oh, Mandisa, Nono was right. How can you be excited by a thing like that? Look at him, short as the path to the faggot just outside the hut.

On my way home, late that night, there he was. He had obviously been lying in wait.

'May I walk you home?'

'I'm not afraid.'

'I want to talk to you.'

'Can't it wait till tomorrow?' Then I remembered Nono's words once again. And the *sangoma*. How long would I keep my life so uninteresting?

'Let's go, then,' I said when he made no move to let me pass. He picked up Mxolisi and we walked back to my *hokkie* with the boy in his arms. The sight of my child seeming so content, head solidly against this man's chest, did something to me.

We spent that night together. And nine months later, Lunga was born. Lungile, his father, had become a permanent fixture in my home although I had made it quite clear, that first night, that I was not looking for marriage.

'See that nail behind the door?' I had said, pointing.

'Mmhh-mmhh?'

'That's for your jacket, each time you come here. And when you leave, I want you to take it with you.'

Lungile was fun. After the initial resistance, Mxolisi adored him. Lungile was patient with him, always trying to figure out what it was he would say, were he to talk. Never getting fed up or hurrying him or giving up when he didn't get whatever the child wanted to convey in his new wordless way.

Soon after Lungile entered our life, the two would often leave me at home and go to the shops or to rugby games together. They went grocery shopping in Claremont together. And even when Lungile's friends came over, as sometimes they did, he would chat away with the boy sitting on his lap, listening, if not saying a word. However, even so, Mxolisi and I still shared what I came to see as Our Private Moments. Before he stopped talking, he liked whispering in my ear when he didn't want other ears hearing what he was telling me. This started when he was still on the breast and people, especially my mother, would say he was too old to be suckled. When he wanted his drink, he would whisper in my ear and tug and pull till I followed him away from prying eyes. The habit persisted past that stage and after he stopped talking, he gave me other signs with which to interpret what he wished to say. So, our 'whispering' stayed on, if changed.

Then Lunga, the baby, came. For a while, the whispering stopped. I didn't notice this at first. In fact, I only remembered that it was so following later events.

When the baby was about three months old, Mxolisi began to wet his bed. This child who was dry and out of napkins by his first birthday, wet his bed. I scolded, I shamed, I ridiculed – all to no avail.

Lungile came up with mice. The idea, that is. Folklore has it that making the bed-wetter eat mice will cure him. But first, we told Mxolisi that if he wet his bed one more time, we were going to catch a mouse, roast it on the open fire, and make him eat it. With everybody, all his friends, watching.

fixture object firmly fixed in place

initial at the beginning

to convey to communicate

to be suckled to be fed with milk from the breast

to tug to pull hard

prying curious

to persist to continue in spite of difficulties

to scold to speak angrily to s.o. because of having done s.th. wrong

to ridicule to make fun of s.o.

lo and behold (humorous) believe it or not
acidy like acid (*Säure*)
stench awful smell
to gag to have difficulty swallowing
to stray to wander away
to crow [krəʊ] to boast
to gnaw [nɔː] (fig.) to keep chewing s.th.
pit (fig.) bottom
stoop to the shoulder lowering of the shoulder
hooded look with the eyelids partially shut
to tell on s.o. *jdn verraten*

His eyes grew large and round. We felt we had scared him enough. Lo and behold, if the same acidy stench did not greet our nostrils the very next morning. That weekend, Lungile made good his threat.

And all the time Mxolisi choked and gagged and finally swallowed the bits we'd chopped the roasted mouse into, his eyes strayed often to his younger brother as though to say: why me alone? What about him? Sure enough, the bed was dry the next morning. But then, even as we were crowing with pleasure at the success of our plan, more awaited us.

'*Uph' owam utata?*' Out of the blue, my son asked, 'Where is my own father?'

I could hardly believe my ears. The dish in my hands dropped to the floor while, mouth agape, I stared. Then, 'What did you say?' I asked.

'*Uph' owam utata?*' Again, Mxolisi said. Clear as clear can be. I had not been mistaken. He who had not said one word in almost two years, had spoken. Such was my joy that I lost sight of the meaning of the words he'd uttered.

Yes, that is Mxolisi. He kept silent for nearly two years. And when he did speak again, it was to ask me a question to which I had no answer. To which I did not know the answer.

'*Uph' owam utata*? Where is my own father?'

But it is not what he said that gnaws the pit of my stomach – every single day. No, it is not what he said that day but what he did not say ... the question he did not ask ... has never asked, that has stayed in my mind. Stayed in my mind, from then and from long before to this very day. Yes, it did. That question he asked only that one time ... asked it twice, within a minute. Never asked it again. Instead, there came a stoop to the shoulder and his suddenly-old-man's hooded look frightened me more than I can say.

'Where is my own father? Where is my own father?'

Yet the bed-wetting stopped soon thereafter. But then, there is the terrible guilt I feel he carries. Mzamo and Zazi. But he never says a word about them. Those friends of his early childhood. Poor children. Died like dogs. Shot by the police. Nobody blamed Mxolisi, he was just a baby then. Nobody blamed him at all. Today, you can kill Mxolisi before he will tell on another. His own sins, he will readily confess. Not another's, no. He would sooner lie than do that, even take the blame himself. But he never tells on someone else, not even his brother or sister. Never. Even with this thing of the Young Lions and the necklacing. Although he is very active in the business of the comrades, himself a student so long in high school, he has denied over and over again that he has had anything to do with necklacing. When Dwadwa and I pointed out, one day, that it was students who went about killing people in this terrible manner, Mxolisi said, 'Not me!' Yes, he said, some of his friends were involved. 'But I am no murderer.' What do those friends of his tell their own parents? As amaXhosa say, *ityal' alingomafutha, alithanjiswa*, guilt is no cream with which one anoints oneself.

Other things happened and time passed and cheer returned to Mxolisi's face. Hugs and kisses, too, returned. And so did our whispers. Mxolisi, who wouldn't finish a bar of chocolate or other sweet without insisting I take a bite. To this very day, of my three children, he is the most demonstrative. However, it worries me that all these years since, he has not once asked for those two boys who used to take him everywhere with them. When he recovered his speech, he did not ask: Where is Mzamo? or, Where is Zazi? Not once since that day long ago when he was all of four has he asked for either boy. Many many times have I asked myself why he has never done that. Why? It is as though he never knew them ... never called their names ... never cried for them not to leave him behind ... never once woke up in the middle of the night crying out for their company. Before he'd said those terrible words: *Nab'ewodrophini*.

At some unguarded moments, however, I have seen the knowledge in his wounded eyes. I have seen the searing knowledge.

When he started talking, Mxolisi had a few months left before he had to start school. However, once he did, it was as though the power of speech had never left him. In school, his progress brought to fruition the earlier promise. Invariably, Mxolisi was top of his class. The only problem, in primary school, came the day he was given corporal punishment because he had not paid his school fees. He was in standard five then. The caning upset him so much he refused to go to school. I cajoled, and pleaded and promised him things I had no business promising him. In the end, though, he agreed to go back.

A few months later, however, Lungile skipped the border, to go and train as a freedom fighter. Once more, I was alone. Difference was, now I had two children. It was not long after this that I discovered that Mxolisi had left school. I came back from work one Friday, to find a brown envelope on my bed. Inside, two crisp twenty-rand notes.

'Where did this come from?' I asked, turning the envelope over. And there, in large black letters hand-written, was Mxolisi's name. As well as the name of the company that had paid him.

He had got sick and tired of being caned for nothing by his teachers, he told me. He didn't have all the books they wanted him to have. Moreover, some of the ones we had bought at the beginning of the year had been stolen. 'Besides,' said my son, 'with Tata gone, I can see how tough things have become for you, Mama.'

Long and hard did I talk to him that night, explaining that he was too young to work. I would manage. I would leave my domestic worker job and start a business or take chars instead of the one steady job with one *mlungu* woman. He had to stay in school, I made him see. Were he to leave school before finishing high school, he would be sorry for the rest of his life. He would be part of the thousands upon thousands of young people who roam the township streets aimlessly

to anoint *salben*

demonstrative showing feelings openly

searing (fig.) burning

to bring to fruition (formal) to attain or realize s.th. worked for or desired

invariably always

corporal punishment punishment by hitting

caning hitting with a cane (stick)

to cajole to try to make s.o. do s.th. by being very nice

to skip (here): to secretly cross

crisp new and unused

rand unit of money in South Africa

to take chars (old-fashioned, BE) to work as a cleaner in a house

day and night. That is how Mxolisi stayed long enough in school to become a high school student.

Unfortunately, it is in that high school that serious problems started. Mxolisi got himself involved in politics. Boycotts and strikes and stay-aways and what have you? Soon, he was a leader in students' politics and many who didn't know his face knew his name.

These children went around the township screaming at the top of their voices: LIBERATION NOW, EDUCATION LATER! and ONE SETTLER, ONE BULLET! And the more involved in politics he got, the less we saw him here at home.

I now had three children, with the arrival of the girl, Siziwe. I had married Siziwe's father, Dwadwa, a homebody. The kind of man that, in my younger days, we used to laugh at and call *imurhu* or a *'skom van ver!* – despising him for his being new in town, his being unschooled in the devious ways of urban living. However, with experience, it was exactly that type of man I wanted in my life. The salt of the earth – solid, steadfast, predictable as the movements of the sun. Might be overcast sometimes, too hot at others, but always there at the set time. There, doing what it has always done, what it was meant to do – from time immemorial. However, the harder we tried to bring Mxolisi closer home, the harder he ran. But then, a thousand, thousand other students his age were doing exactly what he was doing. Here, in Guguletu, as well as all over the country.

homebody person who likes to stay home
to despise to dislike very much
unschooled not experienced
devious dishonest, deceitful
overcast covered with clouds
immemorial longer than people can remember

And in spite of all this politics, two-three weeks ago I could hardly walk anywhere in the whole of Section 3 without being stopped by people whose mouths had no other words to say besides singing Mxolisi's praises. To everyone, he was a hero. People I didn't know from a bar of soap stopped me. Young and old, they stopped me on the street to tell me:

'Mother of Mxolisi, your child is really a child to be proud of. In this day and age, when children do everything but what is decent. We really thank the Lord for you. Yes, we really thank Him because of the son He has given you!'

This Mxolisi! He can make one so proud sometimes. Apparently, he'd gone to the shops over at NY 110 the previous evening to get Dwadwa some fruit. He was gone a long time, a very long time. Of course we scolded him when he eventually returned. It was not till the next morning that we got to know the reason for his delay.

Before five, the next morning, there was a knock at the door. A man and a woman walked in. Both strangers. Before we'd even heard who they were, they began praying and thanking God and Mxolisi and us, his parents.

When he'd got close to the shops, onlookers' stares told Mxolisi something was afoot behind the building. Curious, he asked one of them what was happening.

'Some boys've dragged a girl over there,' the man told him. But the girl was not screaming, he said. Therefore, no one thought to intervene. Because the girl was not screaming. Thanks to Mxolisi, the

afoot happening
to intervene *sich einmischen*

girl had escaped certain rape. 'And who knows what they would have done to her after that?' the mother asked.

'This boy of yours has a good heart,' the girl's father said. Unashamed tears ran down his cheeks. They wanted to give Mxolisi money, but Dwadwa felt that was wrong. Mxolisi had only done what anybody would have done.

'No,' the girl's mother said quietly. 'There were many people there. Looking. Some were even laughing. None stopped the crime, none. Until your son arrived on the scene.'

But now, some of those same people look at me as if I am the one who killed your daughter. Or expressly told Mxolisi to go and kill her.

expressly deliberately, on purpose

Chapter Nine

6 am – Thursday 26 August

At the departure of the police, a host of questions assailed us: Why would the police have come and raided our house at such an ungodly hour? What did they want from Mxolisi? Where was he? Why had he not come home all night? What did the neighbours think of the commotion?

Then, as though the terrible questions were not unsettling enough, hot on their heels an army of answers came flooding us into a state of psychotic paralysis. All at once we knew everything. We had all the answers. The knowledge plunged us into despair, for everything we knew was bad … or worse.

Of course, the police had not told us a thing. Why would they tell us why they were looking for our son? When have the Guguletu Police been known for being reasonable, to say nothing of polite? Courteous? HA! Don't make me laugh.

We were still torturing ourselves with our new-found knowledge, no end to the insights, suggestions, proposals and guesses gushing out of our mouths when, early as the hour was, our very concerned neighbours descended upon us.

'Hey, Mmelwane,' Skonana's eyes were fairly popping out of their sockets. 'What is this *lawaai*, in the middle of the night?'

'As you, no doubt, saw,' replied Dwadwa tartly, 'the police paid us a visit.'

'Oh?'

'Yes,' he said curtly.

Skonana took a step back.

'Said they were looking for this boy, Mxolisi.' And before she could say one word more, Dwadwa added, 'And now that you know as much as we do, may we try and put ourselves together without further interruption? We've had enough of that for one day, wouldn't you agree?'

'I know when I'm not needed,' in a huff, Skonana stormed out. But not before she had flung back, over her shoulder, 'I only came because I thought I should let you know what people on the street are saying!'

'Don't pay him any mind! *Sukumhoya*!' I shouted at the retreating figure. But I didn't get as much as a reply. Skonana did not halt or falter in her step. She did not look back. Her back stiff as though starched, she just kept on walking till she reached the door, opened it, and closed it ever so gently, so softly, you knew she was taking extra care to be civil, making it clear she would not stoop to our level.

I turned on Dwadwa, 'You didn't have to be that crude.'

'Your neighbour can be trying, sometimes,' he retorted. 'Anyway, what does she want? Couldn't she wait, give us some time … God! the police haven't even got to the police station yet!'

'What did she mean by that?'

unsettling making you feel upset and worried
courteous polite and considerate
to gush to pour suddenly
to pop to burst
tartly sharply
curtly abruptly
in a huff in a bad mood
to falter to move unsteadily
to starch *stärken*
civil polite in a formal way
to stoop to lower yourself
crude vulgar
trying very irritating

'By what?' asked Dwadwa crossly.

'What people are saying?'

'Go and ask her, if you really want to listen to gossip.'

That shut me up. That's my husband for you. But the piece about 'Your neighbour' annoyed me. As with the children, if any of our friends or neighbours annoys Dwadwa, he will immediately donate that person to me. 'Your child' and 'Your friend' or 'Your neighbour'. His uncaring back increased my annoyance. There's nothing more irritating than taking offence when the person who is the source of that is oblivious of your anger. Right now, Dwadwa was busy going about his business, while I fumed.

'She is your neighbour too,' I threw at him as I left the bedroom, where the exchange had taken place. I had to see to the children.

Dwadwa did not take me on. And my mind turned on the one child for whom, at that moment, my very arms ached. Where was he? Where was Mxolisi? What had happened to him? And what did the police want him for?

Thank God, Lunga's cuts and bruises turned out to be superficial, more ugly than deadly: a cut lip, a loose tooth, a bump on the forehead busy turning red and blue even as I looked, and what promised to be a king-sized shiner in a couple of hours. The important thing, however, was that we all realized that, no bones broken, he would survive.

Meanwhile, Siziwe, whom the police had hardly touched, was a wreck. Dwadwa took one look at her and opted for the easier task of tending to Lunga, although he himself sported a nasty bruise on the lower right arm, a little above the elbow. Must have got it when he'd fended off a blow aimed at his head.

Just as I was getting myself ready to see to Siziwe, there came a knock, accompanied by: '*Vula, ndim*! Open up, it's me!'

'Me, who?' asked Dwadwa in a voice thick with irritation. 'And is your own house on fire that you should go about waking people up from their sleep?'

'Are you asleep?' came the swift response. From her voice, the woman was genuinely startled. The voice also helped me identify the caller, another of our neighbours, Qwati.

Dwadwa opened the door to admit her, bandaged legs and all, 'I didn't think you would be,' she wheezed as she walked in.

In her early sixties, years of hard toil had left her a legacy – a network of varicose veins so pronounced her legs looked liked the trunks of ancient trees, twisted and gnarled roots choking the life out of them. The veins were perpetually on the brink of bursting, hence the bandages. Chain smoking and heavy drinking hardly improved the situation. Qwati, a very amicable woman, confessed to being diabetic and asthmatic. We all suspected she was alcoholic as well.

'Mother of Siziwe! My Sister, what is this commotion so early in the day?' But before we had answered her, she rattled on. '*Nibanjelwa*

crossly angrily

to take offence to feel insulted
oblivious not aware of
to fume to be very angry about s.th.

did not take me on did not counterattack

bruise [bru:z] blue mark on the surface of the skin resulting from an injury
bump swelling
shiner (coll.) black eye (*Veilchen*)
to opt for s.th. to decide to take a certain course of action
to tend to s.o. to take care of s.o. sick or injured
to sport to display
nasty very bad
to fend off to manage to prevent an attack

to admit s.o. to let s.o. in
to wheeze to breathe noisily
toil work
legacy *Hinterlassenschaft*
pronounced (here): obvious
gnarled [nɑ:ld] twisted and bent
on the brink of on the point of
hence thus
amicable friendly, pleasant
to confess to admit
to rattle on (coll.) to continuously talk about s.th. not important

ntoni, ngenj' ixukuxa? What are you being arrested for, at dog-wash-teeth time?'

If Dwadwa had been abrupt with Skonana, he was downright rude to Qwati and sent her packing in less time than it takes to say How Do You Do! The poor woman hardly got an answer to her first question. Although I didn't necessarily agree with Dwadwa's harsh manner of dealing with our meddlesome neighbours, nonetheless, I had to agree that his method was effective. We certainly had enough on our hands with Mxolisi's absence ... and his being sought by the police.

I walked to the door with her and said, 'Come back later in the morning, Qwati. We have to straighten everything out now, as you can see.'

'I see,' she said, leaving me standing at the door, holding the door open till she went out of the gate. I returned to the business at hand, tending to the two children and putting the house in order again . . . whatever could be righted, those things not broken beyond repair, that is.

In the kitchen, Dwadwa was seeing to Lunga. Siziwe was in the dining-room, and that is where I headed.

Eyes big and round, pushed out as those of a tadpole in a drying ditch, Siziwe squatted on the floor, right in the corner of the room furthest from the door and on the inside wall, the one adjacent to that of the main bedroom. Elbows to knees, she crouched and from deep down her throat came this panicky cooing of a frightened dove. No lifting upward trill. Just a deep dull growl, a trembly sigh, filled with blind despair. On and on and on the terrible wrawl, shoulders heaving horribly. But no tears came from those grotesquely protruding eyes.

Gathering her in my arms, I helped her up and, half-dragging, half-carrying her, took her to my bedroom, where she flopped onto the bed.

Shaking her by the shoulders, I tried to stem the haunted, tearless cry. However, she would neither stop nor answer my call.

'Siziwe! Siziwe! d'you hear me?'

No answer came from her. She just lay there on the bed, shivering. Although the room was far from cold, I took a heavy shawl and covered her with it and went to the kitchen, where I made her a strong cup of black tea.

She took the tea, piping hot as it was, and gulped it down in one go, as though the tea were ice cold or her throat were beyond scalding, nothing living that could burn.

After that, she sat up and, thinking she was about to say something, I waited. Watched her closely and waited.

But she just went on staring, unblinking, quiet as though she had lost her tongue. A few minutes later, she flopped back onto the bed, lay stretched full out, and closed her eyes. Whether or not she was asleep, I couldn't say.

I put my hand against her forehead. No fever there. Relief. Yet, I couldn't bring myself to go ... to leave her alone. Instead, I stood

to send s.o. packing to tell s.o. to leave in a rude manner

meddlesome interfering

ditch *Graben*

to squat to sit on your heels with your knees bent up close to your body

adjacent to next to

to crouch to squat

dove [dʌv] *Taube*

wrawl (dialect, BE) cry, howl

to heave to rise up and down

to protrude to stick out

to stem to stop

haunted (here): tormented

piping hot very hot

to gulp to quickly swallow

to scald to burn yourself with a very hot liquid or steam

unblinking not opening or shutting the eyes

there watching over her as though she were a baby only hours old.

For a while, she tossed, turned and mumbled, fitful in her sleep, if sleep it were. Soon, however, her breathing began to ease, her muscles relaxed. Satisfied she was asleep at last, softly, carefully, I crept out of the room. But left the door ajar.

fitful not continuous
to ease to become less tense

'Mama!' The hoarse cry whipped me round. It took speech away from my throat. I looked at her. Why had she cried out? And why like that ... in that tone of voice? Such heaviness of heart in that cry. As of one in darkest despair.

'What? What is it?' I barked out.

'Oh, Mama!' Now, long fat tears gushed out and galloped down her cheeks, chasing each other to her chin.

'Siziwe, what is the matter?' I yelled, getting no answer. My anxiety level was shooting up. Why had the child called me? What was troubling her?

She shook her head. Then, as though her hands were rags, she scrubbed her face with them; first using the one and then the other. As though the first had become saturated and had to be replaced.

rag a piece of old cloth used for cleaning
to scrub to rub hard
saturated completely wet

I waited. Quite at a loss as to what I could do. Finally, she spoke.

'The police ... Mxolisi was here ... he ... he ... ' then, she stopped; closed her eyes and stopped talking. While the tears gushed down and all over her face.

Again I waited. Held my breath still ... couldn't breathe. As though doing that might frighten her very thoughts away. I held myself upright by the strongest of wills. STAND! I told myself, not saying one word, silently, I told myself to wait, to be patient, to listen to what the child had to say. Indeed, after a while, again she continued.

'He came here, before Mama returned. Came rushing in, went to his *hokkie*, and then left. I think he went to the *hokkie* to hide something.'

'What?'

'I don't know, Mama.'

'Why?'

Siziwe was silent.

'Who was with him? Was he alone?'

Like a shutter, something came over Siziwe's face ... over her eyes. Now, other eyes in another face looked at me. She had not moved. Had not even changed the manner of her sitting. But it was another girl who now looked at me. Cagey as a fox.

shutter *Fensterladen*
cagey (coll.) secretive, not open

Sensing her sudden reluctance, her unwillingness to go on with the conversation, I thought I might be close to some important clue.

'Who was with him, Siziwe?' I coaxed.

to coax (here): to persuade s.o. to talk by being kind

'Mama, I don't know.' I noticed that the tears had dried up. I said nothing. Silently regarded her. Steadily. For a long minute we remained thus locked in each other's gaze; neither of us saying a word.

At last, she broke the uneasy silence.

'Well, I can't say. I wasn't there.'

I knew then I would get nothing more from her. I was left to wonder what it was she had started to tell me ... something that, obviously, made her very uncomfortable ... or, scared. I decided to leave well alone for the time being. That is not to say the matter rested there. Siziwe's words left a hollow feeling at the pit of my stomach. However, more than what she had said, it was that cagey look that had shuttered her eyes that plunged me straight to Hades.

to shutter (here): to close over s.th.
Hades (Greek mythology) land of the dead, (here): hell

From the kitchen, Dwadwa called out he was getting ready to leave.

I left Siziwe in our bed. In her bedroom, we put Lunga, whose bedroom, the *hokkie*, was a complete write-off. He was in the kitchen with his father.

write-off (BE) s.th. completely damaged, normally, as the result of an accident

'Mama, wake me up at eight,' he said, before going in.

'Why, where are you going?'

'To school.'

'School?' What could he be thinking of? School? In his condition? 'Have you seen what you look like?'

Lunga merely nodded and ambled towards the bedroom.

'You should listen to me, sometimes,' I shouted after the receding figure.

to amble to walk in a relaxed manner
to recede to move gradually away

He didn't even pause in his shuffle to the little bedroom, where his sister usually slept.

shuffle walking without lifting your feet

'You're in no fit state to go anywhere, as far as I'm concerned!' I said.

'Yes, Ma!' he said quietly and closed the door.

Dwadwa had put some cream on his bruise, after washing it. Both children had been taken care of. Everyone was fine now, I saw. Everyone, except Mxolisi, of course. But right now, I was thinking only of the three people who had been here when the police came. Suddenly, all the fear and anger I'd kept in check since those men had come and woken us welled up and mingled with this new fear of what Siziwe had almost told me. Or what I feared, and refused to accept, she had been trying to tell me. The whole mystery drained my very bones and tore my heart to shreds. I flopped onto one of the chairs miraculously still upright in the dining-room, put my head down on the table and felt the tears I'd suppressed till then wash my face and fall on the stiff arms beneath it.

in check under control, suppressed
to drain to make empty or dry by removing all the liquid
to tear [teə], **tore, torn to shreds** to tear into tiny pieces

A hand, light as down, fell on my shoulder.

down very soft feather

'It's going to be all right,' my husband whispered softly. 'Please, don't cry, everything will be all right . . . just you wait and see.'

A little while later, the hand on my back lifted. Footsteps. Uncharacteristically soft and quiet footsteps. Moving away. Going in the direction of the kitchen. Soon, came noises that told me Dwadwa was getting ready to go to work.

'Will you be all right?' a while later, Dwadwa asked, shaking me lightly by the shoulder. I tried to peel my eyes open. But the lids refused to cooperate. The lashes fused tight. They felt as though someone had sealed them with cement and it had dried, glueing them forever.

to peel open (here): to open with difficulty
to fuse tight to join together tightly
to glue *kleben*

'That tired?'

'Well,' I nodded in the direction of the voice and, with valiant effort, pried a few of the lashes apart.

'There is that.' Thinly, vaguely, I saw his brow shoot up in question.

'I think I must stay at home. In case ... ' Now it was my tongue that was lethargic. Or was it that it found what I wanted to say ... what I had to say ... too heavy a thing to say?

'In case he comes home.' In a gush, with a mighty effort, I pushed the words out.

'What makes you think he will do that?'

'I don't know ... but ... ' He didn't let me finish.

'What if he doesn't?' My eyes popped wide open then. What did he mean? What did he mean?

'Mxolisi always comes home,' I retorted with a conviction that was fast deserting me.

I could not decipher the look my husband gave me.

'If he doesn't come by lunch time, I'm going to go looking for him.' The words were out of my mouth even before they were in my mind. They flew out of my mouth, shocking me more than they surprised Dwadwa.

'I think you're wasting your time, if you ask me,' he paused, cocked his ear as though listening for something. Then, 'In any event, the police are sure to get to him before you. And he isn't going to come back here ... wherever he is, he must know, by now, that they're looking for him.'

'Why?' I jumped at him. Did he know something I didn't know? something he was keeping away from me?

'Why, what?'

'Why are they looking for him?' I trusted Dwadwa. He is one of very few people I know, who have no guile.

'You ask me?' His brows shot up, chasing the hairline. 'You ask me?' again, he said. 'How long have I told you that this child will bring us heavy trouble one day because of this long foot of his?'

I said nothing. What could I say? Anything I said would just irritate him more. I know my husband. For a moment we looked at each other – he, with one brow raised in query. Well, he could wait as long as he liked for the answer to that question, but he sure wasn't getting the answer from me.

'Also,' I said, shrugging my shoulders, 'let me see how the other two are doing.' The excuse sounded lame to my own ears. The look my husband gave me told me that he saw through the lie.

'No, don't worry yourself about me and my stupid questions,' he said. 'In any event, I've got to be on my way, soon.' Again he was all busyness, all the while mumbling and grumbling to himself. 'Don't say I never told you so, this son of yours ... one *shushu* day, you mark my words, one *shushu* day, wait and see ... he will come here dragging such a thorny bush of a scandal, you won't know what to do with yourself or where to hide your eyes.'

valiant very determined and courageous
to pry (AE), to prise (BE) apart to force open
lethargic apathetic, sluggish, lacking energy
in a gush expressing s.th. suddenly
to pop wide open to suddenly open wide
conviction *Überzeugung*
to desert *verlassen*
to decipher *entziffern*
to cock your ear to move your head so as to listen to s.o. more attentively
guile [gaɪl] dishonest behavior
long foot (here): restlessness
in query questioning
lame (here): not convincing
busyness the appearance of being occupied with a trivial or meaningless activity or labour
to grumble to complain

Chapter Ten

to fuss about to become agitated
swig (coll.) quantity of drink
disdainful contemptuous (*verächtlich*)
flick sudden, quick movement
to pass away a more pleasant way of saying: to die
lean not fat or plump
half-way station (here): a station to resupply ships sailing to India and the Spice Islands
to harrumph to make a slight cough as a sign of disagreement
scorn contempt, lack of respect
the lot (coll.) everything
to rinse to wash away the soap with clean water
over (here): again

There is knowledge with which I was born – or which I acquired at such an early age it is as though it was there the moment I came to know myself ... to know that I was. We sucked it from our mothers' breasts, at the very least; inhaled it from the very air, for most.

Long before I went to school I knew when Tata had had a hard day at work. He would grumble, 'Those dogs I work for!' and fuss about, and take long swigs from the bottle.

Mama's own quarrel with bosses often came on the day when Tata got paid. For some reason, her dissatisfaction with Tata's conditions of employment seemed to deepen on Fridays.

I remember when, one Friday, she exploded:

'*Sesilamba nje, beb' umhlaba wethu abelungu!* We have come thus to hunger, for white people stole our land.' And, with a disdainful flick of wrist, threw the envelope down on the floor. Later, I was to hear those words with growing frequency.' White people stole our land. They stole our herds. We have no cattle today, and the people who came here without any have worlds of farms, overflowing with fattest cattle.'

I never asked Mama what she meant by those words. Besides, who asks her mother what she means when, pointing at the round yellow eye of the blue sky, she teaches, '*Ilanga*! Sun!'?

Then Tatomkhulu, Tata's tata, came to stay with us after Makhulu passed away. Lucky me, that he chose to come to his eldest son.

Tatomkhulu, small eyes in a small lean round face, always had a smile. But one day, soon after he came to us, he asked me what I had learned at school.

'Jan van Riebeeck and his three ships and how he came to build a half-way station at the Cape of Storms and called it the Cape of Good Hope!' As usual, I was showing off, giving more information than was strictly required.

Tatomkhulu's smile left his face. 'Cape of Storms! Cape of Storms!' he harrumphed. 'Go and change your clothes and get something to eat, *Mzukulwana*,' he said.' Then come over here and Tatomkhulu will tell you the truth of what happened. Cape of Good Hope, indeed.'

I did as I was told, wondering at Tatomkhulu's displeasure. My learning was usually a source of praise, not scorn. Puzzled, I hurried and changed into my day dress, grabbed a slice of bread and a glass of ginger beer, gulped the lot down and went out.

'Rinse the dishes you've finished using,' Mama reminded me as I left the house.

As fast as I could, without making her make me do them over, I washed the cup and side plate and put them away. I crept out of the house and went to the back garden, where Tatomkhulu sat on a wooden bunk beside my brother's *hokkie*, sunning himself. That was the beginning of many 'lessons' I learnt, sitting at his knee.

'What did they mean, the Cape of Storms?' he asked.

'Because the sea was often rough and broke their ships.'

'Why then, did they change the name to Cape of Good Hope? Did the sea stop killing them?'

The teacher had not talked of the sea in connection with the renaming of the Cape. Tatomkhulu saw me hesitate. He said:

'Because the sea was no longer as important to them. They had decided to stay here. They were no longer travelling in their ships.' After that, he went on, his voice soft and far-away, as though he were talking to many people, whose ears were filled with nothing else except the sound of his voice.

'Long, long ago,' he began, 'in the times of our ancestors, when *abelungu* first came to this country, they called this the place of storms. They called it that because the great blue river without end ate up their ships. That was more than three hundred years ago. And the chief *mlungu* man who came with his group, one called Vasco da Gama, chose to call it that. The place of storms.

place of storms It was actually called 'the Cape of Storms'

'Did he not know that the biggest storm was the storm they themselves brought?

'They came to find food and water. Then they liked the food so much they stayed. They found people already here. But that did not stop them from staying. And, having stayed, from taking the land from the people they had found here.

'Yes, Mzukulwana,' he sighed, 'the biggest storm is still here. It is in our hearts – the hearts of the people of this land.

'For, let me tell you something, deep run the roots of hatred here. Deep. Deep. Deep.' He was silent, thereafter. Silent for a long minute and so I ventured:

'Why, Tatomkhulu? Why is there hatred in the hearts of the people?' But he wouldn't say. Only patted me on the head. Told me to go and play with my friends before Mama found me something to do or the sun went home to sleep.

to venture (formal) to say in a careful way

to pat to touch lightly to show affection

'Do you remember what I told you the other day, Mzukulwana?' another day, he asked.

'*Ewe,* Tatomkhulu,' I answered.

ewe (Xhosa) yes

'Have your teachers taught you anything about Nongqawuse?'

'*Ewe*, they have, Tatomkhulu.'

'And what did they say?'

'She was a false prophet who told people to kill all their cattle and they would get new cattle on the third day.'

'And did the people do that?'

'*Ewe,* Tatomkhulu.'

'Why?'

'Because they were superstitious and ignorant.'

superstitious *abergläubisch*

Tatomkhulu shook his head, pulled long and strong on his pipe. 'These liars, your teachers,' he said. 'But, what can one expect? After all, they are paid by the same Boer government ... the same people who stole our land.'

He gave me a long look before saying, 'Mzukulwana, listen to me. Listen and remember what you have heard, this day.' Then, in the voice of an *imbongi* of the people, he recited:

tiller farmer who grows crops
fallacious (formal) false, wrong

'Deep run the roots of hatred here
So deep, a cattle-worshipping nation killed all its precious herds.
Tillers, burned fertile fields, fully sowed, bearing rich promise too.
Readers of Nature's Signs, allowed themselves fallacious belief.
In red noon's eye rolling back to the east for sleep.
Anything. Anything, to rid themselves of these unwanted strangers.
No sacrifice too great, to wash away the curse.
That deep, deep, deep, ran the hatred then.
In the nearly two centuries since, the hatred has but multiplied.
The hatred has but multiplied.'

to twinkle to cause to sparkle with amusement

He stopped. Looked at me, a smile playing around his lips, twinkling his eyes.

'Mzukulwana,' he said, 'mark my words. The storm we talked about the other day? About the Cape of Storms?'

I nodded my confirmation.

'Well,' he continued. 'The storm in the heart of a person is more dangerous than howling winds and raging waves. You can run from those and seek shelter elsewhere, perhaps escape them altogether. How does one run away from the heart, one's own or that of another?

'UmXhosa to part with his cattle, is no small matter,' Tatomkhlulu said. 'No small matter, remember that!'

serene calm and peaceful
trifle s.th. of little significance
gourd [gʊəd] container made from the dried shell of a fruit
to tickle *kitzeln*

And, old as I am, those words of my grandfather Marhwanana ring fresh in my ears. His words on the matter of umXhosa and his cattle. Grandfather, his bones long white under the green blanket of the most serene sleep, said to me, that day, a very long time ago:

'Child of the child of my child, a cow or an ox is no trifle. When one is hungry, there is corn in the field or *enyangweni*, *amasi* in the *gourd*, *iinkobe* in the pot, *amarhewu engqayini*. Cattle are not for food, something with which to tickle one's teeth at slightest whim. If meat you must have, there are chickens, pigs, goats and sheep, but in truth cow or ox is no playing thing.'

'But then, Tatomkhulu,' I said, 'why do we keep cattle, at all? Only to give ourselves work, herding them?'

Tatomkhulu laughed, a deep growl of a laugh that came from deep down his enormous, trembly belly.

ridge narrow, raised strip
to jiggle (coll.) to move up and down with short, quick movements
to ruffle *durcheinanderbringen*

'Ah, Mzukulwana,' he chuckled, the ridges of his belly jiggling up and down. 'What questions you ask.' Then, appearing as though he were deep in thought or absentminded, he slowly ruffled my hair and said:

'You are correct in what you say,' he smiled. 'It is no easy work to look after one's herd. Remember though, Mzukulwana, remember, cows give us milk. From them, too, we get dung with which to smear the floors of our huts. We also use the hide from these same beasts to keep us warm and make implements and adornments with their horns.' As he said this, with his one hand, he turned the bangle on the wrist of the opposite arm.

Again he smiled. And then, bending down and ruffling my hair, he continued, 'Wouldn't you agree then that cattle pay for their keep?'

'Oh, yes, Tatomkhulu,' I replied. 'Yes, I suppose they do,' I said, more to dispel the doubt that wouldn't leave me than convince him of his truth.

'Suppose?' he shouted, but there was the gentlest smile on his kindly face. 'Well,' he continued,' let me give you more reasons why I say cattle are important in our lives. These are reasons more important than the milk, the dung, or the hide we get from cattle.

'And here they are, Mzukulwana: First, we keep cattle for a man to offer *lobola* to his in-laws, who in turn, *hlinzeka* him – the blood coming to his family from his intended's a sign, a bond cementing the union; we pay homage to our chiefs, applauding their wise decisions and good governance; we bid farewell to our revered departed and greet and remember the ancestors who protect us; and, in times of war, we give cattle to our enemies in exchange for those unfortunate victims taken by the other side. Cattle are also used as *umlandu* for the services of the healer.' Tatomkhulu was beaming, eyes sparkling with laughter.

'Quite a load there, you will agree. Quite a load that cattle carry in the life of amaXhosa,' he said.

'Imagine then if the whole nation – yes, after much debate, wrangling and verbal mastication – agreed to slaughter all its cattle. Agreed to such an abomination. How deep the resentment to have spurred them to such terrible sacrifice. How deep the abomination, to trigger such a response. UmXhosa, again I tell you, does not lightly part with his cattle.

'However, in 1857, the Xhosa nation killed all its cattle. Not for food. There was no feast or ceremony. No reason at all for the slaughter of even one beast. But all the herds in the nation were killed. The goal was to drive *abelungu* to the sea, where, so the seer had said, they would all drown. All, to the very, very last one.

'Such noble sacrifice. But then, the more terrible the abomination, the greater the sacrifice called for. That is the simple law of cause and effect.

'And they burned their fields. A people who lived off the land, who had no use for the button without a hole, who planted during the planting season, diligently tended their fields – hoeing and weeding – watered the plants and harvested them when the time was ripe. They burned their fields. People with *izisele* high enough for a full grown man to stand upright, so that you couldn't see even a blade of hair from his head, burned their fields. What would they feed those large, hungry *izisele* now? Whence would the corn, pumpkin, beans and other vegetable to be stored come from?

hide skin
implement tool
adornment anything that is decorative
bangle jewellery in the form of a ring
to pay for s.th.'s/s.o.'s keep to bring in enough money to pay for the cost of living
to dispel to make s.th. go away
intended (here): wife to be
to pay homage to s.o. to show respect to s.o. by deed or word
revered [rɪˈvɪəd] greatly respected
departed (formal) dead
to beam to smile with a big, wide smile
to wrangle to argue angrily
verbal mastication (ironic) chewing on words, i.e. arguments
to spur to motivate
abomination disgusting act
seer prophet
button without a hole (fig.) coins, money
diligently with great care and effort
to tend to take care of s.th.
to hoe *hacken*
to weed to get rid of weeds (unwanted plants)
blade (here): single piece

to thrive to flourish
to raze to completely destroy
to sustain to provide enough to live on
amarhewu (Xhosa) maize meal with hot water
tucked folded
appointed chosen
untoward unusual
reversal change so that everything is the opposite of what it was before
preordained (formal) already decided by fate
cob *Kolben*
black-sheened shiny black
reds red-coloured cattle
bullock castrated bull
to ripple to move in waves

'But the same call to kill their cattle had also urged them to burn down their thriving fields. Burn them to the ground. Raze everything. Razed to the ground. Not a stump left standing.

'With neither cattle nor harvest, never having handled the button without a hole, what would they do now? How would they live? How would they survive? Where would they go? How were they to live ... to sustain themselves?'

Tatomkhulu took a sip from the gourd of *amarhewu* Mama had come and put before him.

'Here,' he said, and lowered the gourd for me to drink. I gulped down some *amarhewu* and went back to where I had been sitting on the bare ground with my feet tucked under me. He took another swig and then continued:

'On the appointed day, nothing untoward happened. Nothing unusual. Nothing out of the ordinary. The sun rose in the east. That had been expected. People waited. They waited till it reached the zenith, high noon, when it left no shadow on the ground.

'Eyes unblinking, they looked at the sun.

'Did it move forward?

'No!

'Yes!

'Maybe!

'For a few, very long minutes, they couldn't tell. They went on hoping, though. Their very lives depended on the reversal of things, the natural order turned upside down.

'Soon, soon, tragically soon, there could be no doubt however. The sun was progressing as before, continuing on its preordained path, going forward, forward, and forever forward. As it had done for a million million years. The first sign betrayed. Dared they hope still?

'The sun went and died in the west.

'What of the promise? What of the prophecy? The first sign betrayed, dared they hope still?'

The sun will rise in the east, as usual. It will go up and up and up till it reaches the highest point in the sky. Then, instead of going west, it will turn back, turn back and go and set in the east. The sun will set in the east!

Then, with the rising of the new sun, all the things that had been killed and burned would rise again. New corn, cobs tall and big as the thighs of a maiden; fruit and vegetable – fresh, firm, juicy and sweet – fruit and vegetable known and new to these lands; cattle – pure breeds: black-sheened, reds, nezimfusa, iinco – cows in calf, bulls lowing and strong, bullocks proud, muscles rippling as they, slowly, unhurriedly, moved cattle, sheep, goats, and all other animals of the home, animals useful to folk all these would rise from the ground. Yes, like plants, they would rise from the ground. As it was in the beginning. As it was when Qamata first made all the land and everything in it. As it was Embo, before the people wanted to see Qamata with their own, nothing, naked eyes. The very ones Qamata had given them to see. Things would be as good and unspoiled as they had been Embo, in the very beginning.

'Those eyes now cast about in dire desperation. Where were all these things? The people of Embo looked ... willing the promised miracle into being. And that was not all that had been promised them. No, that was not all they awaited ... not all they hoped for in return for their terrible sacrifice.

'That was not the miracle for which the People of Embo had sacrificed their all. After all, Qamata's good earth was not without wild fowl and beast, not without wild herb and root. Rivers roared galloping downhill, skipped chuckling over boulders, meandered through sleepy fields of *amazimba*, before going to disappear among strange people, villages and villages away.

'Remember now, the biggest miracle, the mother reason for the whole *indaba*, was the promise of a return to the way of before, when the people with hair like the silken threads of corn would be no more:

'A great whirlwind will rise and drive all abelungu to the sea ... where they will all drown.'

'Would that happen? Could it happen even though not one of the other things promised had happened? Could it happen?

'The people looked.

'Where, then, was the sign? Where, the first intimation the prophecy would be fulfilled?

'The people waited. Bile in their mouths. Anxiety grinding their intestines. They waited.

'When not one of the miracles appeared, they wondered. Their eyes large with apprehension, they wondered. Wondered, still hoping. For, is it at a robust tree trunk the drowning man clutches?'

Again, we wet our mouths at the gourd. After that, this time, Tatomkhulu said his voice would go unless he kissed his pipe. 'Take another sip!' he said. I did then, waited as he drew a few more puffs, blew smoke into the air and, eyes closed, sighed in satisfaction.

'The sun set in the west,' he began after the short break. 'The scorched ground remained wounded and black. Not a new blade of grass peeped. No great wind rose to drive *abelungu* to the sea. Not that day. Not the next. Not for all the days that the people waited. Meanwhile, *abelungu* remained stubbornly alive and well, their mines greedily hungry for the strong hands and arms of young men.

'In a few days, the stench rose from rotting corpses of cattle killed in their thousands. Soon thereafter, the stench was of people dying. Old and young. Men and women. Children too. People dying in their hundreds of thousands.

'Like a veld fire, the terrible news travelled. The vultures had heard of the great debate before the slaughter of the cattle and the burning of the fields. Now, the dying of the people of Embo brought them to

dire disastrous
fowl (old-fashioned) birds
herb plants
root plants with roots
boulder large rock
to meander to follow a winding course
intimation (formal) hint or suggestion
bile (fig.) *Galle*
to grind (fig.) *zermahlen*
intestines *Dick- und Dünndarm*
sip small drink
scorched burnt
stench awful smell
veld [velt] open, flat land with grass and no trees, typical of South Africa
vulture (fig.) *Geier*

the villages, Sir George Grey leading the pack. They came. Bringing gifts of food to the starving, dying people. Bringing a golden opportunity never to starve again. "To the mines, to the mines, hasten! hasten and be saved ... Never will you hunger again. Never." '

enticement s.th. that attracts or draws people because of the possibility of money or happiness

For so long, Tatomkhlulu said, the villagers had resisted the enticement. Come to the mines! Come and get paid money, the button without a hole. The button without a hole will make you a very happy people.

Good Volume Bible

'But, long ago, Ntsikane, the Xhosa Seer, had warned the nation of the coming of the people with hair as the silken threads of corn. "They will bring you the Good Volume and the button without a hole.

Take the volume! Take the volume!
But beware the button without a hole!
Do not take the button without a hole!
Do not take it! Do not take it!
Take the volume but not the button without a hole!"

'Therefore, Mzukulwana, at the time of the killing of the cattle, amaXhosa still did not have the hunger for the button without a hole. Among them that hunger was still totally unknown. They had no need for the things the button without a hole could get for one.'

Hayi, ilishwa!
Amabhulu, azizinja!
One settler, one bullet!
By the match stick, we shall free our nation!

'Oh, the road has been long, indeed. The songs came much, much later, I can tell you that. Before the songs, many others tried to rid our nation of the ones without colour, who had come from across the great sea.

'Makana, the Left-Handed, prophesied outcomes similar to Nongqawuse's. His magic would turn the bullets of the guns of *abelungu* to water.

'At Isandlwana, with spear and shield, Cetywayo's *impis* defeated the mighty British army and its guns.

to unleash to let loose

'Bulhoek, in Queenstown, is another example of resistance I can cite. Close to two hundred people murdered. Their sin? They wanted back their land and took possession of it, claiming it as their own. When they wouldn't move, even by force, bullets were unleashed on them.

'But it was all to no avail. All to no avail. To this very day, *abelungu* are still here with us, Mzukulwana. The most renowned liar has not said they are about to disappear.'

fund (here): great store

Tatomkhulu was a fund of facts that, although seemingly different, made a whole lot of sense of some of the things we learned at school. He explained what had seemed stupid decisions, and acts that had seemed indefensible became not only understandable but highly honourable.

1 pm – Thursday 26 August

As from a deep slumber, I dredged myself up. Fog in my head, thick and heavy, made me reluctant to rise to the point where I would open my eyes. Why was I so loath to face the day? A heavy rock sat in the pit of my stomach.

slumber (literary) sleep
to dredge yourself up to pull yourself up from a deep place
loath (formal) unwilling

'Mama, you are awake?' Siziwe was standing at the door leading from kitchen to dining-room. She looked fine. Why did this surprise me? Why was I surprised she looked fine? Vaguely, my mind grappled with the puzzle.

to grapple with s.th. to deal with s.th.

'How are you?'

The smell of fried eggs hit me. Just then, my stomach growled, reminding me it badly needed attention. Behind Siziwe, strong swathes of sunlight flooded the kitchen and yellowed the sink, cupboard, wall and linoleum. The kitchen and everything in it smiled sunnily.

swathe large strip

'I woke up,' Siziwe replied. But there was no smile on the face looking at me.

And suddenly, it all came back. The horror of last night . . . well, early this morning. My eyes flew open and I was just about to ask how her brothers were when, as though she had read my thoughts, she said:

'He has not come back.' She didn't have to say which brother she was talking about.

'And Lunga?' I asked. 'Is he still asleep? How is he?'

'Mama, Lunga has been gone for hours now.'

'But what time is it?'

'One o'clock.'

Hungry as I was, all my appetite suddenly left me. Either seeing or sensing my distress, Siziwe quickly added:

'Some boys came to see him and although I told them he was not well, they insisted on talking to him. They wouldn't go away.'

'Who were those boys? People we know?'

'Yes, Mama.' She was quiet for a minute then added, 'They came by car.' Siziwe looked at me as she imparted this startling piece of news. My mind reeled. Lunga didn't have any friends who had cars. We had no car. Our friends had no cars. We didn't know anyone who owned a car. But, seeing she was getting no response from me, she continued:

to impart to communicate
to reel (here): to seem to spin

'I heard one of them ... I don't know his name but he goes to Langa High School ... I heard him say something about Bhuti Mxolisi.'

That gave me back my voice. And the words. At once alert, I asked, 'They were talking about Mxolisi?'

alert *wach*

'Yes, Mama.'

'What about him? Did they say anything about his whereabouts?'

'No, Mama,' she replied, then stopped and looked at me as though suddenly at a loss as to how to proceed, how tell me some unpalatable intelligence. I remembered the talk we'd had earlier that morning, after the police had left.

edge sharp tone
to inveigle [ɪnˈveɪgl] **itself** (here): to begin to take over by trickery
to do a crazy jiggermammaroll (coll.) to collapse because of shock
accommodating (here): providing enough space
dog-collar (coll.) the white collar that ministers and priests often wear around the neck
mfundisi (Xhosa) preacher, reverend
flock (here): congregation, members of a church
staunch strong and loyal

'What is it?' Again, there was that look. Why was she being secretive? So, I asked:

'What is it? What's the matter, Siziwe?' An edge I had not invited had inveigled itself into my voice.

'Mama, I don't know,' she began, hesitated ... her eyes fell to her feet before she continued. 'I think ... ,' she said, then stopped and started again. 'It seems as though it's something to do with what happened to the white girl yesterday,' she uttered in a rush.

The room spun. It did a crazy jiggermammaroll. Clutching at the arms of the chair near me, I lowered myself onto its comforting, accommodating lap. Slowly, carefully, my body gone all liquid, I watched myself pour it onto the chair. A great sigh escaped from somewhere within that soft, jellified body I couldn't feel. I sighed, for the heart beating painfully against my ribs demanded relief.

'The one who was killed?' I couldn't believe I'd asked that. Why was that the first thing that came to my mind, I wondered. When had I started thinking Mxolisi's absence might be linked to those troubles?

'Yes, Mama,' Siziwe said quietly. She said that and left the room.

I forced myself to eat something – partly so as not to disappoint Siziwe and partly because I realized that whether I wanted to or not I had to eat, I needed the strength food would give me. I had to take strength from eating, as we say.

We had hardly finished our late breakfast when a car stopped outside, right in front of our gate. I jumped to my feet thinking, what now? Then remembering the car that had come for Lunga, I relaxed. Perhaps, the boys were bringing him back. And perhaps, Mxolisi would be with all of them. My heart started pounding at that thought. I went to the window to get a clear look at the car, at who got out of it.

A man I didn't know got out of the car.

'Who is it?' Siziwe asked.

'I don't know.' Just then, I saw that he wore the dog-collar that ministers wear.

'But he is a *mfundisi*,' I added.

At that, Siziwe bounded from where she sat and came to stand right next to me at the window.

'Oh,' she whispered, for the man had gone through the gate and was even then walking up the stoep, approaching the front door.

'Who is it? D'you know him?' There was urgency I didn't intend in my voice. But the man was already knocking at the door.

'Come in!' I said.

'It's *Mfundisi* Mananga of the Anglican Church, in NY 2.'

'*Molweni, aph' ekhaya*!' The Reverend Minister's greeting was in a cheery voice. I wondered what had brought him to my humble house. We were certainly no members of his flock. Marriage to Dwadwa, a staunch Methodist, had meant that I left the Anglican Church, under which I grew up.

After the introductions, Reverend Mananga, in a voice decibels too high, extraordinarily loud, as though he were speaking from the pulpit or deliberately wanted people two doors away to hear what we were talking about, said:

'*Aphi la makhwenkwe alapha*?'

When I told him that both boys were at school, he shook his head, exclaimed that it was a pity they were not home because he had very good news for the older boy.

'It is Mxolisi Ntloko, is it not?'

'Yes, *Mfundisi*,' I replied, 'Mxolisi is my eldest.'

Well, *Mfundisi* went on, the boy and his friends had been to see him the previous day. 'Looking for somewhere to hold their meeting. And now,' he said with a flourish, 'I've found a place for them. Tell Mxolisi to come to the Mission as soon as possible!'

'Thank you, *Mfundisi*, thank you!' I said, trying very hard to keep curiosity and consternation out of my voice, taking care that that voice remained calm and natural as can be.

And that was not as easy as it sounds. For all the while, as he gave his speech, the *Mfundisi* was busy scribbling something on a piece of paper he had fished out of his pocket, nervously looking about him all the time as though he expected someone or something to jump him from one of the rooms. Ceaselessly, his neck swivelled this way and that, rotating as though it had a mind all its own. He was sweating profusely – huge beads of sweat poured down his temples.

Straightening himself up, he passed me the note, nodded and winked as, aloud, he said:

'Tell this boy, Mxolisi, that I will be home all afternoon. He must come and see me. Tell him he can come any time.' And as though answering to something I had said, he went on, 'Yes! Yes, perhaps it is already late for today.' His index finger straight up, he put to his lips, a gesture that I be silent? or, not divulge a secret?

I nodded.

With an answering nod, slow and deliberate, conveying sympathy as I understood, the minister departed, leaving me as puzzled and agitated as ever. On his note he had written:

THATH' ITAXI, EYA EKHAYELITSHA, WEHLE KWISTOP SOKUGQIBELA.

TAKE A TAXI TO KHAYELITSHA, AND GET OFF AT THE LAST STOP.

With speed I would not have imagined was in me at all just a little earlier, I tidied myself up and left. My heart started singing for I was convinced this man was going to lead me to my son. But, as I waited for the taxi, I sobered a little. He had not said he was taking me to Mxolisi, I had assumed that. But then, where would he be taking me? I asked myself. And he had talked about Mxolisi, hadn't he?

The hour of day being what it was, the taxis were slow in coming. However, again because it was not workers' time, when the taxi to

decibel unit of measure to describe how loud a sound is
pulpit *Kanzel*
with a flourish with an exaggerated movement
consternation worry
ceaselessly without stopping
to swivel to turn
profusely in large quantities
temple *Schläfe*
to wink *zwinkern*
index finger *Zeigefinger*
to divulge to reveal, to make known
to sober to become more clearheaded

Khayelitsha eventually came, it was not full and when I got in I even found a seat.

The taxi had gone past two stops when a girl I'd seen at the stop, and whom I'd barely paid attention to, moved from where she was sitting, a few seats behind me and came to stand right next to me. Even then I barely looked at her, taking it she was getting ready to get off and vaguely wondering whether she could not have walked the distance, as we had been on the road but a few minutes. Indeed, we were still in Guguletu's Section Two. My mind was so filled with questions that, had she not dropped the book she was reading, I doubt I would have noticed the girl at all.

to thud to fall with a heavy, dull sound

I looked up when the book thudded right next to my foot. Right then, she bent down to pick it up. A scratch on my foot, just below the ankle, between the ankle and the shoe, surprised me.

I looked down then.

The girl pushed something onto my lap and immediately, without once looking at me, moved away.

frown worried expression

to pleat to make a fold

I could feel a deep frown pleating my brow as I unfolded the little bit of paper, rolled into a tight little roll till it was pencil thin. I looked.

YEHLA KWISTOP ESILANDELA ESI NDEHLA KUSO MNA. GET OFF THE NEXT STOP FOLLOWING THE ONE WHERE I GET OFF.

I looked up. Now, the girl was looking at me as though she had never seen me before. Which, of course, was true. True, but only to a certain extent. We were linked now, were we not? Had she not put this mysterious message at my lap? Who was she? Again, my gaze flew down to the letter and back her way.

With the barest suspicion of a gesture, a slow, ever so slow, narrowing of the eyes, she indicated there was to be no further communication between us.

Again, I looked at the note in my hand. And saw something I had not seen before. The note was in the same, the very same handwriting as the one the *mfundisi* had given me. But then, he had written that one right there before my eyes.

involuntarily unintentionally

fairly almost

Involuntarily, my eyes again flew to the mysterious girl. The note says 'I', I was thinking. Was 'I' the girl? Common sense said yes, that was the case. But, even so, I knew in whose hand the letter had been written. Just then, my thoughts abruptly stopped as my heart fairly flew out of my mouth. The girl was getting off the taxi.

to scramble to your feet to stand up quickly using your hands

Panicked, I scrambled to my feet. This was the last stop in Guguletu, the taxi was headed for Nyanga after this. Wasn't I supposed to get off here? Last stop?

'Wait!' I shouted, for she was the only one getting off at that stop and the taxi had begun to move.

'Wait, I'm getting off!'

screeching making a loud, high, unpleasant sound

'Wake Up!' yelled the taxi driver, 'My taxi is no place to sleep!' he said, bringing the taxi to a screeching halt and provoking grumbles and complaints from passengers thrown from their seats by the abrupt, unceremonious braking.

'I … I'm so … so … sorr … r … ry,' I stammered, realizing my error. The note said to get off the stop after the girl's. What was I thinking, getting off the same stop as her? It was the first note that had mentioned last stop … and that last stop was in Khayelitsha.

The taxi was still arrested from motion. All eyes were now on me. Again I mumbled my apologies. Confused and flustered, I couldn't bring myself to look at the driver or the passengers. Instead, I looked at my feet.

Gears grinding in protest, the taxi took off. I lurched to the side and nearly landed on a short, bearded man sitting on one of the outside seats.

'Sorry,' I gasped, as he gave me a nasty, unamused look of fed-upness. Well, couldn't he see I was not holding on to anything? Did he think I just chose to fling myself on top of his lap? I returned the look with what I hoped was one nastier still and slowly sauntered toward the door. Right then, an unpleasant thought came to my mind. I realized I had the unwelcome task of asking the driver to put me off at the next stop. My tongue weighed a ton.

'Next stop!' an irritated voice yelled from the back. Thankfully, I edged my way to the front.

Then, while waiting for the taxi to arrive at my stop, I threw my eyes to the source of the command, wondering who else was getting off at my stop. But no one was standing yet. That told me we were some ways yet from the next stop.

When the taxi finally arrived at my stop, I was the first one out of that taxi. Two other passengers got out after me. Both men, both elderly. The voice that had shouted 'Next stop' had been a woman's. Young. A girl's voice. What had happened to the owner of that voice? I asked myself. For some reason, this bothered me.

'Mandisa', astounded, I told myself the very next minute, 'you're becoming suspicious. If you're not careful you'll begin suspecting your shadow is following you and attach a sinister reason to that.' Obviously, I now saw clearly, what had happened was that one of the old men getting off had asked for help. Either not trusting his own voice to carry as far as the driver's ears or for whatever other reason, he had asked someone else to alert the driver of his intentions of getting off the taxi. A young woman, perhaps sitting next to one or both of these gentlemen, helped in that little way. What was so wrong with that? Seeing how ludicrous my earlier suspicion had been, I shook my head in exasperation. What had I got myself into? Why this mystery? Where was this *mfundisi* taking me? I said *mfundisi* because I was convinced he was the author of both letters. No two people could form their letters with such close similarity, I was convinced. Where was he sending me? And why the mystery to the destiny?

My immediate problem, I now realized, was that I had no idea where I was going. Hadn't he asked me to go to the last taxi stop in Khayelitsha? What was I doing here, far away from that stop? Why had I allowed myself to be led off the bus? There was quite a differ-

to stammer to stutter

flustered nervous, upset

gears *Gangschaltung*

to grind (here): to make the sound of metal pieces rubbing against each other

to lurch to make an unsteady, sudden movement in a certain direction

to saunter to stroll

to edge your way to s.th. to move slowly and carefully in a certain direction

to attach to connect

sinister evil, harmful

to alert to notify

ludicrous silly

exasperation *Verzweiflung*

destiny (here): goal, end of a trip

ence between the first stop in Nyanga and the last in Khayelitsha. And who was the girl who had passed the note I still held in my hand? Which way did I go now?

to clamour to make a loud outcry

As though in answer to the questions clamouring in my mind right then, a car stopped and the window came down. I stepped back from the road.

'*Ndim, Mama kaMxolisi*, It's me, Mother of Mxolisi!'

Relief washed through me. It was the *mfundisi*. *Mfundisi* Mananga himself. In my state of mind, however, it took me an instant before this fact fully registered. Of course, it did not help any that the *mfundisi* was in a car different from the one he'd had earlier when he'd come to my house. What a lot had happened in the short time since then.

'It is me,' he said, again, for I had made no response to his greeting, or said a word acknowledging him.

to chide to criticize

to hasten to do s.th. to quickly do s.th. without delay

'Good afternoon, again,' I said, convinced he was going to chide me for disobeying his orders. 'A strange thing happened,' I hastened to explain. But, holding his hand up, *Mfundisi* made me stop.

'It's all right,' he said, smiling broadly. 'I'm sorry I can't give you a lift, but I'm going in the opposite direction to you.'

'Oh?' I said. I couldn't, for the life of me, think of one intelligent thing to add, how to go on.

'Wait here,' said *Mfundisi*, adding to my confusion. A woman driving a red car will stop and ask you for directions. The answer you must give her is,' he paused, looked at me and, saying the words very slowly, continued, 'this is what you must say to her: I do not live hereabouts.' Again he looked at me. 'Will you remember that?'

'Yes, *Mfundisi*,' I replied. 'I do not live hereabouts,' I repeated. He nodded his satisfaction.

out and out directly

Fast, confusion turned to alarm in my heart. What was this game this man was making me play? Where was my son? What did I do after telling this woman who would be driving a red car I was not from hereabouts? Why had I not asked *Mfundisi*, out and out, whether all this going up and down in taxis was taking me to Mxolisi? Had he even seen him? Did he know where he was? Why had Mxolisi not returned home last night?

But by now, I was alone at the stop. *Mfundisi* Mananga had driven off as soon as he'd heard me say my piece, repeat the words he had given me.

reverie ['revəri] (formal) daydream

'Mama,' a voice awoke me from my reverie. 'Can you tell me how to get to the airport from here?'

'The airport,' I asked, 'the airport?' Then I saw that the woman asking me the question was driving a red car. My heart lurched so painfully that my hand flew to my chest, holding it back.

'No,' I said. ' No,' frantically trying to recall the exact words *Mfundisi* had given me.

exclamation word, phrase, or sentence spoken with emotion

'Oh?' There was a question to her exclamation. In her twenties, she was very beautiful. And then, I remembered.

'I am not from hereabouts,' I threw in hastily. My palms were clammy from the effort of trying to remember *Mfundisi*'s text. My mind, now that I'd remembered the all-important words, took in this young woman. Teacher or nurse, I was sure. Educated, whatever she was. She looked educated. That skin. Soft sheen. Didn't know hardship. Cheeks glowing with good health ... and eating well. Soft hands, no doubt. Thus went my thoughts.

The back door of the car quietly opened.

'Get in, Mama,' a voice said from the inside of the car. Deep and gruff. Definitely not a woman's voice. In any event, the woman who had asked me for directions was looking at me, her lips still as can be.

I edged towards the car.

'Get in, Mama,' the woman added, smiling, no doubt amused by my hesitation.

I got in. Crouched low on the back seat, was a man in bright white training shoes and a black tracksuit. His face was almost completely hidden inside a black balaclava. As the car roared away, he straightened up, making room for me on the seat.

I cannot tell you what twists and turns that car made. I began to wonder whether this woman, who had not said a word after taking off at great speed, knew where she was taking me or who I was.

At last, the car came to a stop.

'This is the house,' said the man next to me.

'What house?' I asked.

'Where we were told to take you, of course.' Finally, the woman sitting alone at the front had spoken.

'Oh,' I said, scrambling out.

As soon as I closed the door, the car zoomed off and away.

I looked at the house. Orange curtains at the front windows. Drawn. Was there anyone in there? I took a deep breath and walked toward the gate, opened it, and walked up the red, highly polished stoep. I reached the door and raised my hand to knock.

'Come in!' said a hurried voice and the door swung silently in. Surprised at the ready reception, I made my feet take me inside that house where, I could clearly see, I was expected. The house where I feared my son would be. Why? Why was he in hiding? Why here, in this house? What house was this and who were these people who had brought me here? All of them, from *Mfundisi* to the two who had just dropped me off?

Two men were standing near the table in the centre of the room. The woman, who had opened the door, was still holding it open.

'You came just as we were leaving,' she said. 'Please, take a seat.' She showed me to a dark-green sofa near the window and against the wall. 'Take a seat and wait.'

At that the men nodded their greeting and, without another word, all three walked out, leaving me alone.

That I had been awaited at this place was obvious to me. No one had asked me who I was or what I wanted. I perched myself on the

clammy damp

to take in (here): to examine

gruff rough

training shoes shoes for sports

tracksuit *Trainingsanzug*

balaclava (BE) close-fitting woollen hood that covers the ears and neck

twist sharp curve

drawn closed

to perch yourself somewhere (coll.) to sit on the edge of s.th.

to yank (coll.) to pull quickly

purr soft sound

to scurry to run with short, quick steps

dim not loud

recess space that is far away

to charge to rush

sofa, sitting at the edge as though I expected to be yanked out of there at any minute.

Yes, I'd been expected. But now I was alone in the house. What next, I wondered. Would *Mfundisi* make another surprise appearance? Indeed, I half expected him to. My ear, I soon saw, was listening for the purr of a car stopping outside and, a minute later, his hearty greeting. Well, this time, I'd be ready when he came. There were a few questions I would definitely like to address to him.

Full half an hour I sat there. All alone. There did not seem to be one more soul in that house. That still it was. Not even the sound of a mouse scurrying across the floor. I waited, the only noise in the place my own nervous breathing and the drumming of my heart. I waited, my curiosity growing, to say nothing of my anxiety.

I jumped when I heard the door open. An inside door. Although no one had told me so, I had come to the conclusion I was alone in the house. But I'd been mistaken.

Suddenly the room spun. I took a deep breath, fought to steady my reeling senses.

Mxolisi. Wearing clothes I did not recognize. Clean, though he looked as though he could do with a week's sleep.

'Are you alone? Did you come alone?' he asked, casting anxious glances this way and that. I noted that we had not even exchanged greetings yet.

'Yes, I am alone.' We looked at each other, standing on opposite sides of the room.

The next minute, he was in my arms. Or, I in his. Hard to tell at times, especially when they grow this tall. The children we put on our backs, only yesterday. Now, they're men and women. All grown.

I don't know who started crying. But, before the next words were said between us – our cheeks, so close together, wet with tears of an unacknowledged sorrow – I knew we were in deep, deep trouble. I did not remember the last time I had seen my son crying.

'What is it?' I pushed him an arm's length away. I looked at him. 'Why didn't you come home, last night? And what is this? Why are the police looking for you and why are so many people taking all this trouble to hide you?'

Tears now pouring down his cheeks, unashamed, unpretending tears, he looked at me. There was immeasurable fear in those eyes.

'Mxolisi, what are you hiding from? Who are you running away from?'

'They say I did it, Mama!'

Even then, the full horror did not register in my brain.

'They say you did it? Who are they?'

'Everybody. Even the police.'

A dim bell, somewhere in the deep recesses of my mind, began to ring. The question I had avoided asking without knowing that I was doing so, came charging through my lips.

'They say you did *what*? What are you being accused of? *Utyholwa ngantoni*?'

Slowly, haltingly, out came the story of the assault on your daughter. The terrible deed of the previous day. And my son told me:

'Mama, believe me, I was just one of a hundred people who threw stones at her car.'

'But', I said, looking at him full in the face, Skonana's words loud in my ear, '*a knife killed her.*' I heard myself say those words. Words she had said, oh, so long, long ago. Thunk! Fist striking slightly cupped hand. Thunk! I heard it still.

For a long, long minute, Mxolisi did not reply.

'So?'

Finally, with a heavy sigh, he said:

'Even that, Mama, even that ... ', then he stopped. There followed a longish pause I didn't have the strength to bridge, to interrupt, before he continued, '... many people stabbed her.'

Again, I looked at him, my heart pounding out a thousand prayers in different directions all at once.

'Were you one of them? One of the many people who stabbed the girl?' How I prayed, even as I asked the question, how I prayed that the answer would be an unequivocal NO. No, he had thrown stones at her car. And that was the only thing he'd done. Not the knife. He had not plunged a knife into her body. Not even one of many, many knives.

But my son did not answer my pointed question. Even after I repeated it, not once, not twice, but many, many times. No answer denying that he used a knife on the dead girl came from my son's lips. I waited a long time to get that answer, but it would not come. After some time, with a heavy heart, I knew I was not going to hear what I so urgently, so desperately, so fervently, prayed I might hear.

Finally, I said what had to be said. 'Did you do it? Are you the one who killed this white girl? Is it your knife that killed her?'

At that point, I didn't, for the life of me, know what I wanted him to say.

But my son would not answer. He merely looked at me with those eyes glazed with a fear so deep, so big, not even his lies could hide it from me ... could hide it from himself.

'I didn't do it, Mama. I swear, I didn't do it!' He was sobbing. Great, heart-wrenching sobs tearing at his guts.

Wordlessly, I gathered him in my arms and slumped onto the sofa. And let him cry himself on and on till the sobs became dry gasps as of one fighting for air. Then, the weeping subsided. By this time, his head resting on my lap, the skirt of my dress was sopping wet.

After a long while, I realized that he'd calmed a little. For whatever reason, we were now back on our feet, facing each other, eyes searching the others'.

'Why?' I asked. Quietly. No remonstration in my voice. No accusation. I asked, simply because I did not understand how something

thunk sound word

unequivocal *eindeutig*

to plunge (here): to push into s.th.

fervently ardently, passionately

glazed glassy

to sob *schluchzen*

heart-wrenching *herzzereißend*

tearing at his guts (fig.) affecting his innermost feelings

to slump to drop heavily

to subside to slowly stop

sopping wet (coll.) very wet, soaking wet

remonstration (formal) protest

like this could have happened. How he, Mxolisi, could be part of that something … in whatever manner, great or small.

'Why?'

'I said I did not do it, Mama!' his voice high, an edge of anger had crept into it.

Anger? At me? What had I done?

'Then, why is everybody pointing a finger at you?'

No answer.

Again I asked the same question: 'Why you? Why is it you, everybody's picking? Why are they all saying you are the person who did this terrible thing?'

Finally, after I'd repeated the same question (or variations thereof) many times over, Mxolisi burst out: 'I was not the only one there!'

'D'you realize she is never going to come back? Dead, means forever? Do you? Do you? Do you?' Now, I was the one sobbing, hysterical.

'Mama, I was not the only one there!' he shouted. That only infuriated me even more. I was so scared. For him. For me. For all of us – his brother, his sister, Dwadwa. I was so terrified of what the morrow would bring. Now, of course, the earlier visit of the police to our home made sense, horrible sense.They were looking for … for a … The earlier terror returned, only amplified by the new, the realization that my son would be arrested. The police were, even now, looking for a … for him. He would be charged with murder. My mind refused to think beyond that. It balked at even taking a glimpse at what might lie beyond the trial.

'Oh, you fool,' I screamed, totally undone. 'Don't you see what you have done? Don't you see that if your knife has her blood, it doesn't matter if you stabbed her in her thumb! Don't you see that? Mxolisi, don't you see that?'

For a split second, a jamboree of feelings infused my whole being, totally took over. All feeling, no thought, no thought whatsoever. What a state to find myself in. Drifting in a sea of undirected feeling, fear uppermost.

Then, we were in each other's arms. Who was consoling whom? I would be lying if I said I knew. My son patted my back as though I were a baby he was hushing to sleep. Dry sobs racked … which one of us?

A hundred years later, we disentangled ourselves. But still, I held his hand. Spent, I looked into his eyes.

He didn't blink.

I looked into my son's eyes. And saw pain and terror.

to infuriate to enrage

to amplify (formal) to increase
to charge with murder to formally accuse s.o. of murder
to balk at s.th. to try to refuse to accept the possibility of s.th.
undone feeling that all hope has been lost
split very short

jamboree (ironic) large celebration
to infuse (formal) to completely fill

to console *trösten*

to hush to make s.o. quieter
to rack to torture
to disentangle to separate, to disconnect
spent exhausted

Chapter Eleven

But now, my Sister-Mother, do I help him hide? Deliver him to the police? Get him a lawyer? Will that mean I do not feel your sorrow for your slain daughter? Am I your enemy? Are you mine? What wrong have I done you ... or you me?

She had so much to live for ...

Oh, that she had harboured but an ounce of fear! She had a tomorrow. Much to look forward to. Much yet to do, even though she had already accomplished much in her young days.

But, were there no such places where she came from? Places where she could have done good, helped the powerless, and righted what was wrong?

And my son? What had he to live for?

As for these heroes who lash out at my son today, voices raised in indignation, are they not the same who, only yesterday, were full of praise for him? Was he not part of the Young Lions they glorified? Did he not do as they shouted for all to hear?

ONE SETTLER, ONE BULLET!

AMABHULU AZIZINJA!

WITH OUR MATCH BOXES, WE SHALL FREE OURSELVES!

'*Tsaa-ah*! Go for it!' We set the dog on. '*Tsa-aah*!'' It knows what to do, go after the target and grab it by the throat. There is no danger to ourselves. It is the dog we send out that is at risk. It is the dog that takes the risk, that could get hurt. Or killed. Or jailed.

Shame and anger fill me day and night. Shame at what my son has done. Anger at what has been done to him. I am angry at all the grown-ups who made my son believe he would be a hero, fighting for the nation, were he to do the things he heard them advocate, the deeds they praised. If anyone killed your daughter, some of the leaders who today speak words of consolation to you ... mark my words ... they, as surely as my son, are your daughter's murderers. And, in many ways, they're guiltier than my son. They knew, or should have known, better. They were adults. They were learned. They had the key to reason.

Mother of the Slain, you whose heart is torn, know this:

I have not slept since. Food turns to sawdust in my mouth. All joy has fled my house and my heart bleeds, it sorrows for you, for the pain into which you have been plunged. It is heavy and knows no rest.

Other children throw stones at my children. They point indicting fingers at them. I am a leper in my community.

But, even as these voices of concern are raised, calling for what we have not had in the townships for years and years and years, the same winds that gouged dongas in my son's soul are still blowing . . . blowing ever strong. There are three- and four-year olds as well as older

slain killed

to harbour (fig.) to feel, to sense

ounce (fig.) small amount

to lash out at s.o. to criticize in an angry way

indignation *Entrüstung*

to set a dog on s.o./s.th. to get a dog to attack s.o./s.th. with a certain command

to advocate to support s.th. publicly

indict [ɪnˈdaɪt] to accuse, to charge

leper *Aussätzige(r)*

to gouge to make a deep hole with a sharp instrument

donga a steep-sided hole caused by soil erosion

children, roaming the streets of Guguletu with nothing to do all day long. Those children, as true as the sun rises in the east and sets in the west – those young people are walking the same road my son walked.

Does anyone see this? Do their mothers see this? Did I see it? Was I ever scared that it mattered not, on any day, whether my son got out of bed or not?

telling (here): fatal
jumble confused mass

And the police. How can they tell, with absolute certainty, which of those knives that rained on your poor child killed her? How can they tell which hand held which knife, even? They readily admit many fell upon her. Many. How then are they able to tell which hand delivered the telling stab, the fatal blow? Again and again I ask myself, why him? Why do they single him out from the jumble that took your child's life away?

My son! My son! What have you done? Oh, what is this terrible thing that you have done?

lest (literary) for fear that
to perish to die

Father, All-merciful, save me!
Help me! Hurry, help me, Lord, lest I perish.
Help me! Hurry, help me, Lord, right now.

Guguletu, much later

'Who is it?' I asked.

'It's me, *Mmelwane*,' answered Skonana's voice. My eyes filled. What did she want?

'She has people with her, also!' Qwati's asthmatic voice filled the brief silence that had fallen.

With the back of my hand I brushed away the tears, and got up from the side of the bed where I was sitting, my mind all over the place.

'Which side of the house are you?'

'Front,' came a chorus of voices.

Why can't people mind their own business. I opened my eyes wide, to stop fresh tears from starting. Four women stood there when I opened the door. Lindiwe and Yolisa were also from my street.

'We said to ourselves we should come,' said Qwati. 'We talked about this, we asked ourselves: should we not wait till she calls us? But the days have gone on ... '

'Call you?'

'We are people who come to each other's homes when there is a reason,' Lindiwe said. I saw that her eyes had no trouble at all looking into mine. But still, my heart would not be at peace.

'There is neither wedding nor feast at this house.'

'*Mmelwane*,' Skonana quickly jumped in. 'We have come to cry with you ... as is our custom, to grieve with those who grieve.'

to summon to ask to gather
to keen (old-fashioned) to lament
mourner a person who feels and expresses sadness at a person's death

I didn't know what to say or feel. I had not summoned my neighbours. Usually, the keening of mourners calls neighbours to the house that death has visited. I had not called my neighbours – I had not announced the death. Yes, there has been a death. But is it I who may keen? Is it I whom people should help grieve?

'We have come to be with you in this time,' Yolisa's voice said.

And we talked, my neighbours and I. It was like the opening of a boil. Thereafter, I was not so afraid of my neighbours'eyes. I did not immediately see condemnation in the eyes that beheld mine. When some stay away, I do not tell myself they are embarrassed or avoiding me. And even if they do, I know there are some among my friends and neighbours who feel for me – who understand my pain.

It is people such as these who give me strength. And hope. I hear there are churches and other groups working with young people and grownups. Helping. So that violence may stop. Or at least be less than it is right now. That is a good thing. We need to help each other ... all of us, but especially the children. Otherwise they grow up to be a problem for everyone. And then everybody suffers. I pray there may be help even for young people like Mxolisi. That they may change and come back better people.

Oh, My son! My son! What have you done? What is this that you have done?

Your daughter. The imperfect atonement of her race.

My son. The perfect host of the demons of his.

My Sister-Mother, we are bound in this sorrow. You, as I, have not chosen this coat that you wear. It is heavy on our shoulders, I should know. It is heavy, only God knows how. We were not asked whether we wanted it or not. We did not choose, we are the chosen.

But you, remember this, let it console you some, you never have to ask yourself: What did I not do for this child? You can carry your head sky high. You have no shame, no reason for shame. Only the loss. Irretrievable loss. Be consoled, however. Be consoled, for with your loss comes no shame. No deep sense of personal failure. Only glory. Unwanted and unasked for, I know. But let this be your source of strength, your fountain of hope, the light that illumines the depth of your despair.

boil *Furunkel*
condemnation *Verurteiling*
to behold (literary) to see

atonement *Sühne*
host (fig.) *Gastgeber(-in)*

irretrievable that can never be changed or reversed

Chapter Twelve

glaring bright and unpleasant
void [vɔɪd] (literary) large, empty space
intimately privately
stoop condition of being bent forward and downwards
huddled gathered close together
ragged in old, torn clothes
gnarled twisted
brazier ['breɪziə] large metal container filled with burning wood or coal to keep people warm
to dwell to live
employ work
abode home
posh elegant, fashionable
to forsake to abandon, to desert
to wither to decay, to shrivel, to become ever more run-down
stark grim, harsh, bleak
signpost (fig.) sign at a road that gives directions and distances
stillborn born dead
lumpen (literary) poor workers

And my son? What had he to live for?

My son. His tomorrows were his yesterday. Nothing. Stretching long, lean, mean, and empty. A glaring void. Nothing would come of the morrow. For him. Nothing at all. Long before the ground split when he pee'd on it, that knowledge was firmly planted in his soul ... it was intimately his.

He had already seen his tomorrows; in the defeated stoop of his father's shoulders. In the tired eyes of that father's friends. In the huddled, ragged men who daily wait for chance at some job whose whereabouts they do not know ... wait at the corners of roads leading nowhere ... wait for a van to draw up, a shout, a beckoning hand that could mean a day's job for an hour's wage, if that. He had seen his tomorrows – in the hungry, gnarled hands outstretched toward the long-dead brazier, bodies shivering in the unsmiling, setting sun of a winter's day. Long have the men been waiting: all day. But chance has not come that way today. Chance rarely came that way. Any day. Chance has been busy in that other world .... the white world. Where it dwelt, at home among those other beings, who might or might not come with offers of a day's employ. Where it made its abode – in posh suburbs and beautiful homes and thriving businesses ... forever forsaking the men looking for a day's work that might give them an hour's wage. The men from the dry, dusty, wind-flattened, withering shacks they call home. Would always, always call home. No escape.

Such stark signposts to his tomorrow. Hope stillborn in his heart. As in the hearts of all like him. The million-million lumpen, the lost generation. My son. My son!

Guguletu, late afternoon, Wednesday 25 August

The yellow Mazda drives up NY 1, from the Bellville side going north towards the Lansdowne side of Guguletu. The five young people inside are singing. All along the street, little groups of people walking, talking, or just standing, perhaps waiting ... for someone ... or for a taxi. The pedestrian traffic is thick and heavy, workers are coming back from work, schoolchildren from school, women at home scurrying from the shops to get back and start that evening meal.

congestion state of being overcrowded

Over there, near the Police Station, there is almost a congestion, the crowd is thickest here. There is a bus stop. Also, taxis to and from Langa and Nyanga stop here. So do some employers, fetching or bringing back labourers. There are several churches located in this area, as are a number of schools.

gait [geɪt] manner of walking
to shamble to walk in a lazy way dragging your feet

Here, Mxolisi's group changes both tune and gait. Gone the toyi-toyi, the freedom songs, and the marching. Shambling, is more like the step the group now adopts. All singing has stopped. Brief consultations are held, reiterating the next day's plans and bidding each other goodbye.

The larger group splits. A few of the young people, less than a hundred, walk down the street, towards the car fast approaching.

There is nothing setting the car apart. Nothing proclaiming it as special, peculiar, or marked. It is just one car among several driving up or down this particular stretch of NY 1, at this time, on this day. Past the shopping centre at NY 110. Past NY 132, where three buildings squat inside a high wire fence. This is Zingisa Higher Primary School. It is silent now. All the students and teachers are gone. If they ever were in today. The buildings are silent now. Empty. To the left over the other side of NY 132 and well away from the road, beyond a lush green patch of lawn, there is a Shell garage, with three little pumps, red and white. The yellow car is now headed for NY 112. Nothing sets it apart. Nothing. Until you look inside.

At the corner of NY 1 and NY 109, the group of students divides into two: the Langa crowd heads west, to Netreg Train Station while their Guguletu comrades splinter into smaller groups of two, three, or four, each heading home.

About midway between the garage and the second set of shops, smaller than the one at NY 110, the car comes to a reluctant stop. Three hundred metres ahead, the lights at the intersection of NY 1 and NY 108, also known as Klipfontein Road, have turned red. Several vehicles – delivery trucks, lorries, cars – between ten and twelve, are ahead of the little yellow car.

Mxolisi's little group is chatting idly. He can see his home, this side of the Police Station, a mere hundred metres from where he stands. Why, were he to hail someone standing at his gate, they'd hear him, it's that close. They'd see him too, if he waved and they happened to be looking his way.

Your daughter taps the steering wheel. The singing has long trailed to a stop. The engine purrs softly, idling.

A casual glance from a passer-by. Instantaneous ignition.

'*Kwi*Mazda! *Kwi*Mazda! *Kukh' umlungu kwi*Mazda! In the Mazda! In the Mazda! There is a white person in the Mazda!'

ONE SETTLER! ONE BULLET!

The cry rings out, sending a shock-wave through the hordes all around this part of NY 1. Not yet a crowd. Nothing binds them yet, but of course Operation Barcelona is in the air.

Others pick up the cry, repeat it and send it along. More and more re-echo it.

ONE SETTLER! ONE BULLET!

The tremor flashes and spills over to all within hearing. And all who hear it are riveted. Heads swivel this way and that.

The cry pulls women from their busy kitchens, stops in their tracks tired workers returning from work; children's play comes to

to squat (here): to be low and broad
lush with thick, healthy plants and grass
patch small area
to splinter into s.th. (here): to break off into a smaller group
reluctant unwilling
intersection *Kreuzung*
idly without any specific purpose
to tap to hit lightly and quickly
to trail to gradually stop
to idle *leer laufen*
casual incidental, not showing much care or thought
ignition (fig.) start of a fire
horde vast crowd, mob
tremor (fig.) shock wave
to flash (fig.) to suddenly burst out
riveted attracted and completely attentive
to stop in your tracks to immediately stop walking

to baptise (fig.) *taufen*
to meld to combine, to blend
disparate (formal) different, various
to verify to confirm
ignition key *Schlüssel für die Zündung*
implication possible effect or result of an action
to elicit (formal) to cause, to call forth
to dismiss to reject
hoax joke
lout idiot, dolt
to stir things up to cause trouble
to disintegrate (fig.) to break into small pieces
epicenter (fig.) the centre of an earthquake
oddity s.o. or s.th. strange or unusual
accelerator *Gaspedal*
to emit (formal) to send out

an abrupt halt; and the other drivers stopped at this point check that their doors are locked.

'Over here! Over here, in the yellow Mazda!'

The car has been singled now. It has been set apart. Noted.

The same baptising cries meld the disparate individuals and little groups, isolated but a minute before, into a one-minded monster. A group. A crowd, with one aim, one goal – at first, far from sinister, just to verify what the ears have heard, see if it is true. Could it be? How could it be?

Yet, doubting still, their feet all turn and point toward the car that has been marked. The yellow Mazda.

'Drive on! Drive on!' urges one of your daughter's passengers, one of the girls she is giving a lift back home.

Lumka groans, clenching and unclenching her jaw, fisting and unfisting her right hand. The hand is warm and sweaty.

'Drive on!' the first girl's voice is hoarse with fear.

Your daughter turns the ignition key. Crawls the space of one parked car. Stops. Stops because there is no going further, a car blocks her way.

ONE SETTLER! ONE BULLET!

Mxolisi's group, what remains of it, are they deaf not to hear the cry? Are they crazy not to see the implications? Only one thing could have elicited the cry. One. Somewhere, nearby, some white person has been spotted.

Incredible.

A white person. Here in Guguletu? In these times? After what happened to that KTC *mlungu* woman only yesterday? No way! Most dismiss the cry as a hoax, the work of some bored lout, looking to stir things up.

But the cry comes back again. Louder, this time, with more voices added.

The pack races towards the source of the cry, as one, echoing: 'One settler, one bullet.' Although they have not seen the stimulus for the cry.

ONE SETTLER! ONE BULLET!

Mxolisi's crowd quickly disintegrates, each person going full speed to the epicentre, searching for the one thing that will jump out, the oddity.

'Please, don't stop! Please, don't stop! Drive on!' Frantic, her friends shout.

She steps on the accelerator. The yellow car leaps ahead, emitting a surprised groan. After three car lengths, however, it again halts. Engine running but nowhere to go. Blocked by the car before it. By all those before that.

The young men who, a minute before, were standing at the corner of NY 1 and NY 109, have reached the mob surrounding the car.

By now, the cry has become frenzied. From throats haphazardly all around the milling crowd it comes incessantly:

ONE SETTLER, ONE BULLET! ONE SETTLER, ONE BULLET!

There is a thickening in the long, bleak road. A knob of bobbing and weaving heads, all around the yellow car. Hands reach out, playfully, at first. They rock the car. Those inside shudder, but there is no going forward. The car is totally immobilised.

Then, suddenly, the rocking stops.

Relief.

BANG! CRASH!

Relief quickly shattered. The windscreen wrinkles as a million-million little web-cracks paint themselves on it.

A scream escapes from someone's throat just as a second rock comes flying through a window, showering sparkling shards on face and neck and arms and legs and feet.

Don't panic, she tells herself, silently. Her lips tightly pressed together, jaw clenched, she tells herself, keep calm. You can get out of this. Keep your head.

ONE SETTLER, ONE BULLET!

From throat to throat the cry gaily goes; carried by the unthinking winds. It becomes a joyous refrain, voluntary and instinctive in its cruelly careless glee.

Another spray of broken bits of glass. The affronted flesh sprouts surprised eyes that open unseeingly. Red tears slowly ooze out of those eyes, and slowly trickle and join each other for solidarity. Red petals on shirt, on pants, and on legs and onto shoes.

An earthquake rocks the car.

'Drive on!' There is a crazed tone to the voice, urging the impossible.

Red petals in her eyes. Red petals blinding her to a halt.

The dilemma of the passengers in the yellow Mazda is a spur to the mindless crowd outside. The chant grows. Rocks rain upon the car. They come flying through, into the car and onto its fragile cargo, clearly endangered now.

Blocked, the car cannot move.

Blinded, your daughter cannot escape. Not by driving on. 'Let's run to the garage!' the young man cries out.

NO! NO! DRIVE ON!

The debate stops short as another earthquake rocks the car. In the darkened stomach of the car, all light is blocked by the mob of bodies all around it, pushing from all sides, pushing and yelling and stamping their feet, fists raised. Arms reach inside through the now naked, unglassed windows. The five young people are frozen scared. They are beside themselves with dread.

AMANDLA!

But now, inside the car, the so-loved, familiar cry triggers fear and panic.

frenzied very emotional and violent
haphazardly with no particular plan
milling moving about
incessantly constantly
bleak *trostlos*
knob knot, round lump, bunch
to bob and weave to quickly move up and down and to the side
to wrinkle to form lines or folds
web (fig.) *Spinnwebe*
shard piece of broken glass
clenched tightly pressed together
glee delight, happiness
to affront (fig.) to insult, to offend
to sprout (fig.) to cause to appear
to trickle to flow slowly in a thin stream
spur motivation
fragile *gebrechlich*
to be beside yourself with s.th. to be completely overwhelmed by s.th.

to yield to s.th. to give way to s.th., to accept s.th.
inevitable unavoidable
bid attempt
haven safe place
debris ['debri:] rubbish, things no longer wanted
to fall on reason to use reason as an argument
paltry very small, meagre
searing (fig.) explosive, burning
fervid (formal) intensely passionate
to dwell on s.th. to consider carefully
to brew (here): to cause
animosity hostility
to bear, bore, borne (here): to feel
compassion *Mitleid*
blanket general
irrevocable (formal) irreversible

Yielding to the inevitable, your daughter turns the car engine off. In one last desperate bid for freedom, all five fly out of the car in a mad dash for the three petrol pumps – the building – yellow, gold, white. A haven. Safety.

Smelling the climax, the pack is hot on their heels. Those with knives in their pockets, reach for them. Those unarmed cast their eyes about in the forever debris-rich dirt of Guguletu they're bound to find something useful.

The students from the university run.

The mob, like hounds, give chase, yelling and screaming in glee.

'Don't! Please, don't hurt her!' pleads Lumka.

'She's just a university student,' another of your daughter's friends screams, putting herself between her and her attackers. But 'university student' falls on deaf ears. The mob cares nothing for these words. My son and his friends and all those mobbing around your daughter's car, they know nothing of universities.

Your daughter falls on reason. 'Please don't do this. You don't want to do this. You can't do this. You can't do this to me. Please, don't. DON'T! Do-oo-hn-on-nt!'

But her pleas fall on deaf ears.

That unforgiving moment. My son. Blood pounding in his ears. King! If for a day. If for a paltry five minutes ... a miserable but searing second.

AMANDLA! NGAWETHU! POWER! IT IS OURS!
AMANDLA! NGAWETHU! POWER! IT IS OURS!

Thus rose the cry. Rose and fell to the cheering answer from the crowd. *Amandla*! a few cried out, their clenched fists high in the air. *Ngawethu*! came the unhesitating response from the fervid crowd. *Ngawethu*! Transported, the crowd responded; not dwelling on the significance of the word. Deaf and blind to the seeds from which it sprang, the pitiful powerlessness that had brewed this very moment

And the song in my son's ears. A song he had heard since he could walk. Even before he could walk. Song of hate, of despair, of rage. Song of impotent loathing.

AMABHULU, AZIZINJA!
AMABHULU, AZIZINJA!
BOERS, THEY ARE DOGS!
BOERS, THEY ARE DOGS!

Oh, that her goodness had not blinded her to the animosity of some of those for whom she bore such compassion! That her naiveté had not tricked her into believing in blanket, uniform guiltlessness of those whom she came to help.

That irrevocable moment! The crowd cheers my son on. One settler! One bullet! We had been cheering him on since the day he was born. Before he was born. Long before.

Nongqawuse saw it in that long, long-ago dream: A great raging whirlwind would come. It would drive *abelungu* to the sea. Nongqawuse had but voiced the unconscious collective wish of the nation: rid ourselves of the scourge.

She was not robbed. She was not raped. There was no quarrel. Only the eruption of a slow, simmering, seething rage. Bitterness burst and spilled her tender blood on the green autumn grass of a far-away land. Irredeemable blood. Irretrievable loss.

One boy. Lost. Hopelessly lost.

One girl, far away from home.

The enactment of the deep, dark, private yearnings of a subjugated race. The consummation of inevitable senseless catastrophe. I do not pretend to know why your daughter died ... died in the manner in which she did. Died when the time and place and hands were all in perfect congruence; cruel confluence of time, place and agent.

For that is what he had become at the time when he killed your daughter. My son was only an agent, executing the longsimmering dark desires of his race. Burning hatred for the oppressor possessed his being. It saw through his eyes; walked with his feet and wielded the knife that tore mercilessly into her flesh. The resentment of three hundred years plugged his ears; deaf to her pitiful entreaties.

My son, the blind but sharpened arrow of the wrath of his race.

Your daughter, the sacrifice of hers. Blindly chosen. Flung towards her sad fate by fortune's cruellest slings.

But for the chance of a day, the difference of one sun's rise, she would be alive today. My son, perhaps not a murderer. Perhaps, not yet.

scourge [skɜːdʒ] misfortune, curse, plague
eruption outburst
to simmer (fig.) to cook just below the boiling point
to seethe (fig.) to boil
irredeemable not able to be recovered, irreparable
irretrievable not able to bring back
enactment carrying out
yearning *Sehnsucht*
to subjugate to oppress
consummation fulfilment, achievement
congruence (formal) coming together, coinciding, confluence
agent s.o. or s.th. that carries out an action
to execute (formal) to successfully carry out
to wield to hold a weapon ready for use
to plug to tightly fill a hole with s.th.
entreaty plea, earnest request
to fling, flung, flung to throw with force
sling *Schleuder*

Additional Notes

page	line	
4	1	**Fulbright scholar** a student, teacher, or scientist of special merit who is given a grant to study abroad by the US government sponsored Fulbright Program, designed to promote understanding among the peoples of the world
	2	**Guguletu** township near Cape Town established in the 1960s for native Africans, especially the Xhosa – It was the scene of numerous upheavals after the end of apartheid in the early 1990s.
	15	**Andrew Goodman** (1943 -1964) civil rights activist murdered in Mississippi by the Ku Klux Klan
	23	**apartheid** [əˈpɑ:taɪt] official government system of racial and political segregation in South Africa from 1948 to the early 1990s that led to frequent violent opposition – Compare with Jim Crow and the concept of "equal but separate," especially in the American South, and the treatment of Aborigines in Australia.
5	11	**Xhosa** (here): a Bantu language of formerly cattle-rearing Africans who lived chiefly in South Africa
	36-37	**Langa, Nyanga, Khayelitsha** additional townships similar to Guguletu
7	8-9	... **the cup You have given me** ... Cf. Mathew 26: 42-43 "My Father, if it is not possible for this cup to pass me by, thy will be done." The cup symbolizes the bitter fate that Jesus will have to suffer on the cross and which He, for a moment, wishes to avoid.
8	top	**Mowbray** affluent suburb of Cape Town with mostly white English-speaking people
9	7	**hokkie** (Afrikaans) shack – Afrikaans is a variation of Dutch that was spoken by the first Dutch settlers in South Africa in the 17th century and has since developed separately from the Dutch spoken in Holland. It is also spoken by 2 percent of the native population of South Africa.
11	25	**Congress of South African Students** anti-apartheid student organisation founded in 1979 – It supported young workers and the unemployed.
	26	**Operation Barcelona** On the Monday before Amy Biehl's death in August 1993, the student wing of the African National Congress announced a programme it called Operation Barcelona, encouraging youngsters to destroy Government vehicles and property in support of striking teachers.
12	14	**bajita** (Tsotsitall, a street gang language) a form of greeting to more than one person
	15	**mjita** (Tsotsitall) greeting to one person
	22	**NY 1** townships often do not have street names but only letters and numbers
	26-27	**St Mary Magdalene** Anglican church in the parish of Guguletu

page	line	
13	8	**UWC** the University of the Western Cape – It was originally founded for Coloured (mixed raced) people only and was involved in resistance to the policies of apartheid. Since the end of apartheid it has been open to all races.
14	4	**Young Women's *Manyano*** missionary organisation of The Methodist Church of South Africa with the goal of helping the sick and unemployed
	36	**we overcome** Cf. the civil-rights protest song "We shall overcome" in America – Note how the rest of the song is more or less accurately sung towards the end of the chapter.
	40-41	**Ngubani lo?** (Xhosa) Who is this?
		NguMandela! It's Mandela!
		Uyintoni? Yinkokheli! What is he? He is a leader!
		Nelson Mandela (1913 – 2013) a Xhosa ['kɔ:sə], who played a key role in the opposition to apartheid – After 26 years in prison he was freed and later became President of South Africa, 1994-1999.
16	30	**NguSobukhwe!** It is Sobukhwe!
		Robert Mangaliso Sobukhwe (1924 – 1978), a black African, was actively opposed to apartheid and founded the Pan Africanist Congress.
	31	**Baziintoni?** What are they?
		Ziinkokheli! They are leaders.
19	4	**click** Clicks are a common sound of spoken Xhosa.
	39	**war of the Boers** It refers to The Second Boer War (1899 – 1902) between Great Britain and Afrikaans-speaking settlers (Boers) in the Transvaal Republic and the Orange Free State. The immediate cause of the war was the discovery of gold. In the end the Boers were defeated. Mandisa, however is probably referring to WW II.
21	28	**Soweto** The Soweto Uprising in 1976 was a series of protests in the form of strikes and boycotts in response to the forcible requirement that Afrikaans be used as a language of instruction. The protest was put down by brutal action taken by the police that resulted in numerous deaths. Since that time protests continued, with the South African government becoming increasingly unstable, and losing its legitimacy in the eyes of the world as well. Later students from Langa, Gugulethu and Nyanga in Cape Town organised protest marches that were put down by the police. School buildings were destroyed by fire.
22	32	**Johannesburg** The city started as a result of the discovery of gold nearby in 1884. The hard work of extracting the gold was done by Chinese immigrants and Africans.
23	26	**the Flats** This area – that included District Six – was from where Africans were forced to leave, though they had lived there for generations. They had to resettle in townships such as Guguletu from the early 1950s.
25	40	**Malay slaves** Dutch settlers imported slaves from Malay (Indonesia) in the 17th and 18th centuries.

page	line	
26	12	**Bantu** a general term for native Africans in South Africa and their languages
27	36	**tata** (Xhosa) father
37	24-25	**one settler one bullet** slogan first used in rallies by the Pan Africanist Congress when fighting apartheid in the 1980s – Even after the abandonment of apartheid in 1991 the slogan was used in rallies to apply to whites in general, although "settlers," was originally restricted to whites who supported apartheid. This slogan was used to whip up a Black mob to such a frenzy that the American, Amy Biehl was murdered.
	26	**necklacing** a method of executing s.o. by placing a tyre filled with petrol around a person's arms and chest and setting the tyre on fire – This method of execution was primarily used by native Africans to kill informants, corrupt officials, and Black policemen from the 1980s to 1990s, a time of numerous upheavals.
38	34	**isityhwentywe** (Xhosa) stew of innards and vegetables, especially potatoes, carrots, onion
39	10	**oonongobozana** (Xhosa) (plural) watercress (*Kresse*)
41	20	**tikoloshes** (Xhosa) evil gnomes, usually found by the riverside, with a hairy, long tail – They were used by witches.
44	8	**Eropleyni!** Aeroplane!
	9	**Zundiphathel' iorenji!** Bring me an orange!
	10	**Zundiphathel' ipesika!** Bring me a peach!
	23	**Uza kuwa! Uza kuwa!** He'll fall! He'll fall!
	32	**Bhasopha! Bhasopha** Look out! Look out!
46	36	**Tyhini** Gosh!
	46	**I-iish!'** Jee!
47	6	**NKQO-NKQO!** Knock-knock!
50	22	**imfecane** (Xhosa) exodus, (here): people fleeing Shaka
		Shaka (1787 - 1828) a major warlord who, for a time, ruled the Zulu Kingdom as a kind of monarch – He was known for his innovative and exceptionally brutal war tactics. White supporters of apartheid depicted Shaka as a monster to justify their own brutal treatment of Africans, whereas some Africans perceived him as a kind of hero.
54	31-32	**In 1976, students rose in revolt** ... cf. Soweto Uprising of 16 June 1976.
55	42	**They burnt a nun – in East London** The Irish nun Dr. Elsie Aidan Quinlan was killed in East London, Cape Province, South Africa on Nov. 10, 1952. She was shot in the head, stoned, and burned to death in the car she was driving by a frenzied mob of Africans within the context of a weekend of rioting. The nun wanted to deliver food and clothing for needy children.
57	16	**The Young Lions** not a distinct political group – meant just to describe young people opposing apartheid
	21	**gogga** (Afrikaans) insect

page	line	
58	28	**pass** Since the 18th century non-whites have often been required to carry a pass. Especially in the 20th century, a pass system was used to restrict the movement of non-whites within South Africa.
60	19	**izithunzela** spirits of dead people whom a witch has raised
61	9	**skollie** (Afrikaans) gangster
62	30	**Steve Biko (1946 – 1977)** South African political leader who founded 'a black consciousness' movement – After being arrested he died in prison as a result of maltreatment.
64	28	**andaz'** (Afrikaans) someone else
71	4	**mmelwane** neighbour
73	15	**Sowuvukile?** Are you up already? Have you got up?
		Unjan' ukuvuya, nivala? Aren't you glad school's closing?
	40-41	**Kalok' umam' akho akakho apha** Your mother is not here . . . understand [that].
74	16	**baas** (Afrikaans) boss – a form of address formerly used by Africans for whites
75	25	**mzukulwana** (Xhosa) grandchild
82	10	**utakelwe** (Xhosa) jumped into; the sperm went into her without her having been penetrated.
91	27-28	**benyuke nengalo** (Xhosa) said of the family of a young man who has 'damaged' a maiden ... they will go up from the hand ... that is, go the whole way up, marry her instead of just paying damages for impregnating her.
	44	**lobola** (Xhosa) what the groom/his family offers to the bride's family, used to be cattle but is now more often money ... bride offering
96	20	**ululant** (Xhosa) one who ululates
	23	**KIII-II-KIIKIIIIKII! HALALAA! HA-AALAA-AALAA!** Xhosa words of ululation
97	24-25	**Nohehake, Hehake** expression of surprise or distress; like saying: "Oh, look! What a mess!" So, to name someone that way means she is an unpleasant surprise.
	36	**Molokazana** daughter-in-law
99	13	**makoti, umakoti** new wife
103	8-9	**abakhozi** in-laws
	15	**shushu** (Xhosa) hot
105	19	**imfumba, qashi-qashi** game where a player guesses in which hand something is hidden; the one who hides s.th. says, 'qashi-qashi,' which means 'guess-guess!'
	33-34	**boycotting classes** In the 1970s schools were boycotted by young Africans because of the poor quality of education and the forced introduction of Afrikaans as the language of instruction for half of the subjects. Cf. Steve Biko and Black consciousness, and the Soweto uprising – also compare with 'equal but separate' with regard to education in the South up to the 1960s

page	line	
105	36	**Unganyebelezeli, kuza kudlalwa!** Don't hide yourself, the game is on! – meaning the fight is on, i.e. calling out to others not to flee but fight
	37-38	**the Comrades** what the young people called themselves – later also used by more radical groups
107	39	**malume** (Xhosa) uncle
115	1	**amaXhosa** (plural) the Xhosa, singular: **umXhosa** a Xhosa
116	13	**imurhu** (Xhosa) village simpleton lately come to town
	13-14	**'skom van ver** (derog., Afrikaans) he who has come from far away
118	20	**lawaai** (Afrikaans) noise, din
124	27	**Jan van Riebeeck** (1619 – 1677) Jan van Riebeeck, along with 90 other persons from Holland, set up the first permanent European settlement in 1652 at Table Rock on the Cape of Good Hope. It was a provisioning station for the Dutch East India Company. He soon began trading with the local Khoikhio, gave Europeans land to establish farms, and brought in slaves from Africa and Malaysia. By 1662 the European population numbered 250 near the Cape. Gradually they moved inland, with Stellenbosch being founded in 1679. Research the Dutch East India Company. Where did the Dutch establish settlements in America?
	28-29	The name 'Cape of Good Hope' was actually given by King John II of Portugal (1455 – 1495). Before that it was named the 'Cape of Storms' by the Portuguese explorer Bartolomeu Dias in 1488, not by the Portuguese navigator, Vasco da Gama (1469 -1524).
125	35	**Nongqawuse** In 1854, after being soundly defeated in several wars by white settlers, another tragedy struck: Xhosa cattle were largely decimated by a lung disease imported from Europe (bovine pleuropneumonis). Not surprisingly, the Xhosa fell under the influence of several prophets, most notably a sixteen-year-old girl, Nongquawuse. In 1856 she and another girl claimed they had met two men who had died many years before. These dead men instructed them to tell the Xhosa to slaughter all their remaining cattle, to no longer plough the land, and to destroy all their grain. This sacrifice would bring about the destruction of the white settlers. Dead Xhosa would return with cattle and fresh grain. The mass slaughter of cattle and destruction of grain followed. The prophecy was to be fulfilled on February 18, 1857. But the expected results never came to fruition; massive starvation ensued. The British governor of British Kaffraria, Sir George Grey exploited the situation to make land now depopulated by starvation available to a group of German immigrants. Surviving Xhosa were left with no choice but to work as labourers on white farms or in diamond mines ten years later. Compare with the Native-American, Wovoka (1856 – 1932), who envisioned the return of the dead and the elimination of whites.

page	line	
126	3	**imbongi** (Xhosa) a composer and orator of poems praising a chief or other figurehead
	31	**enyangweni** in the storeroom, a hut used for food as well as goods
		amasi sour milk with curds and whey
	32	**iinkobe** boiled loose kernels of maize
		amarhewu engqayini cold, thick drink made from mealie-meal porridge, sour in taste, fermented, but non-alcoholic
127	15	**hlinzeka** slaughter in celebration of s.o.
	21	**umlandu** money or goods offered to a witch doctor or healer for his/her services
	44	**izisele** underground cellars
128	41	**nezimfusa** the fawn-coloured (yellowish-brown) ones, i.e cattle or other animals
		iinco cattle of red and white colour
	46	**Qamata** God
		Embo whence people originated, place
129	12	**amazimba** sorghum
	15	**indaba** affair, event
130	6	**Come to the mines!** Actually, diamond mining didn't begin until 1867, and gold mining until 1886.
	29	**Makana, Makhanda Nxele** (? - 1819) Xhosa warrior and prophet, who advised an attack against a British garrison at Grahamtown in 1819. He claimed that British bullets would turn to water. It should be noted that there were constant wars between the Xhosa/Zulus and white settlers in the 19th century.
	32	**Cetywayo (1826 – 1884)** King of the Zulu kingdom, who defeated the British in the Battle of Isandlwana in 1879. Cf. the film *Zulu* (1964)
		impi Zulu regiment
	34	**Bulhoek, in Queenstown** In Bulhoek on May 20, 1921 a police and military force attacked a group of Xhosa religious fanatics led by Enoch Mgimia, who had allegedly settled illegally on a piece of land. About 200 people were killed.
132	41	**The Anglican Church** in South Africa is associated with the Church of England. Its most famous primate (head) was Desmond Tutu, who was active in the fight against apartheid in the 1980s.
	42	**Molweni, aph' ekhaya!** (Xhosa) Hello, here at home ... (a friendly greeting from someone entering a home)
133	5	**Aphi la makhwenkwe alapha?** (Xhosa) literally: Where are the boys of here/ of this home?
142	19	**mmelwane** (Xhosa) neighbour

page	line	
146	25-26	… **happened to that KTC mlungu woman only yesterday** … KTC, Kakaza Trading Company, is a grocery/goods shop situated on the border of Guguletu and Nyanga. The area there is now known as KTC. A white woman had been attacked there on August 4, the day before the Biehl murder. Luckily, people intervened and she escaped unharmed.
149	22	**slings** Notice how the words *flesh*, *arrow*, *fortune*, *slings*, and *consummation* are used at the end of the novel. Cf. Hamlet's soliloquy (Act III, Scene 1): To be, or not to be, that is the question: Whether 'tis nobler in the mind to suffer The slings and arrows of outrageous fortune, Or to take Arms against a sea of troubles, And by opposing end them. To die – to sleep – No more; and by a sleep, to say we end The heartache, and the thousand natural shocks That flesh is heir to. 'Tis a consummation Devoutly to be wish'd. […]

Sindiwe Magona

Sindiwe Magona was born on 23 August 1943, in the village of Gungululu in rural Eastern Cape (formerly Transkei). The first born of eight children, Magona earned her secondary and undergraduate degree by correspondence, and later won a scholarship to study for her Master's Degree in Social Work at Columbia University in the United States of America.

Ms Magona is one of many internationally prominent South African writers whose work is informed by her experience of impoverishment, femininity, resistance to subjugation and being a domestic worker. She traversed South Africa's racially-defined socio-cultural-economic spaces while simultaneously being a mother, wife and community leader in a township. These interlaced themes and realities are pronounced throughout her literary career.

A former primary school teacher and civil servant, she is a prolific author who has produced nine books, among them an autobiographical work, a collection of short stories, novellas and an anthology of poetry.

She has produced various plays and continues to lecture and deliver key addresses at universities and conferences, both locally and internationally. Until her retirement in 2003, she contributed immeasurably in various capacities to the work of the United Nations (UN), an organisation she served for 20 years.

Even in retirement, she continues to pen literary works, to initiate writers' conferences, lead women's rights advocacy groups and write children's educational books. Among her internationally acclaimed works are *Beauty's Gift; Living, Loving, and Lying Awake at Night; To My Children's Children; Teach Yourself Xhosa; and Push-Push and Other Stories*. Her plays include *I Promised Myself a Fabulous Middle-Age* and *Vukani*.

Ms Magona is the recipient of numerous awards, including the Molteno Gold Medal for Lifetime Achievement for her role in promoting isiXhosa, the Permio Grinzane Terre D'Otrantro, and the Department of Arts and Culture Literary Lifetime Achievement Award (all three received in 2007); the Bronx Recognises Its Own Fiction Award in 2000; a Fellowship for Non-Fiction from the New York Foundation of the Arts; the Xhosa Heroes Award; and the UNdimande Grand Prize. The Hartwick College of New York conferred her with an honorary doctorate in 1993. She was shortlisted for the Commonwealth Writer's Prize in 2009.

She remains an accomplished motivational speaker, author, poet, playwright and storyteller in South Africa. Many of Ms Magona's essays, short stories and poems have been anthologised. She has been published in, among other publications, the *New York Times*, *The New Internationalist, Fair Lady, Oprah Magazine* and *Femina*.

She is also recognised for her work in women's issues, the plight of children and the fight against apartheid and racism. Ms Magona is the founder and Executive Director of South Africa 2033. A worker for peaceful change during the years of struggle in South Africa, she was one of the founding members of the Women's Peace Movement in 1976.

With her inspiration and encouragement, the Gugulethu Writers' Group meets once a month and nurtures new writers. The group has already published a collection of short stories, *Umthi ngamnye unentlaka yawo,* and won First Prize in the Maskew Miller Longman Story Competition in 2009.

In recognition of her literary and humanitarian contribution, the State President, Jacob G Zuma, conferred Sindiwe Magona with the Order of Ikhamanga in Bronze on 27 April 2011.

Her latest novel, *Chasing the Tails of My Father's Cattle* is to appear in October 2015.

© 2015 Professor Dr. Dianne Shober, Head of the English Department, University of Fort Hare, South Africa
reprinted with the permission of Dr. Shober

Some Useful Literary Terms

Allegory: a narrative in verse or prose form in which specific characters and actions represent abstract ideas or moral qualities – An allegory can be literal, or real, and have symbolic levels of meaning.

Alliteration: the repetition of consonant or vowel sounds at the beginning of words

Allusion: a reference to a person, place, event, or written work such as the Bible that the author expects the reader to recognize

Ambiguity: the state of having more than one possible meaning or interpretation

Anaphora: the repetition of the same word or words at the beginning of successive phrases, clauses, or sentences

Antagonist: the character or force that opposes the protagonist or hero in a conflict

Archaism: a word or expression that is out of date

Argumentation: writing or a speech that tries to convince the reader of the logic and merits of a particular viewpoint by giving specific reasons and examples

Asyndeton: the omission of a conjunction between the parts of a sentence

Characterization: the means used by the author to develop the character, e.g. by description, what the character thinks or says, how he/she reacts or speaks, and how the other characters react or describe the character; the character may be superficially described: flat, or made to seem very real and complex: round.

Chiasmus: two parallel phrases with a reversal of the order of words with antonyms in the second of two phrases – 'He came in triumph and in defeat departs.'

Climax: the turning point of the story, the crisis, after which there seems to be no other possible way for the plot to continue – The part of the plot before the climax is often called rising action and that after the climax falling action.

Commentary: The author or narrator inserts his or her own comments or views.

Complication: the point in the story at which the conflict is introduced, thus giving the plot a new impetus

Conflict: the clash between opposing forces – It can involve ideas, persons, the forces of nature and be in the mind or external.

Dénouement: the part of a story when all questions are answered, secrets are revealed, conflicts are resolved – It is also called the resolution or outcome.

Description: The author tries to give the reader a mental image of what can be seen, felt, or heard by giving concrete descriptions, often to create a certain atmosphere.

Dialogue: what the characters actually say

Diction: the choice of words used by the author to produce a certain effect on the reader

Dramatic Irony: when a character says something without realizing the true significance of what was said, however, it is obvious to the reader

Euphemism: the substitution of a mild or less negative word or phrase for a direct one, as in the use of "to pass away" instead of "to die"

Exposition: the part of a story, usually at the beginning, that gives essential background information for an understanding of the unfolding plot

Flashback: a scene in a story that interrupts the action to show what happened in the past – The opposite is a flashforward or prolepsis, whereby an event that will occur in the future is revealed beforehand.

Foil: character who is the opposite of another character in order to point up the strengths or weaknesses of the other character

Foreshadowing: a hint that something, usually bad, is going to happen later

Frame Story: a story with a framework, for example a narrator who, from a later point of time, describes what happened in the past, or a story within a story

Historical or Historic Present/Narrative Present: the present tense used to narrate past events for the purpose of highlighting a section of the plot, or to make a scene have a direct effect on the reader

Hyperbole: an exaggeration

Imagery: vivid sensory details that arouse certain emotions or feelings in the reader

Irony: when the author or a character means the opposite of what he/she actually writes or says

Metaphor: a direct comparison between two apparently different things, ideas, or persons without using *as* or *like*, i.e. She had rose lips.

Motivation: the force that drives a character to take a certain course of action

Mood: overall atmosphere of a work that can be created by a purposeful description of the setting, and how and what the characters say

Open Ending: when it's not clear how the plot will continue

Oxymoron: the combining of two terms that contradict each other, e.g. a cold fire

Paradox: a statement that seems to be contradictory

Peripateia: sudden change of fortune, sudden reversal

Personification: giving human or even animal qualities to objects or things

Plot: the plan and arrangement of related incidents within a story, it can be chronological, or be interrupted by flashbacks, or in the opposite direction by a flashforward (prolepsis)

Point of View: the manner in which the author presents the events and characters in a story

1. first-person narrator: the story is told by a character in the story, the "I" in the story – The question remains how reliable the narrator is.
2. limited third-person narrator who focuses on one character
3. omniscient third-person or an all-knowing observer who can describe and comment about everything and everyone in the story

Polysydeton: a rhetorical device whereby a conjunction, often *and*, is used repeatedly – It is frequently used in the Bible or by the American writer, Ernest Hemingway.

Protagonist: the main character in a story on whom the action centres

Register: the kind of language used in a specific social setting – Examples of register are slang, colloquial, old-fashioned, literary, and formal. The kind of register used often reflects the social status of the character or may be purposely used in the wrong context or setting.

Repetition: repeating a word or phrase in a sentence to produce an effect – Sometimes a string of synonyms is used for special emphasis.

Sarcasm: the use of ironic remarks to show you dislike s.o./s.th.

Satire: the use of sarcasm or irony to show the moral weakness of people, an idea, a movement, a country, etc.

Setting: the surroundings, location where the action takes place – The setting can be used to establish mood or inner feelings of the characters.

Simile: a direct comparison between two basically different things, ideas, or persons using *as* or *like*, i.e. She had lips like a rose.

Stock Character or Stereotype: a character with typical characteristics who keeps reappearing in literature, such as the jealous husband, the all-knowing but silent butler, the absent-minded professor, the hypocritical preacher, the naïve American

Stream of Consciousness: often considered the same as interior monologue – the thoughts and impressions of a character which are set down just as they occur in his/her mind

Suspense: the feeling of uncertainty and anxiety as the plot rises towards its climax

Symbol: anything that has a meaning in itself, but also stands for something larger than itself

Topos, plural Topoi: a traditional theme or motif, such as the jealous husband, young lovers, good overcoming evil, the servant of several masters (picaroon) who is able to trick them all, the beautiful woman who bewitches all men, the mad scientist, the devil buying souls

Timeline

4th century
Bantu-speakers from the north settle south of the Lipopo River, joining the indigenous San and Khoikhoi people.

1487
The Portuguese navigator Bartholomeu Dias is the first European to travel round the southern tip of Africa.

1497
The Portuguese explorer Vasco da Gama lands on the Natal coast.

1652 – 1795
Jan van Riebeeck, representing the Dutch East India Company, founds the Cape Colony at Table Bay to resupply ships. Khoikhoi is conquered. Slaves are imported from India, Ceylon and Madagascar.

1795
British forces seize the Cape Colony from the Netherlands.

1803
The territory is returned to the Dutch.

1806
Britain reconquers the Cape Colony.

1815
Frontier Boers rebel. It is known as the Slagtersnek rebellion.

1816 – 1828
Shaka founds and expands the Zulu empire. He creates a formidable fighting force.

1820
British settlers arrive in the Cape Colony.

1834 – 1835
The Xhosa are defeated by British and colonial forces.

1835 – 1840
The Boers leave the Cape Colony in the 'Great Trek' and found the Orange Free State and the Transvaal.

1852
The British grant limited self-government to the Transvaal.

1856
Natal separates from the Cape Colony.

In the late 1850s Boers proclaim the Transvaal a republic.

1856 – 1857
Xhosa cattle killing

1860 – 1911
Arrival of thousands of labourers and traders from India

1867
Diamonds are discovered at Kimberley.

1877
Britain annexes the Transvaal.

1879
The British defeat the Zulus in Natal after losing a regiment at Isandhlwana.

1880 – 1881
The Boers rebel against the British, sparking the first Anglo-Boer War. The conflict ends with a negotiated peace. The Transvaal is restored as a republic.

1886
Gold mining begins on the Witwaterstrand. The Gold Rush begins. Mining becomes an important source of wealth for South Africa.

1895 – 1896
Leader Starr Jameson leads an unsuccessful raid into the Transvaal.

1899
British troops gather on the Transvaal border and ignore an ultimatum to disperse. The second Anglo-Boer War begins.

1902
The Treaty of Vereeniging ends the second Anglo-Boer War. The Transvaal and the Orange Free State are made self-governing colonies of the British Empire.

1910
Formation of the Union of South Africa by former British colonies of the Cape and Natal, and the Boer republics of the Transvaal and the Orange Free State

1912
The Native National Congress is founded and later renamed the African National Congress (ANC).

1913
The Land Act is introduced to prevent Africans, except those living in the Cape Province, from buying land outside reserves.

1914 – 1918
As a member of the British Empire, South Africa sides with the British in World War I.

1914
The National Party is founded.

1918
The Secret Broederbond (brotherhood) is established to advance the Afrikaaner cause.

1919
South West Africa (Namibia) comes under South African administration.

1934
The Union of South Africa parliament enacts the Status of the Union Act, which declares the country to be 'a sovereign independent state.'

1939 – 1945
South Africa sides with the Allies in World War II.

1948
The Afrikaaner National Party wins a general election and implements its policy of apartheid.

1950
The Population Registration Act classifies people by race: white, African, Coloured, and Indian. The Group Areas Act is passed; it requires each race to live in a special zone. The Communist Party is banned. The ANC responds with a campaign of civil disobedience, led by Nelson Mandela.

1959
The Pan-Africanist Congress (PAC) is founded.

1960
Sixty-seven African demonstrators are killed at Sharpeville. The ANC is banned.

1961
South Africa is declared a republic and leaves the Commonwealth. Mandela heads the ANC's new military wing, which launches a sabotage campaign.

1960s
International pressure against the government begins. South Africa is excluded from the Olympic Games.

1964
The ANC leader Nelson Mandela is sentenced to life imprisonment.

1966 September
Prime Minister Hendrik Verwoerd is assassinated.

1970s
More than 3 million people are forcibly resettled in black settlements.

1976 – 1977
More than 600 people are killed in clashes between African protesters and security forces during an uprising which starts in Soweto.

1984 – 1989
Township revolt: a state of emergency is declared.

1986
The Pass laws are repealed.

October The US Congress passes the Comprehensive Anti-Apartheid Act over President Reagan's veto. New investments and banks loans are banned and a wide range of imports from South Africa is prohibited.

1989
FW de Klerk replaces PW Botha as president. He meets Mandela. Public facilities are desegregated. Many ANC activists are freed.

1990
The ANC and the PAC are unbanned, and Mandela is released after 26 years in prison. Namibia becomes independent.

1991
Multi-party talks begin. De Klerk repeals remaining apartheid laws. International sanctions are lifted. Major fighting occurs between the ANC and the Zulu Inkatha movement.

1993
An interim constitution is agreed on.

1994 April
The ANC wins the first non-racial elections. Mandela becomes president. The Government of National Unity is formed, and Commonwealth membership is restored. Remaining sanctions are lifted. South Africa takes a seat in the UN General Assembly after a 20-year absence. Crime escalates.

1995
The Truth and Reconciliation Commission chaired by Archbishop Desmond Tutu begins hearings on human rights crimes committed by the former government and liberation movements during the apartheid era.

1996
Parliament adopts a new constitution. The National Party withdraws from the coalition, saying it is being ignored.

1998
The Truth and Reconciliation Commission report declares apartheid to be a crime against humanity and finds the ANC accountable for human rights abuses.

1999
The ANC wins the general elections, and Thabo Mbeki takes over as president.

2000 December
The ANC prevails in local elections. The recently formed Democratic Alliance captures nearly a quarter of the votes. The Inkatha Freedom Party wins 9%.

2001 December
The High Court rules that pregnant women must be given Aids drugs to help prevent the transmission of the virus to their babies.

2002 July
The Constitutional Court orders the government to provide key anti-Aids drugs at all public hospitals. The government had argued the drugs were too costly.

2002 October
Bomb explosions in Soweto and a blast near Pretoria are thought to be the work of right-wing extremists. Separately, police charge 17 right-wingers with plotting against the state.

2003 May
Walter Sisulu, a key figure in the anti-apartheid struggle, dies aged 91. Thousands gather to pay their last respects.

2003 November
The government approves a major programme to treat and tackle HIV/Aids. It envisages a network of drug-distributon centres and preventative programmes. The cabinet had previously refused to provide anti-Aids medicine via the public health system.

2004 April
The ruling ANC wins a landslide election victory, gaining nearly 70% of the votes. Thabo Mbeki begins a second term as president. The Inkatha Freedom Party leader Mangosuthu Buthelezi is dropped from the cabinet.

2005 March
Investigators exhume the first bodies in a Truth and Reconciliation Commission investigation into the fates of hundreds of people who disappeared in the apartheid era.

2005 June
President Mbeki sacks his deputy, Jacob Zuma, in the aftermath of a corruption case.

2005 August
Around 100,000 gold miners strike over pay, bringing the industry to a standstill.

2006 May
Former Deputy President Jacob Zuma is acquitted of rape charges by the High Court in Johannesburg. He is reinstated as deputy leader of the governing African National Congress.

2006 September
Corruption charges against former Deputy President Zuma are dismissed.

2007 April
President Mbeki, often accused of ignoring widespread crime, urges South Africans to join forces to bring rapists, drug dealers and corrupt officials to justice.

2007 May
Cape Town mayor Helen Zille is elected as the new leader of the main opposition Democratic Alliance (DA).

2007 June
Hundreds of thousands of public-sector workers take part in the biggest strike since the end of apartheid. The strike lasts for four weeks and causes widespread disruption to schools, hospitals, and public transport.

2007 December
Zuma is elected chairman of the ANC, placing him in a strong position to become the next president. Prosecutors bring new corruption charges against him.

2008 May
A wave of violence directed at foreigners hits townships across the country. Dozens of people die and thousands of Zimbabweans, Malawians and Mozambicans return home.

2008 September
A judge throws out a corruption case against the ruling ANC party chief Jacob Zuma, opening the way for him to stand as the country's president in 2009.

President Mbeki resigns over allegations that he interfered in the corruption case against Mr Zuma. ANC deputy leader Kgalema Motlanthe is chosen by parliament as president.

2008 December
A new political party is launched in Bloemfontein, in the first real challenge to the governing ANC. The Congress of the People - or Cope - is made up largely of defectors from the ANC and is headed by the former defence minister Mosiuoa Lekota.

2009 January
The Appeals Court rules that state prosecutors can resurrect their corruption case against ANC leader Jacob Zuma, opening the way for Mr Zuma's trial to be resumed, just months before the general election.

2009 April
Public prosecutors drop the corruption case against Jacob Zuma.

The ANC wins the general election.

2009 May
Parliament elects Jacob Zuma as president.

2009 July
Township residents complaining about poor living conditions, mount violent protests.

2010 August
Civil servants stage a nationwide strike.

2011 May
In local elections the opposition Democratic Alliance nearly doubles its share of the vote since the last election.

The opposition Democratic Alliance picks an African woman – Lindiwe Mazibuko – as its leader in parliament.

2011 November
The ANC suspends its controversial and influential youth leader, Julius Malema, for five years for bringing the party into disrepute.

The National Assembly overwhelmingly approves an information bill accused by critics of posing a threat to freedom of speech. The ANC says it is needed to safeguard national security.

2012 July
A member of a white extremist group is found guilty of plotting to kill Mandela and trying to overthrow the government.

2012 August – October
Police open fire on workers at a platinum mine in Marikana, killing at least 34 people, and leaving at least 78 injured and arresting more than 200 others. In September, prosecutors drop murder charges against 270 miners after a public outcry, and the government sets up a judicial commission of inquiry in October.

2012 September
Former ANC youth leader Julius Malema is charged with money laundering over a government tender awarded to a company partly owned by his family trust. Mr Malema says the case is a politically motivated attempt to silence his campaign against President Zuma, in particular over the Marikana shootings.

2012 October
Platinum mine owner Amplats fires 12,000 striking miners because of a wave of wildcat strikes.

2012 December
President Zuma is re-elected as leader of the ANC.

2013 October
Members of a white supremacist group are accused of bombings in Johannesburg's Soweto township in 2002, and of plotting to murder Nelson Mandela. They are found guilty and given long sentences.

2013 December
Nelson Mandela dies, aged 95.

2013 March
President Zuma is accused of using public funds for a twenty million dollar upgrade to his private home.

2014 May
The ruling ANC party wins a majority in general elections.

2015 February
President Zuma announces plans to limit farm sizes and ban foreign farmland ownership in an attempt to redistribute land to African farmers – a longstanding ANC pledge.

2015 March-April
A series of anti-immigrant attacks leaves several people dead.

Nelson Mandela Blasts Apartheid in His Speech held at His Trial in 1964 (excerpt)

to blast to severely criticize

On April 20, 1964 Nelson Mandela, 45 years old, gave his famous anti-apartheid speech at his second trial. Already convicted to a prison term of five years, he was again put on the stand as part of the so-called Rivonia Trials, named for the Johannesburg suburb where South African police had arrested 19 ANC leaders. Mandela, charged with three counts of sabotage, directed his speech not only at South Africa but the world. He would remain in jail for another 26 years.

to convict (law) *verurteilen*
to put s.o. on the stand (law) to require that s.o. appears in court
count (law) *Anklagepunkt*

I hold a Bachelor's Degree in Arts and practised as an attorney in Johannesburg for a number of years in partnership with Oliver Tambo. I am a convicted prisoner serving five years for leaving the country without a permit and for inciting people to go on strike at the end of May 1961.

At the outset, I want to say that the suggestion made by the State in its opening that the struggle in South Africa is under the influence of foreigners or Communists is wholly incorrect. I have done whatever I did, both as an individual and as a leader of my people, because of my experience in South Africa and my own proudly felt African background, and not because of what any outsider might have said.

[...] I must deal immediately and at some length with the question of violence. Some of the things so far told to the Court are true and some are untrue. I do not, however, deny that I planned sabotage. I did not plan it in a spirit of recklessness, nor because I have any love of violence. I planned it as a result of a calm and sober assessment of the political situation that had arisen after many years of tyranny, exploitation, and oppression of my people by the Whites.

I admit immediately that I was one of the persons who helped to form *Umkhonto we Sizwe*, and that I played a prominent role in its affairs until I was arrested in August 1962.

[...] we believed that as a result of Government policy, violence by the African people had become inevitable, and that unless responsible leadership was given to canalize and control the feelings of our people, there would be outbreaks of terrorism which would produce an intensity of bitterness and hostility between the various races of this country which is not produced even by war. Secondly, we felt that without violence there would be no way open to the African people to succeed in their struggle against the principle of white supremacy. All lawful modes of expressing opposition to this principle had been closed by legislation, and we were placed in a position in which we had either to accept a permanent state of inferiority, or to defy the Government. We chose to defy the law. We first broke the law in a way which avoided any recourse to violence; when this form was leg-

attorney lawyer
to incite to encourage s.o. to do s.th. violent or illegal
outset beginning
recklessness showing no regard for danger or the consequences
sober (here): careful
assessment judgement
Umkhonto we Sizwe (Xhosa) 'The Speer of the Nation' – the militant arm of the ANC
to defy to resist the authority of s.o.
recourse making use of s.th.

to resort to s.th. to make use of s.th. as the only possibility left

to bear out to confirm

to curtail (formal) to limit

to adhere to s.th. to follow exactly

grievance complaint about s.th. unfair

to dissolve to break up

unremitting constant

toil hard work

to bear, bore, borne fruit to succeed

islated against, and then the Government resorted to a show of force to crush opposition to its policies, only then did we decide to answer violence with violence.

But the violence which we chose to adopt was not terrorism. We who formed *Umkhonto* were all members of the African National Congress, and had behind us the ANC tradition of non-violence and negotiation as a means of solving political disputes. We believe that South Africa belongs to all the people who live in it, and not to one group, be it black or white. We did not want an interracial war, and tried to avoid it to the last minute. If the Court is in doubt about this, it will be seen that the whole history of our organization bears out what I have said, and what I will subsequently say, when I describe the tactics which *Umkhonto* decided to adopt. I want, therefore, to say something about the African National Congress.

The African National Congress was formed in 1912 to defend the rights of the African people which had been seriously curtailed by the South Africa Act, and which were then being threatened by the Native Land Act. For thirty-seven years – that is until 1949 – it adhered strictly to a constitutional struggle. It put forward demands and resolutions; it sent delegations to the Government in the belief that African grievances could be settled through peaceful discussion and that Africans could advance gradually to full political rights. But White Governments remained unmoved, and the rights of Africans became less instead of becoming greater. [...]

In 1960 there was the shooting at Sharpeville, which resulted in the proclamation of a state of emergency and the declaration of the ANC as an unlawful organization. My colleagues and I, after careful consideration, decided that we would not obey this decree. The African people were not part of the Government and did not make the laws by which they were governed. We believed in the words of the Universal Declaration of Human Rights, that 'the will of the people shall be the basis of authority of the Government,' and for us to accept the banning was equivalent to accepting the silencing of the Africans for all time. The ANC refused to dissolve, but instead went underground. We believed it was our duty to preserve this organization which had been built up with almost fifty years of unremitting toil. I have no doubt that no self-respecting White political organization would disband itself if declared illegal by a government in which it had no say. [...]

In the light of our political background the choice was a logical one. Sabotage did not involve loss of life, and it offered the best hope for future race relations. Bitterness would be kept to a minimum and, if the policy bore fruit, democratic government could become a reality. This is what we felt at the time, and this is what we said in our Manifesto [...]:

'We of *Umkhonto we Sizwe* have always sought to achieve liberation without bloodshed and civil clash. We hope, even at this late hour, that our first actions will awaken everyone to a realization of the disastrous situation to which the Nationalist policy is leading. We hope that we will bring the Government and its supporters to their senses before it is too late, so that both the Government and its policies can be changed before matters reach the desperate state of civil war.'

The initial plan was based on a careful analysis of the political and economic situation of our country. We believed that South Africa depended to a large extent on foreign capital and foreign trade. We felt that planned destruction of power plants, and interference with rail and telephone communications, would tend to scare away capital from the country, make it more difficult for goods from the industrial areas to reach the seaports on schedule, and would in the long run be a heavy drain on the economic life of the country, thus compelling the voters of the country to reconsider their position.

drain burden
to compel (formal) to force

Attacks on the economic life lines of the country were to be linked with sabotage on Government buildings and other symbols of apartheid. These attacks would serve as a source of inspiration to our people. In addition, they would provide an outlet for those people who were urging the adoption of violent methods and would enable us to give concrete proof to our followers that we had adopted a stronger line and were fighting back against Government violence.

In addition, if mass action were successfully organized, and mass reprisals taken, we felt that sympathy for our cause would be roused in other countries, and that greater pressure would be brought to bear on the South African Government. [...]

reprisal action taken in revenge
to rouse to stimulate, to awaken
to bring to bear on s.o./s.th. (formal) to make use of s.th. to make s.o./s.th do s.th.

Already scores of Africans had died as a result of racial friction. In 1920 when the famous leader, Masabala, was held in Port Elizabeth jail, twenty-four of a group of Africans who had gathered to demand his release were killed by the police and white civilians. In 1921, more than one hundred Africans died in the Bulhoek affair. In 1924 over two hundred Africans were killed when the Administrator of South-West Africa led a force against a group which had rebelled against the imposition of dog tax. On 1 May 1950, eighteen Africans died as a result of police shootings during the strike. On 21 March 1960, sixty-nine unarmed Africans died at Sharpeville.

scores (plural) very many
friction (here): conflict
imposition act of introducing a new law

How many more Sharpevilles would there be in the history of our country? And how many more Sharpevilles could the country stand without violence and terror becoming the order of the day? And what would happen to our people when that stage was reached? In the long run we felt certain we must succeed, but at what cost to ourselves and the rest of the country? And if this happened, how could black and white ever live together again in peace and harmony? These were the problems that faced us, and these were our decisions. [...]

The ideological creed of the ANC is, and always has been, the creed of African Nationalism. It is not the concept of African Nationalism expressed in the cry, 'Drive the White man into the sea.' The African Nationalism for which the ANC stands is the concept of freedom and fulfilment for the African people in their own land. The most impor-

creed set of principles

blueprint masterplan

to perpetuate (formal) to allow s.th. bad to continue for a long time
hollow (here): without substance
to repeal to make invalid

Gold Law Africans were not allowed to own gold mines, or keep a large quantity of gold.

the Petition of Right short-lived civil rights law passed by Parliament in 1628
to hold in veneration to greatly respect

impartiality neutrality

drought-stricken seriously affected by lack of rain
labour tenant worker who rents a flat or house
squatter (here): person living under primitive conditions
serf *Leibeigene(r)*
impoverished very poor

tant political document ever adopted by the ANC is the 'Freedom Charter.' It is by no means a blueprint for a socialist state. It calls for redistribution, but not nationalization, of land; it provides for nationalization of mines, banks, and monopoly industry, because big monopolies are owned by one race only, and without such nationalization racial domination would be perpetuated despite the spread of political power. It would be a hollow gesture to repeal the Gold Law prohibitions against Africans when all gold mines are owned by European companies. In this respect the ANC's policy corresponds with the old policy of the present Nationalist Party which, for many years, had as part of its programme the nationalization of the gold mines which, at that time, were controlled by foreign capital. Under the Freedom Charter, nationalization would take place in an economy based on private enterprise. The realization of the Freedom Charter would open up fresh fields for a prosperous African population of all classes, including the middle class. The ANC has never at any period of its history advocated a revolutionary change in the economic structure of the country, nor has it, to the best of my recollection, ever condemned capitalist society. [...]

The Magna Carta, the Petition of Right, and the Bill of Rights are documents which are held in veneration by democrats throughout the world.

I have great respect for British political institutions, and for the country's system of justice. I regard the British Parliament as the most democratic institution in the world, and the independence and impartiality of its judiciary never fail to arouse my admiration.

The American Congress, that country's doctrine of separation of powers, as well as the independence of its judiciary, arouses in me similar sentiments.

I have been influenced in my thinking by both West and East. All this has led me to feel that in my search for a political formula, I should be absolutely impartial and objective. I should tie myself to no particular system of society other than of socialism. I must leave myself free to borrow the best from the West and from the East . [...]

South Africa is the richest country in Africa, and could be one of the richest countries in the world. But it is a land of extremes and remarkable contrasts. The whites enjoy what may well be the highest standard of living in the world, whilst Africans live in poverty and misery. Forty per cent of the Africans live in hopelessly overcrowded and, in some cases, drought-stricken Reserves, where soil erosion and the overworking of the soil makes it impossible for them to live properly off the land. Thirty per cent are labourers, labour tenants, and squatters on white farms and work and live under conditions similar to those of the serfs of the Middle Ages. The other 30 per cent live in towns where they have developed economic and social habits which bring them closer in many respects to white standards. Yet most Africans, even in this group, are impoverished by low incomes and high cost of living. [...]

Poverty goes hand in hand with malnutrition and disease. The incidence of malnutrition and deficiency diseases is very high amongst Africans. Tuberculosis, pellagra, kwashiorkor, gastro-enteritis, and scurvy bring death and destruction of health. The incidence of infant mortality is one of the highest in the world. […]

The complaint of Africans, however, is not only that they are poor and the whites are rich, but that the laws which are made by the whites are designed to preserve this situation. There are two ways to break out of poverty. The first is by formal education, and the second is by the worker acquiring a greater skill at his work and thus higher wages. As far as Africans are concerned, both these avenues of advancement are deliberately curtailed by legislation.

The present Government has always sought to hamper Africans in their search for education. One of their early acts, after coming into power, was to stop subsidies for African school feeding. Many African children who attended schools depended on this supplement to their diet. This was a cruel act.

There is compulsory education for all white children at virtually no cost to their parents, be they rich or poor. Similar facilities are not provided for the African children, though there are some who receive such assistance. African children, however, generally have to pay more for their schooling than whites. […] The quality of education is also different. According to the Bantu Educational Journal, only 5,660 African children in the whole of South Africa passed their Junior Certificate in 1962, and in that year only 362 passed matric. This is presumably consistent with the policy of Bantu education about which the present Prime Minister said, during the debate on the Bantu Education Bill in 1953:

'When I have control of Native education I will reform it so that Natives will be taught from childhood to realize that equality with Europeans is not for them . . . People who believe in equality are not desirable teachers for Natives. When my Department controls Native education it will know for what class of higher education a Native is fitted, and whether he will have a chance in life to use his knowledge.'

The other main obstacle to the economic advancement of the African is the industrial colour-bar under which all the better jobs of industry are reserved for Whites only. Moreover, Africans who do obtain employment in the unskilled and semi-skilled occupations which are open to them are not allowed to form trade unions which have recognition under the Industrial Conciliation Act. This means that strikes of African workers are illegal, and that they are denied the right of collective bargaining which is permitted to the better-paid White workers. The discrimination in the policy of successive South African Governments towards African workers is demonstrated by the so-called 'civilized labour policy' under which sheltered, unskilled Government jobs are found for those white workers who cannot make the grade in industry, at wages which far exceed the earnings of the average African employee in industry.

malnutrition poor health because of lack of proper food
deficiency not enough vitamins
pellagra disease of the skin because of malnutrition
kwashiorkor [ˌkwɒʃiˈɔːkɔ] disease caused by lack of protein
gastro-enteritis illness of the stomach
scurvy *Skorbut*
to curtail to limit
subsidy *Subvention*
matric ordinary-level exam
sheltered protected
to make the grade to reach the necessary standard

The Government often answers its critics by saying that Africans in South Africa are economically better off than the inhabitants of the other countries in Africa. I do not know whether this statement is true and doubt whether any comparison can be made without having regard to the cost-of-living index in such countries. But even if it is true, as far as the African people are concerned it is irrelevant. Our complaint is not that we are poor by comparison with people in other countries, but that we are poor by comparison with the white people in our own country, and that we are prevented by legislation from altering this imbalance.

The lack of human dignity experienced by Africans is the direct result of the policy of white supremacy. White supremacy implies black inferiority. Legislation designed to preserve white supremacy entrenches this notion. Menial tasks in South Africa are invariably performed by Africans. When anything has to be carried or cleaned the white man will look around for an African to do it for him, whether the African is employed by him or not. Because of this sort of attitude, whites tend to regard Africans as a separate breed. They do not look upon them as people with families of their own; they do not realize that they have emotions – that they fall in love like white people do; that they want to be with their wives and children like white people want to be with theirs; that they want to earn enough money to support their families properly, to feed and clothe them and send them to school. And what 'house-boy' or 'garden-boy' or labourer can ever hope to do this?

Pass laws, which to the Africans are among the most hated bits of legislation in South Africa, render any African liable to police surveillance at any time. I doubt whether there is a single African male in South Africa who has not at some stage had a brush with the police over his pass. Hundreds and thousands of Africans are thrown into jail each year under pass laws. Even worse than this is the fact that pass laws keep husband and wife apart and lead to the breakdown of family life.

Poverty and the breakdown of family life have secondary effects. Children wander about the streets of the townships because they have no schools to go to, or no money to enable them to go to school, or no parents at home to see that they go to school, because both parents (if there be two) have to work to keep the family alive. This leads to a breakdown in moral standards, to an alarming rise in illegitimacy, and to growing violence which erupts not only politically, but everywhere. Life in the townships is dangerous. There is not a day that goes by without somebody being stabbed or assaulted. And violence is carried out of the townships in the white living areas. People are afraid to walk alone in the streets after dark. Housebreakings and robberies are increasing, despite the fact that the death sentence can now be imposed for such offences. Death sentences cannot cure the festering sore.

to entrench to fix more firmly
menial task job requiring no training
breed race
to render to make
liable to s.th. legally subject to
surveillance [sɜːˈveɪləns] observation
brush (here): encounter
illegitimacy being born of unwed parents
to impose *auferlegen*
festering sore (fig.) infected wound

Africans want to be paid a living wage. Africans want to perform work which they are capable of doing, and not work which the Government declares them to be capable of. Africans want to be allowed to live where they obtain work, and not be endorsed out of an area because they were not born there. Africans want to be allowed to own land in places where they work, and not to be obliged to live in rented houses which they can never call their own. Africans want to be part of the general population, and not confined to living in their own ghettoes. African men want to have their wives and children to live with them where they work, and not be forced into an unnatural existence in men's hostels. African women want to be with their menfolk and not be left permanently widowed in the Reserves. Africans want to be allowed out after eleven o'clock at night and not to be confined to their rooms like little children. Africans want to be allowed to travel in their own country and to seek work where they want to and not where the Labour Bureau tells them to. Africans want a just share in the whole of South Africa; they want security and a stake in society.

to endorse (here): to remove

widowed (here): without one's husband

stake (here): share

Above all, we want equal political rights, because without them our disabilities will be permanent. I know this sounds revolutionary to the whites in this country, because the majority of voters will be Africans. This makes the white man fear democracy.

disability handicap

But this fear cannot be allowed to stand in the way of the only solution which will guarantee racial harmony and freedom for all. It is not true that the enfranchisement of all will result in racial domination. Political division, based on colour, is entirely artificial and, when it disappears, so will the domination of one colour group by another. The ANC has spent half a century fighting against racialism. When it triumphs it will not change that policy.

enfranchisement right to vote

This then is what the ANC is fighting. Their struggle is a truly national one. It is a struggle of the African people, inspired by their own suffering and their own experience. It is a struggle for the right to live.

During my lifetime I have dedicated myself to this struggle of the African people. I have fought against white domination, and I have fought against black domination. I have cherished the ideal of a democratic and free society in which all persons live together in harmony and with equal opportunities. It is an ideal which I hope to live for and to achieve. But if needs be, it is an ideal for which I am prepared to die. [own bold print]

dedicated devoted

to cherish *schätzen*

Martin Luther King's Acceptance Speech, on the Occasion of the Award of the Nobel Peace Prize in Oslo, December 10, 1964 (excerpt)

[…] After contemplation, I conclude that this award [Nobel Prize] which I receive on behalf of that [civil rights] movement is a profound recognition that nonviolence is the answer to the crucial political and moral question of our time – the need for man to overcome oppression and violence without resorting to violence and oppression. Civilization and violence are antithetical concepts. Negroes of the United States, following the people of India, have demonstrated that **nonviolence is not sterile passivity, but a powerful moral force which makes for social transformation.** [own bold print] Sooner or later all the people of the world will have to discover a way to live together in peace, and thereby transform this pending cosmic elegy into a creative psalm of brotherhood. If this is to be achieved, man must evolve for all human conflict a method which rejects revenge, aggression and retaliation. The foundation of such a method is love.

The tortuous road which has led from Montgomery, Alabama to Oslo bears witness to this truth. This is a road over which millions of Negroes are travelling to find a new sense of dignity. This same road has opened for all Americans a new era of progress and hope. It has led to a new Civil Rights Bill, and it will, I am convinced, be widened and lengthened into a super highway of justice as Negro and white men in increasing numbers create alliances to overcome their common problems.

[…]

I believe that wounded justice, lying prostrate on the blood-flowing streets of our nations, can be lifted from this dust of shame to reign supreme among the children of men. I have the audacity to believe that peoples everywhere can have three meals a day for their bodies, education and culture for their minds, and dignity, equality and freedom for their spirits. I believe that what self-centered men have torn down men other-centered can build up. I still believe that one day mankind will bow before the altars of God and be crowned triumphant over war and bloodshed, and nonviolent redemptive good will proclaim the rule of the land. 'And the lion and the lamb shall lie down together and every man shall sit under his own vine and fig tree and none shall be afraid.' I still believe that we shall overcome!

[…]

antithetical [ˌæntɪˈθetɪkl] in direct opposition

pending waiting to happen

elegy poem or song expressing sorrow

tortuous (fig.) long and complicated

Montgomery scene of Rosa Parks' refusal to give up her seat in a bus in 1955, and the three Selma to Montgomery civil rights marches in 1965

Civil Rights Bill Civil Rights law that ended segregation in public accommodations and strengthened the right to vote

prostrate lying on a surface face down

to reign supreme (fig.) to predominate

audacity boldness

redemptive suffering that is later compensated

to proclaim to announce

vine tree *Weinrebe*

fig tree *Feigenbaum*

And the lion and the lamb … cf. Isiah 11: 6-8

Compare with Nelson Mandela's 1964 speech at his trial.

Amy Biehl and Her Killers' Gift to South Africa – the Enduring Power of Restorative Justice

enduring lasting for a long time

by Marianne Thamm 29 Jul 2015 South Africa

Seventeen years ago on 28 July 1998, the Truth and Reconciliation Commission granted amnesty to four young men who had been sentenced to jail terms for killing American Fulbright scholar Amy Biehl in Gugulethu in 1993. The manner in which her parents, Peter and Linda Biehl, chose to deal with her death as well as their decision to forgive and engage with the killers, provided a much-needed example of restorative justice. In a country torn apart at the time by racial tension and violence, the Biehls taught us how to step out of the eye of the tempest and seek a common humanity.

tempest (literary) violent storm

Who knows where Amy Biehl would have been today or what she would have done with her life. She would have turned 48 this April. She visited South Africa in 1991 and returned in 1993 after studying international relations at Stanford University. South Africa was then on the cusp of transitioning from a racially-exclusive and authoritarian state to a democratic one.

Stanford University renowned private university in California
on the cusp of on the verge of

Whatever path Amy's life might have taken, those of us who knew or encountered her during her brief stay, are certain she would have made a difference to the lives of others wherever she would have ended up. She was due to leave Cape Town for the US to finish her doctorate in African affairs three days after she died. Had she survived, said her mother, Linda Biehl, she would have wanted to be "just a number" and not famous.

Amy was only 26 when she was killed after being caught up in a protest action in Gugulethu on the afternoon of 28 July 1993. The killing was shockingly brutal. Cape Town had been tense for some time and that afternoon had seen an upsurge in protests in the townships, much of it related to the South African Democratic Teachers' Union. Operation Barcelona – aimed at preventing any deliveries being made in the area – had also been launched. Young protesters thronged the streets, pelting cars and trucks with stones. News bulletins warned motorists to stay away from the area.

upsurge sudden increase
to launch to start
to throng to gather in large numbers somewhere
to pelt to attack by throwing things

Amy, who had been working at the Community Law Centre at the University of the Western Cape, had been giving a lift to colleagues in her old, orange Mazda and drove straight into one such protest. She had often visited Gugulethu, unlike most white South Africans at the time, and believed she had nothing to fear.

However, the streets were filled with angry crowds chanting 'One settler, one bullet.' Vusumzi Samuel Ntamo, Ntombeki Ambrose Peni, Mzikhona Eazi Nofemela and Mongesi Christopher Manqina were part of the 200-strong crowd, fired up after attending a Pan African

Student Organisation (Paso) meeting in Langa. Peni, Nofemela and Manqina, all scholars and in their teens, were Paso members.

In that moment Amy Biehl came to represent, for some in the enraged crowd, collective white South Africa. A group of people spotted Amy. She stood out with her blonde hair and blue eyes. They surrounded her car. She fled, was chased, tripped up and brutally beaten with bricks and stones before she was stabbed to death while her friends desperately tried to save her life, telling the men who were killing her that she was 'a comrade.'

to trip up to make s.o. fall

Her horrific death was not 'senseless' in the essential sense of the word. It was cruel, mindless and brutal but not senseless. The tragedy is it made perfect sense in the eye of that political storm in that particular moment. And in many ways it shocked us out of our hot rage.

In the immediate aftermath of the killing – when we understood what had happened, when we grasped that a chant like 'One settler, one bullet' was not a harmless political slogan but could result in a tragedy – we paused and took stock. Amy's death made international headlines and various political and religious leaders called for calm and reason.

to take stock to stop and think about what has happened

And then Amy's parents, Linda and Peter Biehl, a couple filled with truly awesome grace and compassion, did something that stunned many. They announced that they had forgiven the men who had killed their daughter. There were many who were outraged at the Biehls' capacity to try to understand and forgive.

awesome amazing

But in that moment, the gesture was hugely symbolic for South Africans both black and white. Linda and Peter Biehl helped to pioneer the thorny path, along with many others, to a reconciliation that continues today.

The four killers were all sentenced to 18 years for Amy's murder and later applied for amnesty, supported by the Biehls. Over the years many have continued to remark on the Biehls' remarkable capacity for forgiveness. But should we have been that surprised when countless numbers of ordinary black South Africans were asked to do the same, and did, during the gruelling and flawed Truth and Reconciliation Commission (TRC) established in 1995?

gruelling exhausting, difficult
flawed with defects
Truth and Reconciliation Commission commission established by Mandela to deal with the crimes of apartheid and unite the country – Archbishop Tutu was appointed chairman.

Nofomela later said he had not wanted to give testimony at the TRC, believing it was a 'sell out.'

'But then I read in the press that Linda and Peter had said that it was not up to them to forgive: it was up to the people in South Africa to learn to forgive each other. I decided to go and tell our story and show remorse. Amnesty wasn't my motivation. I just wanted to ask for forgiveness. I wanted to say in front of Linda and Peter, face to face, 'I am sorry, can you forgive me?' I wanted to be free in my mind and body. It must have been so painful for them to lose their daughter, but by coming to South Africa – not to speak of recrimination, but to speak of the pain of our struggle – they gave me back my freedom,' he said.

to give testimony *aussagen*
sell out betrayal
remorse deep regret

recrimination the act of returning an accusation

There were other white people who later followed the Biehls' example. Ginn Fourie immediately springs to mind. Fourie's 23-year-old daughter, Lyndi, was killed during an Azanian People's Liberation Army attack on the Helderberg Tavern, also in 1993.

Ginn had attended the trial of Lyndi's killer, Pan Africanist Congress member Letlapa Mphahlele, and it was there that she was able to begin to understand the circumstances that led to his decision to attack the establishment. Since then Fourie and Mphahlele have shared many platforms across the world speaking on reconciliation.

Linda and Peter Biehl (who died in 2002) established the Amy Biehl Foundation in the US in 1994 and the Amy Biehl Foundation Trust in South Africa.

In October this year Linda Biehl and Ntobeko Peni, who now works for the Amy Biehl Foundation, will talk about the power of restorative justice at an event at Whittier College in Southern California. In September last year Peni and Nofemela (who also works with the foundation) travelled to Mexico's CG Jung Institute to deliver a lecture on restorative justice.

The foundation, established in 1994, continues to operate in the Western Cape and is involved in a variety of initiatives from education, health, sport and job creation.

While Amy Biehl found herself in the wrong place at the wrong time, the gift of her life has been the ongoing inspiration this young individual continues to provide across the world.

The story and the subsequent brave journey undertaken by Amy's parents and those who took her life continues to inspire and serve as an example of what can be accomplished, even in the face of great tragedy, when anger and rage do not drive human interaction.

Just last month poet Antjie Krog, delivered a keynote address at the 2015 Sunday Times Literary Awards. Titled *An Inappropriate Text for an Appropriate Evening*, Krog controversially suggested a second Radical Reconstruction Period in South Africa as the country is 'facing a disaster in the absence of a crucial social unifying vision of a humane society. The times are pitiless. No vision is coming to save us. Let us dirty our hands with the tactics of the kind of communality needed to create openings into which new rhythms, new language and new modes of being human can be poured.'

reconstruction period a period of the state reforming the social structure analogous to 'the Reconstruction' in the American South after the Civil War

Amy Biehl, her parents and the men who killed her have helped, in a way, to create those very openings for these new rhythms, languages and modes of being human. And for this we thank them.

posted at
http://www.dailymaverick.co.za/article/2015-07-29-amy-biehl-and-her-killers-gift-to-south-africa-the-enduring-power-of-restorative-justice/#.Vb0vgvk9ZMk

The Literary Bridges of Sindiwe Magona (excerpt)

by Dianne Shober

[...] Although Magona intends for the novel to be a tool of reconciliation, **Mother to Mother** is also a book of revelation, revealing the results of apartheid's humiliating and dehumanizing laws that bred angry young men who could mutilate a helpless young woman simply because she was white. Further, it identifies the fathers whose sperm spawned another generation, but whose bodies are forced to work in mines or factories thousands of kilometers away from the children they will never see or know. Finally it provides a voice to the anguished African mothers who couldn't raise their children because they were acting as surrogate mothers for their white employers [...]

Magona states later in an interview:

> *The mother who abandons her children is a story that has not been told in South Africa. The majority of the women we saw in the urban areas during the era of the passes, wearing overalls and aprons and caps and wide smiles that labeled them as domestic workers, were in the cities without their children. These are the mothers who were busy being mothers to white babies and white children and being servants to white families so that their children back in the village could barely survive.*

Through her sensitive portrayal of real-life heartache, Magona becomes as former Archbishop Desmond Tutu describes himself 'a wounded healer.' Says Magona: 'It is not in loving our neighbor that we become better human beings: the challenge before us is in learning to understand and perhaps one day love our enemy.' Through her personal migrations of discovery, Magona creates in her writings a conscious textual bridge between the two cultures and two spiritual traditions (Western and African), thus enabling the proprietors of each group to share ideas and achieve understanding and appreciation of the other while finding for herself a secure place under the protection of the Trinity and her ancestors.

Even her writing style unites two distinct literary forms, incorporating both the oral African tradition as well as the western conventional style through its use of 'realism, linear plot and first-person narrative.' This dual cultural and literary staging provides a multi-vocal and multi-focal canvas on which to place her characters and the tragedy and triumph of their lives while at the same time making 'the insights of one culture accessible to another.' Magona also carefully interweaves together the two, sometimes three South African languages of Xhosa, Afrikaans, and English to form an intricate tapestry of linguistic beauty. Through the interrogation of her life his-

revelation the uncovering of s.th. that was unknown before
to breed, bred, bred (fig.) to create
to spawn to produce
surrogate a person acting as a substitute
proprietor owner, possessor
Trinity a reference to the Christian idea of the Trinity: Father, Son and Holy Spirit to indicate that Sindiwe Magona engages with both Christian and traditional faith practices
to incorporate to include
canvas (fig.) *Leinwand*
intricate [ˈɪntrɪkət] detailed
tapestry (fig): *Wandteppich*

tory and the stories of her people, Magona enlightens the global and local reader of the tragedies and triumphs of her Xhosa people as they strive to secure a sense of personhood and purpose in a society fraught with distancing discourse. […]

distancing discourse (literary) a dialogue that tends to separate rather than unite in a common understanding

© 2014 Professor Dr. Dianne Shober, reprinted with permission
for the complete working paper: www.ifeas.uni-mainz.de/Datien/AP 149.pdf
excerpt from
Working Paper 149
Working Papers of the Department
of Anthropology and African Studies
Johannes-Gutenberg-Universität, Mainz

Students in South Africa Protest Slow Pace of Change

by Norimitsu Onishi September 8, 2015

CAPE TOWN – It was only when he landed at the University of Cape Town, a bastion of the fight against apartheid, that Ramabina Mahapa became truly conscious of his race.

bastion (fig.) bulwark, stronghold

Mr. Mahapa, 23, grew up in a village with only black South Africans, and he graduated at the top of his high school class. But when he got to the University of Cape Town, the gap between black and white students became clear to him: Of the 15 people who owned cars in his dorm, only one was black. When the first test results came in, the black students ranked at the bottom.

dorm (coll.) dormitory building where students can live
to rank to have a certain position in a list

"That's why I then started feeling black," said Mr. Mahapa, who was born two years before the end of apartheid and is now a third-year psychology and philosophy major, as well as the president of the university's student government.

"Even when I occasionally would see pictures on TV about apartheid, you never internalized it or thought about it – up until you come to a space where you actually experience it," he added.

Mr. Mahapa stood recently outside the student government office, which demonstrators had occupied in the latest of a series of protests that have made this liberal campus a potent symbol of the lack of change in post-apartheid South Africa. The numbers, in a country where 80 percent of the population is black, are stark: Black South Africans make up less than a quarter of the university's student body, and they account for just 5 percent of members of the faculty.

potent [ˈpəʊtnt] powerful
stark grim

The protests that roiled this campus, the country's most prestigious public university, have quieted for now. But they have spread to other institutions with similar problems, including Stellenbosch University, whose campus less than an hour east of here has been dominated by demonstrations in the past week.

to roil to stir up, to cause great agitation

The student actions have shed light on a much broader national dissatisfaction with the glacial pace of transformation, as South Africa's policy of giving blacks equal representation is called.

to shed light on s.th. (fig.) to reveal, to make known
glacial [ˈgleɪʃl] (fig.) slow like the movement of a glacier (*Gletscher*)

In today's South Africa, forged in negotiations between the African National Congress and the former apartheid government in 1994, whites retain disproportionate power over the economy and other important sectors, like higher education. Transformation is widely seen as having greatly benefited a small, politically connected black elite, while bringing much less to the broader population.

to forge to create
to retain (formal) to keep
disproportionate (here): too much compared to the percentage of whites in the total population

"During the protests, you had a lot more people questioning the project of 1994, and condemning it," said Rekgotsofetse Chikane, 24, another student leader at the University of Cape Town, adding that the criticism extended to former President Nelson Mandela. "If Mandela wasn't safe, no leader was."

to extend to s.th. to also include

Mr. Chikane took part in protests and in the occupation of administrative buildings, where students held marathon reading sessions of Frantz Fanon, an anti-colonialist author, and Steve Biko, the South African leader of the black consciousness movement.

The protesters' rallying cry is the need to "decolonize" the university. They are calling for more black faculty members, continued affirmative action policies to increase the number of black students, and a curriculum that is less Eurocentric and more African-oriented.

"It's a combination of national, political unresolved issues and the students' own personal search for issues of identity and meaning," said Xolela Mangcu, an associate professor of sociology at the university and one of the national leaders in the debate over transformation in higher education.

The slow pace of change at the nation's 26 public universities – where only 14 percent of full professors are black – has more far-reaching consequences for South Africa than does transformation in other institutions, critics say.

Malegapuru William Makgoba, who leads the government's transformation oversight committee on higher education and was formerly principal of the University of KwaZulu Natal, said that white administrators and senior faculty members, who continue to wield power over hiring, promotion and the curriculum, resisted change. A generation after the end of apartheid, in 1994, white South Africans want to keep molding the nation's future leaders, he said.

"The only way they can legitimize themselves is to befriend black people who can be their spokespersons and who can drive their values," Mr. Makgoba said of white South Africans.

"What happens, in essence, is that you change the government from white to black, but you choose the blacks who will protect white values," he added.

Here at the University of Cape Town, widely considered the continent's best institution of higher learning, discontent among black students had been brewing for years. But the recent protests here – as well as elsewhere in the country – were set off by an unusual act of defiance.

In March, a student threw excrement at a statue of Cecil Rhodes, the British imperialist who donated land to the university. Students here and elsewhere call their movement "Rhodes Must Fall."

The statue, at the heart of the campus, had long been the object of student protests. But things were different this time.

Dr. Max Price, the vice chancellor of the university, said he had been surprised by the enduring reaction against the statue, given that earlier demonstrations had fizzled.

"It tapped into – and a statue was a perfect way of articulating – the sense of alienation that black students feel on this campus," he said. "The culture of the place feels white. The architecture is a European, Oxbridge architecture. Obviously, the language of instruction is English. The culture of what's held up to be excellent universities and

Frantz Fanon (1925 – 1961) born in Martinique he was influential in the field of post-colonial studies and supported numerous liberation movements

rallying cry slogan to arouse followers

to wield power to exert or maintain power

promotion advancement

to mold (fig.) to form

to drive (here): to support and further

to brew (fig.) to be in the process of forming

defiance bold resistance

Cecil Rhodes (1953 – 1902) British colonial financier and Prime Minister of the Cape Colony – He made a fortune in diamond and gold mining.

enduring lasting a long time

to fizzle to fail after a promising start

to tap into s.th. to make use of s.th. as a source

alienation feeling of not belonging

to emulate (formal) to strive to be equal or better
to aspire to be s.th. to have a strong desire to be s.th.
the Ivy League universities the elite universities in America
to highlight to bring notice or emphasis to s.th.
to gravitate to s.th. to be drawn to s.th.
to pluck (fig.) to quickly take
to rise through the ranks to acquire increasingly higher positions
assessment judgement, evaluation
critical mass (fig.) the smallest amount necessary to bring about a change
intellectual discourse (here): intellectual communication among scholars
to simmer (fig.) to be about to break out
to go into your face (slang) to say directly
to expel to make s.o. officially leave
trust fund a large sum of money set aside that can be used after reaching a certain age
gated community group of houses surrounded by a fence, with a guarded entrance
marginalized group *Randgruppe*

excellent science, and what we emulate and aspire to be, are the Ivy League universities and European universities."

Dr. Price pointed to signs of progress since the end of apartheid. The number of students from other African nations has risen sharply, highlighting the university's increasing ties with the rest of the continent. The percentage of black South African students has also risen, to 24 percent last year from 18 percent in 1994, although the increase has been held back by South Africa's weak primary and secondary schools, he said.

The single area in which the university has "failed completely," Dr. Price said, is in hiring more black members of faculty. Talented black South Africans do not gravitate to academia, he said, but are often plucked instead by the government or the private sector.

"What's more," Dr. Price said, "it simply takes time for an academic to rise through the ranks to become a full professor. It would take one more generation for blacks to make up a majority of full professors at South Africa's public universities," Dr. Price said, "and two generations to match the percentage of the South African population that is black."

Mr. Mangcu, the sociologist and a leading critic of the lack of change at South Africa's universities, agreed with Dr. Price's assessment. But he said that changes in hiring and promoting could quickly establish "a critical mass" of black faculty members who would change the environment and intellectual discourse on the campus.

The recent protests drew a diverse group of black students, and class divisions simmered below the surface.

Lindokuhle Patiwe, 18, grew up in a poor township outside Cape Town. He lived with his family – his mother, a brother and two cousins – in a public housing unit that his mother, a child-care worker, bought in 2000. On the 25th of each month, the mother's payday, the family went out to eat at McDonald's.

"For someone from the townships, coming from there to here is a huge change," Mr. Patiwe said. "No one goes into your face and says, 'You're not welcome here.' No one says that you don't belong here. But it's just that the structure, and the environment itself, says that I'm not welcome here."

Mr. Patiwe's mother worried that participating in the protests would get him expelled. "She was not impressed at all," he said. "I don't have a trust fund to go back to."

For Mr. Chikane, the 24-year-old student leader, and his family, post-apartheid South Africa has brought great opportunities. The son of a famous anti-apartheid leader, the Rev. Frank Chikane, he grew up in Soweto, the township outside Johannesburg. But he had attended private schools as a child, and his family had moved to a gated community north of the city.

Just as the protests drew Mr. Chikane and Mr. Patiwe, they also attracted the participation of gay people, students of mixed race, anarchists and other marginalized groups.

"The elephant in the room was class," Mr. Chikane said. "Class was never discussed. It was neatly swept underneath the rug."

"I knew that if you bring up class too early in this organization, all you would do is to split the black students," he added. "Then it would be blacks-who-have and blacks-who-don't-have. And at U.C.T., you can see that quite blatantly."

blatantly obviously

The movement has held together, at least for now. The students realized their first goal by pressing the university to remove the statue of Rhodes. A few days later, though, students woke up to see that a shadow had been painted on the ground, as if cast by the fallen monument.

http://www.nytimes.com/2015/09/09/world/africa/student-protests-in-south-africa-highlight-dissatisfaction-with-pace-of-change.html?emc=edit_th_20150909&nl=todaysheadlines&nlid=69748495

© 2015 New York Times reprinted with permission

Suggestions for Additional Reading and Viewing

Cry the Beloved Country by Alan Paton, 1948

novel with insights into the tragedy of apartheid

The Second Hut by Doris Lessing, 1951 in **The Many Voices of English**, Diesterweg, 2005

short story that contrasts the attitudes of British and Boer settlers towards Africans in Southern Rhodesia

The Help by Kathryn Stockett, 2010

novel about racism in Mississippi in the early 1960s – many parallels with racism in South Africa

Black Like Me by John Griffin, Diesterweg, 2009

Originally published in 1961, this autobiography provides insights into racism in the southern United States by a writer who travelled through the South with his skin dyed black.

Small Island by Andrea Levy, 2005

wonderful novel about Jamaican immigrants in Great Britain before, during, and after WW II

A History of South Africa by Leonard Thompson, Yale University Press, New Haven, 2014

readable, concise history of South Africa

Other works by Sindiwe Magona are mentioned in the biography.

Film:

Gandhi 1982 two scenes at the beginning of the film are of special interest:

1. when Gandhi, as a young lawyer trained in England, is thrown off a train in South Africa because he is an Indian sitting in a first-class compartment with a first-class ticket

2. when he organizes a nonviolent protest demonstration in South Africa against the requirement of passes for Indians

These articles are also of interest:

http://www.theguardian.com/commentisfree/2015/sep/07/spirit-africa-art-business-creativity

The spirit of Africa's people will transform the continent
by Ben Okri, 7 September, 2015

Our nations were shaped by outside forces and faced instability from their creation. But from art to business I can see the resilience and creativity that will help us overcome the challenges.

For most of the 20th century Africa made an epic journey: from its original way, through the trauma of colonialism and into the flawed daylight of independence. It made a journey in 50 years that it took other continents centuries – and, in some nations, thousands of years – to accomplish.

We all know that the terms of African independence were flawed at birth; Africa stepped on to the world stage with its hands tied, the contract of nations negotiated against its favour. It was joining a game in which all the contestants had been in training for centuries, had set the rules of the game, and had all the best facilities and the bias of the ages; and it was joining this game with broken arms and legs, confidence shattered, spirit scattered. [...]

---

http://www.nytimes.com/2015/08/21/us/george-houser-freedom-rides-pioneer-dies-at-99.html?hpw&rref=obituaries&action=click&pgtype=Homepage&module=well-region&region=bottom-well&WT.nav=bottom-well

George Houser, Freedom Rides Pioneer, Dies at 99
by Margalit Fox, 20 August, 2015

The Rev. George M. Houser, a founder of the Congress of Racial Equality who was believed to be the last living member of the inaugural Freedom Ride — the volatile, sometimes violent bus trip through the South by a racially mixed group in 1947 — died on Wednesday in Santa Rosa, Calif. He was 99. [...]

Mr. Houser, who in 1952 helped found the group Americans for South African Resistance, became the executive director of the American Committee on Africa in 1955. In that post, which he held until his retirement in 1981, he worked to abolish apartheid and to end colonial rule throughout Africa.

For his work, Mr. Houser received the Oliver R. Tambo Award from President Jacob Zuma of South Africa in 2010. Named for the former African National Congress president who spent three decades in exile, the award recognizes foreign nationals for service to South Africa. [...]